Flux Leadership

Real-Time Inquiry for Humanizing Educational Change

EDITED BY

Sharon M. Ravitch
Chloe Alexandra Kannan

Foreword by Christina M. Grant

TEACHERS COLLEGE PRESS

TEACHERS COLLEGE | COLUMBIA UNIVERSITY
NEW YORK AND LONDON

Published by Teachers College Press®, 1234 Amsterdam Avenue, New York, NY 10027

Library of Congress Cataloging-in-Publication Data
Names: Ravitch, Sharon M., editor. | Kannan, Chloe Alexandra, editor.
Title: Flux leadership : real-time inquiry for humanizing educational change /
    Edited by Sharon M. Ravitch, Chloe Alexandra Kannan ; Foreword by Christina Grant.
Description: New York, NY : Teachers College Press, [2022] | Includes bibliographical references and index. | Summary: "In these times of rapid change, including a global pandemic, educational leaders need tools and frameworks that can adapt to evolving shifts in real time. What might happen if a leadership framework could make sense of this complexity in ways that are humane, ethical, culturally responsive, and multifaceted? This book examines how a flux leadership mindset and corresponding tools promote the conditions for educational change that uplift stakeholders and generate contextualized data during emergency situations. The educational leaders at the heart of this book employed a flux leadership tool through a process called "rapid-cycle inquiry," which allows for collaborative inquiries to take place in real time to answer tough questions and surface stories that are often silenced in times of sudden change. Featuring narratives of what happened to schools during COVID-19, Flux Leadership introduces a generative framework for agile, responsive, anti-racist, trauma-informed, healing-centered leadership for times of crisis and beyond. Book Features: ·Provides a framework and set of real-time strategies for leaders to engage in critical leadership practice and crisis leadership with attention to equity. ·Addresses vital school and district-based leadership issues in various contexts, including reflexivity, identity, positionality, racial literacy, brave space leadership, equity-focused professional development, and critical collaboration. ·Covers a range of vantage points and intersectional social identities in succinct, accessible, and pragmatic ways. ·Creates a new approach for leaders to get at context and drive homegrown metrics that speak back to and challenge top-down metrics in schools and districts"— Provided by publisher.
Identifiers: LCCN 2021037085 (print) | LCCN 2021037086 (ebook) |
    ISBN 9780807766248 (hardcover) | ISBN 9780807766231 (paperback) |
    ISBN 9780807780671 (ebook)
Subjects: LCSH: Educational leadership. | Educational change. | Educational equalization. | Culturally relevant pedagogy.
Classification: LCC LB2806 .F58 2022 (print) | LCC LB2806 (ebook) |
    DDC 371.2/011—dc23
LC record available at https://lccn.loc.gov/2021037085
LC ebook record available at https://lccn.loc.gov/2021037086

ISBN 978-0-8077-6623-1 (paper)
ISBN 978-0-8077-6624-8 (hardcover)
ISBN 978-0-8077-8067-1 (ebook)

Printed on acid-free paper
Manufactured in the United States of America

We Dedicate This Book to Critical Race Theory

Contents

Foreword

In March 2020, educators became superheroes overnight as they navigated the new realities of transforming schools and education systems while fighting a new war with a microscopic enemy: Coronavirus. While managing the precarity of our own lives, we learned new technologies, designed rigorous curricula, and figured out how to love, reach, and teach our children—from our homes to theirs. We managed our fears about the unknowns while encouraging our students, staff, and communities to be strong and believe in the power of education and relationships to carry them through. As we faced these daily, weekly, and monthly unknowns, including, for many, managing our own families in confined spaces—we showed up for our children. We did this because, like superheroes in the movies, we needed to save the day. So many people depended on us—and still do.

Within the seemingly relentless terror of the COVID-19 global pandemic, the long-known yet insidious enemy of structural racism took hold of our public consciousness. We saw the systematic dehumanization of Black, Brown, and Indigenous bodies become foregrounded in an unprecedented way in the United States media and consciousness. From a shared social uprising came stories of intense and wide-ranging lived racism and discrimination—Black@ pages from students of color storied their pain and marginalization at the hands of educators and our education system. We have learned a great deal in these times about the felt inequities of schooling; these students' brave stories of their oppression are a collective outcry for radical change in education and schooling—from conception to implementation and back again.

These times and the social movement they have emboldened create new and long overdue accountability for leaders, schools, and the education system as a whole. This new accountability has precipitated a sweeping influx of Diversity, Equity, and Inclusion (DEI) programs and antiracism initiatives in schools. Accountability is a good thing, and it is *long* overdue. This new presence of accountability for educational bias and discrimination requires that leaders bring new mindsets, skills, and strategies to the foreground and lead for equity in their districts, schools, and communities. It also means that we need applied research and inquiry to flow from practitioners and communities to academic and policy circles in ways that foreground and affirm practitioner and student knowledge, insight, and experience.

As education leaders, we must center critical learning about ourselves as a vital source of professional learning. Taking an inquiry stance on our practice allows us to make meaning of experience in ways that help us to improve our practice and create spaces for others to do the same. We have never before needed to center our learning, make meaning of our identity-based experiences and stresses, and learn from each other as we do now. Though we find ourselves emerging from this global pandemic and feel the comfortable return of familiar routines, we will be—we need to be—actively learning from and leaning on each other, now and for many years to come. This uncomfortable first step is necessary to create the conditions for us to unpack everything that we have experienced while serving our students, and while learning from our students and teachers and communities what they've been through and its meaning. Inquiry must be our love language as we come together as a collective to process, to learn, and to heal.

Through the rapid-cycle inquiries at the heart of this book, written by educational leaders who are doctoral students in the Mid-Career Doctoral Program in Educational Leadership at the University of Pennsylvania Graduate School of Education, I hope you find glimpses of your courageous leadership. Allow yourself to sink into the affirming reflections on all that you have learned and experienced as a leader over these last 2 years. I hope you embrace your humanity and can unpack some of the challenges and fears you've faced as an educational leader during the pandemic and *all* the rest. Amid unspeakable fears and ever-changing daily realities that we could never have conceived or planned for—we led. *You led.*

We use terms like "essential workers" and "on the frontlines" to describe medical practitioners and public health leaders during the pandemic. This term applies to educators who taught and led through constant change and under duress throughout the pandemic. We led the frontlines and learned as we went, proving that educators are essential to the livelihood and progress of this country. As our own experiences and the leader inquiries at the heart of this book show us, inquiry is not a luxury. Inquiry is a necessity for the betterment of our children and transformation of our systems as we work to get to the other side of all of this.

A flux leadership approach, as you'll see throughout every chapter of this groundbreaking, practitioner-focused book, surfaces real-time, actionable lessons for leaders as we serve children and families in these times. *Flux Leadership: Real-Time Inquiry for Humanizing Educational Change* brings it all together through sharing live leader inquiries that illuminate what story-based inquiry and our inquiry stances can teach us as leaders. The book offers a model of collaborative inquiry that is actionable in real time and, further, that can lead us to a more equitable future one school and district at a time, all at once.

As we move forward, we must look back and appreciate ourselves as leaders. *We. Did. It.*

Apart and together, we have changed the course of educational history. If this moment marks the first time sitting in that truth, please let that wash over you. Let it sink in. *Breathe.* Steady yourself, break open your paper-based journal or journaling app and allow yourself to freely write and reflect on this unique and unprecedented time in your leadership journey. Keep your pen and journal nearby as you turn these pages. Let this text be a source of resonance, dynamic reflection, and an active site of inquiry within and for your practice and leader healing.

I wish you strength and pedagogical love on this next leg of your leadership journey, and I hope that you sow the seeds of your humanization as you read each chapter. May we heal and grow from all that has happened to and around us. Let us use this growth to build a better future together. This book—each of the stories within it—offers that reflexive path forward.

—Christina M. Grant, Ed.D.,
State Superintendent of Education,
Washington, D.C., June 28, 2021

Acknowledgments

To all the contributing authors, you are why this book exists—we watched you, we saw you, we felt you lead with such tenacity, bravery, deep care, and responsiveness, even as your own pandemic fates and those of your families were unclear. We will always hold that in our hearts with you. We saw the trauma on your faces on March 13, that fateful night we all came together online, just after you had closed your buildings for lockdown. We will always know the heroes you are, and we thank you for your service. Each of you embodies the ideals of this book and gives us hope for the future of education—and humanity. We love you one and all. Thank you for your courage and your leadership in these times.

We are grateful for the Mid-Career Program in Educational Leadership at Penn GSE, specifically Mike Johanek, Kathy Rho, Martha Williams, Joseph Jackson, Gerald Campano, Diane Waff, Rand Quinn, John D'Auria, and the students and alumni who make Mid-Career so dynamic and generative.

Thank you to Teachers College Press and visionary editor Brian Ellerbeck, who encouraged us throughout this project in ways that really improved the book. Thank you to the entire TC Press team—Caritza Berlioz, Karl Nyberg, Nancy Power, Mike Olivo, and Emily Fryer. Sincere appreciation to Kaley Ciluffo for your skillful editing—you are a light in this project. Lulu Cossich, thank you for organizing pieces in *Perspectives on Urban Education* on the way to these full-length chapters. Ari Burstein, thank you for creating the flux tables for us on the fly.

Sharon's Acknowledgments

Chloe, I marvel at the depth and dynamism of all that is you and love thinking and writing with you! Your empathy and compassion and your active need to press for justice in every space and place is part of why conceptualizing and writing this book together was such a creatively transforming joy. I appreciate you and your deep humanity and kindness, your generous mind and receptive sensibility, your brilliance. I respect, appreciate, and love you my sister, Miigwech.

I am deeply grateful to my thought and action partners: my job coach, north star, and father, Carl Meir Ravitch—apple and tree, אבא, apple and tree. Appreciation to the brilliant and kind game-changers in my professional life: Katie Pak, Michael Nakkula, Howard Stevenson, Susan and Torch Lytle, Carol Gilligan, Nicole Mittenfelner Carl, Annie McKee, Dana Kaminstein, Marsha Richardson, Laura Colket, Christina Grant, Reima Shakeir, Michael Baker, Usama Mahmud, Antonio "Tono" Baltodano, Alejandra Rodriguez, Rosa Rivas, Gowri Ishwaran, Janet Salmons, Sherry Coleman, Gloria Fernández-Tearte, Nimet Eren, Mala Pandurang, Creutzer Mathurin, Vanneur Pierre, Wagner Marseille, Lilian Ajayi-Ore, Cecelia Cardesa, Leland McGee, William N. Thomas IV, Preston Cline, Lonnie Rowell, Alice Goldberg Debbs Ryan, Liza Herzog, Perri Shaw Borish, Tim Foxx, Jen Murphy, Deborah Melincoff, Amy Leventhal and Marc Diamond, and Ariana Maria Ravitch—blessings to and from our ancestors.

To my first and best leaders, my parents, Arline and Carl Ravitch, thank you for giving me deep roots and strong wings, deep faith, connection to Our People, and abundant love for humanity. Your love keeps me strong and focused and I am grateful for you every day in every way. Ari and Lev, my sons, may you grow a more just world and have the will, tenacity, and vision to imagine and effect change. Be leaders of justice and work for *tikkun olam*, healing the world. Andy, best friend and ex-husband, thank you for being an amazing co-parent and confidante, and for always having my back. And finally, Don Duilio Baltodano, one of the most influential leaders of my life, died as I began writing this book. Duilio, you will always, even in death, be our night lantern. Siempre amaré a tu amada Nicaragua. Inspired gratitude for the writings of Yung Pueblo, a healing prophet. Thank you to my students—current and past, near and far—you ignite my curiosity and desire to heal the world each and every day.

Chloe's Acknowledgments

Sharon, you are a glimmering light of research, practice, guidance, and humanity. There is another story-based inquiry that can be written about our partnership, friendship, and sisterhood. Your wisdom is the glitter that falls from the sky and the fire that burns slowly in my heart. May we continue to write on napkins and think intensely about the issues facing educational leadership on comfy couches. Zaagi'idiwin. Always.

I am grateful to the Educational Leadership RAC at the University of Pennsylvania Graduate School of Education for their reflections and contributions in both influencing my leadership practices and my thinking about the field more broadly: Katie Pak, Sarah Gudenkauf, Laura Ogburn, Nimet Eren, Amanda Jones-Lyman, Jennifer Kobrin, Meg MacDonald, Chenelle Boatswain, Serrano Legrand, Sia Brown, Rand Quinn, and Mike Johanek.

I also want to deeply thank the Columbia Summer Principals Academy 2012 NOLA Cohort for their wisdom. As one of the youngest leaders in that cohort, I learned so much on how to be a better and more responsive educational leader from you all. It was such a gift to learn alongside you and from you. I will always carry your leadership lessons with me.

To the other thought partners in my life (research and practice)—Andy Danilchick, Mike Nakkula, Joy Esboldt, Karla Venegas, Ricki Ginsberg, Mike Mannix, Harris Sokoloff, Andy Malone, Gerald Campano, Carol Alter, Velicia Pernell, Rohit Kumar, Bindiya Hassaram, Andrea Wood, Frances Nan, Megan Gildin, Olivia Harris, and the Sault Ste. Marie Tribe of Chippewa Indian Traditional Medicine Department—thank you for your love and support in my journey to push back against the status quo for more humanizing narratives of leadership and education.

Thank you to my parents (Ravi and Shelley Kannan) who taught me that you must work hard, love what you do, and keep humanity front and center in how we approach our work. Zac, thank you for our intellectual conversations that keep me going in the work that I do. I am also grateful to friends who are family: Elizabeth Wilson, Stephanie Wordes, Rachel White, Sarah Pendergast, Sara Steinhurst, Austin Lowes, and Faraz Ahmed. Thank you for your love and strength. And to Christina Zajicek, who passed away before this book could be published: you have a piece of my heart, always. Nick, my best friend, thank you for almost a decade of the most intense debates on both teaching and learning and educational leadership. I am better for those conversations. Thank you, Dr. Craig Richards, for teaching me that educational leadership is the heart and soul of this work. I will continue to fight to make it better no matter where I go. And lastly, to every student I have ever taught in K–12: your perspectives matter and they are worth fighting for.

Storying the Gaps

Transforming Schools
Through Story-Based Inquiry

Sharon M. Ravitch and Chloe Alexandra Kannan

With all that's transpiring in the world and in people's lives, educational leaders need new skills and supports that help them to identify, examine, and challenge limiting beliefs and assumptions—their own and others—in mission mode and as a central leadership remit. Today's school leaders must be able to critically examine their mindsets, implicit beliefs, and tacit internalized knowledge hierarchies in responsive and actionable ways that they can articulate with criticality. This kind of leader learning agility requires leader reflexivity—critically reading and adjusting the self in real time with disciplined, curious, and compassionate humility. Ultimately, we argue, this requires as it supports the creation of *brave-space inquiry processes* through storytelling.

Taking an inquiry stance (Cochran-Smith & Lytle, 2009), which is foundational to flux pedagogy (Ravitch, 2020b), requires that leaders engage a reflexive learning stance on identity, mindsets, practices, and the contexts—near and far, personal and societal—that shape their practices and organizations. Intentional, societally contextualized self-reflection questions what leaders know and how they know it and opens up possibilities for authentic leader learning. As each chapter illuminates, an inquiry stance helps leaders upset normative knowledge hierarchies to make room for and inform more equitable education possibilities. *Flux Leadership: Real-Time Inquiry for Humanizing Educational Change* offers restorative possibilities through intentional and equitable inquiry for educational leaders; it shares transformative promise for humanizing and antiracist leading, teaching, schooling, and learning.

LEADER INQUIRY STANCE

Working from an inquiry stance (Cochran-Smith & Lytle, 2009) means that leaders show up—as their raison d'être—as reflective, curious, and engaged learners who engage in humble inquiry as their mission mode (Schein, 2013) rather than showing up as knowledge droppers or unilateral experts from on high. This intentional shift in power dynamics around expertise, when leaders centralize the wisdom of everyone around them and leverage shared wisdom to push into knowledge hierarchies, constitutes a *distributive wisdom approach*. In a distributive wisdom approach (to be discussed in depth in Chapter 3) all wisdoms are foregrounded, brought into the conversation, and hybridized. Co-creating intentional processes and practices for individual and shared knowledge generation elevates everyone in schools and communities. In this fraught extended moment, in which most people feel helpless and depleted, education leaders need to learn how to create the conditions in which people can be agentic in sharing their perspectives, experiences, ideas, and concerns; this agency is vital for learning, healthy development, and positive educational experiences and outcomes (Ravitch, 2020a).

Leaders working from an inquiry stance position everyone as "legitimate knowers and knowledge generators, not just implementers of others' knowledge" (Cochran-Smith & Lytle, 2009, p. 18). A *critical inquiry stance* extends an inquiry stance precisely by questioning why, in White-dominated Western educational contexts, knowledge (epistemology) is even valued over values (axiology) and ways of being (ontology). That this itself—the preoccupation of knowledge as the highest form of human capital—is to many a neutral backdrop speaks volumes to the sedimented White Western bias in this country's approach to education and schooling (Ravitch, 2020a). A critical inquiry stance upsets traditional notions of what constitutes valid knowledge and who is a knower; it enables leaders to identify and challenge traditional learning beliefs and practices. The eye of the challenge is the ways that these traditional practices are steeped in Westernized White values and norms yet normalized and imposed on everyone universally without any real accountability for the dire outcomes for BIPOC (Black, Indigenous, People of Color) students and communities.

A *critical inquiry stance* exposes the invisible-yet-pervasive imposition of Western hierarchical logics, including the devaluation of emotion, nondominant values and priorities, and Indigenous wisdoms (Chilisa, 2020; Ravitch, 2020a). As Nobel Prize–winning economist Amartya Sen (2004) implores, "It is important to reclaim for humanity the ground that has been taken from it by various arbitrarily narrow formulations of the demands of rationality" (p. 51). The moment to reclaim these stolen grounds—literal, metaphorical, educational—is now. We must stand together against current narrow formulations of the demands of "rationality" and their harmful reverberations within schools, across our education systems, and in the research of those systems (we write this acknowledging that we work and live on occupied Lenape land). The term "rationality" could be replaced with the words "colonial violence." The United States of America must decolonize educational leadership, education, and schooling once and for all.

To save U.S. education from its intergenerational commitment to racist social reproduction, leaders must make decisions that take down the master's houses with new tools (Lorde, 1988). To build and access these new tools, we must inquire into and understand how we have been socialized to misunderstand our current tools in education—to count rather than connect, to make competition from collaboration, to reduce transformation into transaction. The ability to identify and upset the tacit beliefs and value systems into which leaders (and those they supervise and serve) have been socialized requires the willingness to question our indoctrination into systems of performance and evaluation based on proscribed forms of social, cultural, and educational capital that reflect and perpetuate an imagined White ideal. This undermines authentic connection and collaboration in schools, classrooms, and communities.

This critical questioning of an oppressive system and its hold on us is what scholar-activist bell hooks (1994) refers to as *teaching to transgress*—creating the conditions to push against the grain of normative White Western value systems. This liberation is framed (and punished) as transgression. hooks and other critical pedagogues (Brayboy, Faircloth, Lee, Maaka, & Richardson, 2015; Davis, 2020; Paris & Alim, 2017) teach us that, in reality, such so-called "transgression" is, in actuality, radical self- and community-care that is vital to well-being—a liberation from the long-term and daily indoctrination that separates leaders (and students, practitioners, and communities) from the sources of our own most imaginative learning and authentic engagement, and from equitably supportive educational ecosystems (Ravitch, 2020b).

In this fraught global and national moment, educational leaders face constant battles and complex stress in their schools and communities as a result of a twin pandemic moment: COVID-19 and racial reckoning in the United States that has reached its arm into schooling with few guides that are customizable to context in real-time ways. As U.S. public schools face rapidly changing demographics and the national landscape becomes more polarizing, educators are faced with exponentializing challenges of how to lead and level up their own skills amidst the current tyranny of the urgent. Alongside civil unrest that ebbs and flows, prioritizing relational authenticity by pushing into established hierarchical norms, foregrounding local wisdoms and kinds of expertise (e.g., activist expertise, student voices, community wisdom), and engaging multiple perspectives and funds of knowledge (González, Moll, & Amanti, 2005) within an ethic of interdependent care is vital for the well-being of everyone in schools. Most importantly, enacting this relational authenticity through the willingness to lead into a *critical inquiry stance* is necessary to lead these times of new accountability.

As a leader, a critical inquiry stance creates humanizing and relational possibilities instead of sustaining useless, divisive, and even harmful knowledge hierarchies and binaries that shape how leaders understand the world and show up. Binaries are reductive and generally false. Moreover, they can do harm (e.g., gender binaries marginalize gender fluid and nonconforming individuals, Black/White racial binaries in conversations about racism oversimplify what is lived in complex intersectional ways and invisibilize people). Identity binaries preclude resonant conversations about intersectionality (Crenshaw, 2021), justice, and equity (Pak & Ravitch, 2021).

Further, disrupting the "expert-learner binary" (Ravitch & Tillman, 2010) that confers dominance on a narrow knowledge hierarchy and marginalizes the experiences, wisdoms, and knowledges of people and groups farthest from dominant power is vital to antiracist leadership and equitable decision making. In shifting to a *distributive wisdom approach*, leaders build a receptive sensibility and create possibilities for dialectics of mutual growth and reciprocal transformation (Nakkula & Ravitch, 1998; Ravitch, 2020a; Ravitch & Carl, 2021). These new communication pathways, norms, and processes, and the meaning frameworks underneath them, help leaders to interrupt the daily transactionalism of schools and, in its place, to offer transformative possibilities through collaborative thought, planning, and action. But how do leaders disrupt the old and harmful and rebuild the new and liberatory, especially when everyone is *exhausted*?

STORYING THE GAPS

School communities—and those who lead and teach in them—must learn to identify and *story the gaps* between our humanity and education as liberation. These gaps in contextualized information, assets-based understanding, and humanizing pedagogy are created by power and the political nature of schooling and broader social and political life. One antidote to the issue of this missing critical information, which serves as a portal to compassion and care in education and schooling, is storytelling. Storytelling can be emancipatory. But all of us, leaders and practitioners, must remember that stories are told and heard within webs of power, context, and axes of structural oppression. These forces shape and constrain possibility in ways that are often invisible and hidden, even to the storytellers themselves given the vicissitudes of oppression and its colonization of how we understand ourselves *and* the world and ourselves *in* the world (Crenshaw, 2021; Ravitch & Carl, 2021).

Schools do not know what to do with stories because the schooling paradigm is not set up for them yet. And, moreover, people often do not share their stories authentically, given that it is often unsafe. If they do, these stories are often not affirmed or engaged with in ways that meet them with affirmation, understanding, and compassion. So many people in schools are misunderstood or never even asked for their opinions, never truly engaged, and therefore rendered invisible. Students and those who teach them are often mischaracterized in stories—their own stories and stories about them—because no racial literacy or brave norms for storytelling exist to support the process, so it does more harm than good. Flux pedagogy situates storytelling within equity praxis to transform ordinary educational moments into portals to healing, connection, and learning (Ravitch, 2020b).

Storytelling, when situated as an intentional enactment of a *brave-space inquiry stance*, helps leaders and organizations become communities of practice engaged in shared inquiry, reflection, and meaning-making. Stories are portals into people's interpretive processes and an empathic understanding of diverse experiences and perspectives. While in some educational circles, storytelling seems new, it is not. As storytelling inquiry is introduced in schools, leaders should name and lift up the long oral traditions of Indigenous peoples, BIPOC (Black, Indigenous, and People of Color) communities, and a range of cultures and groups. Storytelling is increasingly centralized in the education of traditionally minoritized communities as a tool to center their wisdoms, to affirm and contest false narratives of their histories, and to ground and foment critical consciousness and political resistance (Khalifa, 2018). As NativeCrit scholar Bryan Brayboy (2005) shares, "many Indigenous people have strong oral traditions . . . stories remind us of our origins and serve as lessons for the younger members of our communities; they have a place in our communities and in our lives" (p. 439). Amidst grand narratives of deficit, counter-storytelling serves as an analytical tool for challenging dominant narratives and dominating stories by foregrounding the stories of marginalized people and communities (Solórzano & Yosso, 2002).

Similar to these culturally embedded and responsive storytelling approaches, testimonios are first-person accounts, a form of narrative inquiry used in Latinx communities as a tool to center their bespoke knowledges, insights, and histories. By default, testimonios also share and affirm collective, group, and individual experiences. Rosales Montes and Peynado Castro (2020) draw on El Ashmawi, Sanchez, and Carmona (2018) as they explain: "Through our *testimonios*, we explore our lived experiences and bear witness to advance our own liberation, build bridges to reclaim and produce a collective account that is told by us and that is centered on our agency to overcome oppressive barriers" (p. 5). These approaches to intentional storytelling link liberatory approaches to inquiry with storytelling and personal narrative-building and foreground the role of community and relationships of deliberate care in healing-centered engagement processes (Ginwright, 2018).

Storytelling evinces the ways that the personal is political (Hanisch, 1970) and is a profoundly generative approach to leadership, learning, team building, collaboration, and mentorship. When done with fidelity to equity, storytelling creates powerful opportunities for schools to build decolonizing third spaces (Bhabha, 2004) that center critical inquiry, identity expression, affirmation, and preservation for all learners. Storytelling is particularly powerful when focused on re-storying, testimonios, counter-storytelling, and the development of counter-narratives in BIPOC, LGBTQ, disability, and trauma-informed communities. This is so because of the dire need to push back on dehumanizing grand narratives of deficit that infiltrate and constrain people's lives. Often, these dehumanizing narratives circulate within harmful school policies, programs, and pedagogies that uphold dominant and deficitizing values and norms. These narratives can lead to distrust, pain, and opportunity costs for members of our communities (Ravitch, 2020a). How do we begin to tell and listen to liberating stories within our schools given how inequality and racism manifest in the national landscape? This is where brave-space pedagogy and an inquiry stance meet. It is where story-based inquiry is born.

STORY-BASED INQUIRY

Story-based inquiry is a game changer for leaders, teachers, and school communities. When integrated within the processes of brave-space pedagogy, story-based inquiry provides an inquiry framework for schools to engage in the tenets and processes of storytelling. Story-based inquiry centrally acknowledges the unequal power dynamics that exist within and outside school communities that are marked by race, class, gender, religion, and other identity intersections. Story-based inquiry allows for the centering of equitable process and communication norms through a group process approach called *brave spaces* (Arao & Clemens, 2013).

Brave-space pedagogy, central to flux pedagogy and described in depth in Chapter 2, is an approach that helps groups to consciously identify, name, and disrupt daily inequalities disguised in so-called safe-space language with concepts that center and privilege White male priorities and communication norms. Traditionally, these communication norms create conditions that allow only those with proximal power to communicate authentically. This proximal power is shaped by social identity hierarchies as they play out in organizations and teams. Thus, it is an acceptable, if implicit, norm that those from nondominant groups and identities must engage in emotional labor (Hochschild, 1983). Emotional labor refers to the ways that people—most often people of color—must regulate and manage their authentic reactions and emotional expressions at work in order to maintain a veneer of "appropriate" professional conduct. These unspoken-yet-enforced rules are proscribed by dominant White male norms policed through racialized and gendered expectations of what constitutes professional communication and behavior.

Brave-space pedagogy disrupts these pernicious and constraining norms in schools and classrooms. It enables groups to create authentic and equitable communication norms through explicit acknowledgment of, and reckoning with, how people show up in teams, classrooms, and organizations. Creating brave-space norms (Arao & Clemens, 2013), and critiquing the status quo as a foregrounded driver of the process, surfaces critical insights, diverse resources and needs, and lived experiences that may otherwise be neglected, silenced, erased, misunderstood, or relegated to the margins. In these times of radical flux and shared (yet distinct) human suffering, educational leaders must know how to support and work toward brave spaces. They must also have the skills and reach to co-create the conditions for story-based inquiry that promotes healing and centers counter-narratives that are restorative in school communities. *A story-based inquiry approach requires the cultivation of a brave-space inquiry stance.*

Across approaches to storytelling are possibilities for restorative learning and growth, the building of personal and group authenticity and resiliency, self-learning, relational learning, and world learning. Stories, when engaged within a brave-space inquiry stance, become a pedagogical and relational portal into resonant inquiry, contextually engaged insight generation and knowledge production, racial socialization, and positive identity and history affirmation (Stevenson, 2014). Storytelling helps leaders and teams cultivate a sense of agency and hope for critical transformation—personal, group, community—in ever-widening spheres of connecting influence and connection. Stories help groups dismantle deficit thinking and ways they take this on themselves and project it onto other people and groups through deficit educating (Valencia, 2010). In brave-space inquiry, across time and place, storytelling is positioned as a vital process for *undoctrination* from socialized knowledge hierarchies and logics that constrain connection, authenticity, and learning possibilities (Ravitch, 2020a).

Stories are an embodied invitation into our own and each other's critical consciousness (Freire, 1973) and to our liberated being and becoming (Ravitch & Carl, 2021). Brown (2017) offers that "we are socialized to see what is wrong, missing, off, to tear down the ideas of others and uplift our own. To a certain degree, our entire future may depend on learning to listen, listen without assumptions or defenses." Story-based inquiry helps leaders create the conditions for this kind of empathic listening and perspective-taking within schooling contexts. It helps leaders understand that their assumptions and defense mechanisms are human. More important, these defense mechanisms and assumptions are *moveable* with practice. As people, we are always on the way; we are in a process of becoming. This book offers a way to embrace our becoming through a *radical growth mindset* that enables a *distributive wisdom approach* that helps leaders level up without negative self-talk or defensiveness (Ravitch, 2020; Ravitch & Carl, 2021).

BRAVE-SPACE INQUIRY STANCE

A *brave-space inquiry stance*, a process concept central to this book, is an intentional approach to cultivating intra- and interpersonal awareness, racial literacy, and actionable communicative accountability and radical compassion for oneself and others (Ravitch, 2020a) through learning into experiences through stories. Story-based inquiry processes—which include a range of participatory approaches to sharing and listening to individual and group stories—helps leaders make deeper and broader (i.e., more critical) sense of the rootedness of our ideologies and beliefs, and the historical and contextual moorings of our current mindsets, beliefs, and stances. Storytelling within a brave-space inquiry process helps leaders create the conditions for critical examination of our belief systems and the broader social, cultural, political, and structural forces and narratives that shape them (Solórzano & Yosso, 2002). School leaders must exhibit a brave-space inquiry stance for story-based inquiry to transpire in ways that lead to building trust and paving the way for effective and long-lasting change. As Brown (2017) avers, "Liberated relationships are one of the ways we actually create abundant justice, the understanding that there is enough attention, care, resource, and connection for all of us to access belonging, to be in our dignity, and to be safe in community" (p. 18). We must understand each other to engage in this kind of shared future-building.

Story-based inquiry is an intentional storytelling and story-listening model. When situated within a brave space (Arao & Clemens, 2013) remit, it offers a means of learning, confirming, and contesting reality. Story-based inquiry builds and preserves community while conveying knowledge, values, beliefs, and emotions; it allows practitioners and students to engage in grounded and contextualized self-reflection and to become constructively critical of self *and* society and self *in* society (Khalifa, 2018; Stevenson, 2014). As scholar and public intellectual Salman Rushdie (1991) avers, "Those who do not have power over the story that dominates their lives— the power to retell it, rethink it, deconstruct it, joke about it, and change it as times change—truly are powerless, because they cannot think new thoughts" (p. 480). The need to learn to tell our own stories underscores the power stories can have over us and illuminates the power we regain when we engage our stories—individual and collective—through critical inquiry processes.

Through intentional and participatory storytelling processes, leaders learn to identify, reflect on, examine, and re-examine experiences, histories, and values (Khalifa, 2018). And further, leaders, and those they work with, serve, and lead, can learn skills to explore and challenge the meaning, authenticity, and validity of the information they have, to reflect on assumptions, experiences, actions, and inactions to identify motivations and contextual mediators. Finally, intentional storytelling processes help leaders examine how context and history inform thought and behavior patterns in both visible and tacit ways in the daily life of students, teachers, and school communities (Solórzano & Yosso, 2002).

Storytelling within a brave-space inquiry stance is a powerful leadership approach—it constitutes a potent tool for identity-based learning and development. Since this process of telling stories is intentional, reflexive, and relational, it helps to co-create the conditions necessary for leaders to identify, consider, and work to understand their ways of being in communities of challenge and care. Over time, it helps to make sense of the familial and broader social, cultural, educational, and ideological contexts that shape leaders' sense-making and decision making through how they interpret themselves and their experiences in the world (Nakkula & Ravitch, 1998; Stevenson, 2014). As Chimamanda Ngozi Adichie (2009) offers in *The Danger of a Single Story*, "Many stories matter. Stories have been used to dispossess and to malign. But stories can also be used to empower and to humanize. Stories can break the dignity of a people. But stories can also repair that broken dignity" (p. 2). Leaders can engage stories and storytelling to repair all the broken dignity in and around a school. The job of the leader is to shepherd, create and hold space for, engage, and lead from these unique and diverse stories in all of their range and complexity. The job of a leader is to take on the responsibility for centering and bringing stories into the light and moving stories once marginalized or unheard from the gaps and margins to a new center of critical intersectional inclusivity (Pak & Ravitch, 2021).

Given that people's authentic stories are often not spoken, heard, or viewed as important data in the life of schools or in overarching approaches to school improvement and educational leadership, story-based inquiry within brave spaces is a necessary leadership and organizational approach to storying the gaps in schools and in education more broadly. There is a moral and ethical imperative for educational leaders to fill existing gaps of understanding with meaningful and contextualized data rather than top-down metrics, especially in moments of crisis and ever-changing classroom, school, and district conditions. There are tremendous equity gaps in who is heard—often, it is not practitioners; more often, it is not even students, and this is biased along racial and social class lines. And we see in our work that even educational leaders are often not heard—the primacy placed on academic versions and visions of leadership has made more authentic leader narratives hard to find (Pak & Ravitch, 2021).

RAPID-CYCLE INQUIRY

Story-based inquiry is a practical and robust approach to storying the gaps in research and practice and building bridges—through the cultivation of inquiry and the sharing of disciplined stories (Pugach, 2001)—to policy and school change. This book stories these gaps through firsthand accounts of school leaders, in a time of multifaceted crisis and change, engaging in story-based inquiry through a method we have termed *rapid-cycle inquiry* with each other, teachers, students, staff, and communities in a pandemic. Rapid-cycle inquiry provides a robust and sustainable way to engage in story-based inquiry that bridges research and practice in transformative ways, thus moving schools into better places and third spaces. The leaders at the heart of this book enact a brave-space inquiry stance as they work to surface the stories and contextualized data that are all too often either lost or erased, or never sought out in the first place, especially in crisis moments. Appendixes A–D offer process considerations and templates to enact your own rapid-cycle inquiry processes.

A significant point here is this: Stories and storytelling are far from neutral and should not be viewed as such. We must always pay attention to power—the critical understanding that those with the closest proximity to dominant power (i.e., White upper-class power holders) benefit from that proximal power. Specifically, students and communities of color are most often storied without their permission—both living and in textbooks, their stories are sublimated by White narratives and projections, which are most often essentializing and deficit-based, ignoring student and community funds of knowledge (González et al., 2005) and the intragroup variability that exists within every social identity and group (Erickson, 2004; Ravitch & Carl, 2021). BIPOC students and communities are misrepresented and misunderstood through the stories told by researchers and policymakers who most often do not examine or understand contextual mediators or approach their work with criticality about the relationship and role of intersectional identities and structural racism as they shape and mediate students' educational experiences and outcomes (Crenshaw, 2021).

Students of color, and to some extent all students in the United States, are silenced and placed at the margins of their education. Consequently, their stories most often remain untold and unlistened to, which constitutes a huge knowledge gap, even in these dire times when this kind of isolation costs students so very much. Teachers, too, are often storied as a monolith and in ways that deprofessionalize them and keep them siloed and undersupported rather than viewing them as agentic change-makers and transformative intellectuals (Giroux, 1988). Even educational leaders find themselves unstoried, particularly BIPOC leaders—there is a gap of leader inquiry stories that can illuminate the ways educational leaders can transform their practice and make daily decisions that support antiracist pedagogy, equity awareness, and brave-space communication (Arao & Clemens, 2013).

Dominant stories dominate—phrase by phrase, image by image, subjective value by subjective value (disguised as objective values)—and become a purview and a storyboard, forming a sense of self, identity, and trajectory. This formation happens to such a significant (though unconscious) degree that it takes considerable intention and self-reflection to learn to identify and then work to uncover and address how they shape and sediment within our mindsets, ideologies, and behavior patterns (Ravitch, 2020b). Storytelling and inquiry go hand in hand to help leaders and those they serve to construct and enact humanizing approaches to racial literacy development, antiracist professional development, and culturally responsive and humanizing engagement.

Merging storytelling and inquiry helps leaders, and those they serve, build self-literacy that leads to increasing inner calm, a sense of agency, and an ever-growing practice of self-compassion, in relationship, for community/ies, and for the world. Ultimately, this process of reflection, understanding, and addressing internalized, socialized values through storytelling helps leaders re-story and recast themselves and their intersectional identities in bespoke, authentic, and agentic ways (Anderson & Stevenson, 2019).

THIS BOOK: HUMANIZING LEADERSHIP THROUGH INQUIRY

In work during the pandemic, we have found deep and generative inspiration in this inquiry with educational leaders making sense of rapid change and its reverberations. *Flux Leadership: Real-Time Inquiry for Humanizing Educational Change* emerged from a flux leadership community of practice, which was formative to this catalytic approach. We invite you to join us in thinking about *story-based inquiries as timely brave-space inquiry narratives that can push the field forward one school at a time all at once.*

The rapid-cycle inquiries in this book, in all their depth, range, and variation, illuminate the expansive possibilities of story-based inquiry and brave-space schooling contexts. This approach supports the idea of critical leadership praxis as the center of humanizing leadership, whether in crisis or not (Pak & Ravitch, 2021). Praxis is the process of enacting, embodying, and embedding knowledge from lessons, skills, and theories, in/to/for transformational action (Freire, 1985). Each chapter illuminates praxis as part of the inquiry itself, an ongoing process of moving between practice and theory through and in our research (Eikeland, 2012). The educational leader-authored chapters constitute praxis counter-narratives that speak back to and push against top-down narratives that deficitize students and teachers of color, flatten identity complexity, and make growth, healing, and belonging secondary to transactional goals like efficiency, standardization, and strict measurement. The leaders at the heart of this book enacted rapid-cycle inquiries to *story the gaps* in available information so that they could understand how to best serve their constituencies in a time of unimaginable suffering. Rapid-cycle inquiry became a collaborative data-driven mechanism necessary to make decisions for stakeholders in real time.

The educational leaders at the heart of this book were new students in an executive leadership doctoral research seminar when COVID-19 hit. As mentioned, rapid-cycle inquiry was a collaborative method of story-based inquiry utilized in real time in order to answer tough questions, and surface stories that leaders felt had been silenced or erased in times of rapid change in their contexts. Alongside the rapid-cycle inquiries of what happened to its schools and stakeholders during the pandemic, this book explains and details two essential equity-oriented frameworks to teaching and learning and leadership more broadly that supported these leaders in their work: *flux pedagogy* and *flux leadership*. These integrated praxis frameworks allow for stories to be centered in school improvement work. This book provides practitioner-scholars and educational leaders a new way of thinking and taking informed action. Specifically, this approach supports educational leaders' thinking on how and why schools should be utilizing stories to gather data that deeply inform leader and practitioner decisionmaking in times of rapid change.

The collective power of these leader-led inquiries humbles us. Even before the twin pandemics, educational leaders faced an ongoing tyranny of the urgent and needed new tools to navigate the moment. We are excited to introduce a living framework for educational leaders that helps cultivate the kinds of story-based inquiry and brave-space community work that schools need now more than ever. Each story will inspire you to lead with even more compassion for yourself and those you serve and rely upon. These stories will renew your commitment to organizational justice born through shared inquiry and intentional reflection in/on practice.

CHAPTER OVERVIEWS

Chapter 1: Storying the Gaps: Transforming Schools Through Story-Based Inquiry

In this chapter, Ravitch and Kannan share the concept of storying the gaps as a portal into understanding the generative relationships between antiracist pedagogy and leadership, story-based inquiry, brave-space pedagogy, and school transformation. They challenge leaders to take an inquiry-based stance to make the invisible visible. Through this lens of human development, this chapter incites critical action, using this newly constructed positionality to re-story how we see the world and understand whose knowledge matters/must matter within it. To do this, the authors introduce rapid-cycle inquiry, a framework that bridges theory and practice in sustainable and transformational ways. The chapter evinces understanding that when leaders understand self in this way, we actively invite others to do the same—to create brave, humanizing inquiry spaces.

Chapter 2: Flux Pedagogy

In this chapter, Ravitch and Kannan share flux pedagogy as a conceptual framework and action approach for cultivating antiracist, inquiry-based, healing-centered trauma-informed, compassionate, and racially literate pedagogy and responsive school cultures. This pedagogical framework evinces a humanizing alternative for building and sustaining culturally responsive teaching and learning environments. Flux pedagogy recognizes the ways that educators themselves live in a constant state of flux and encourages leveraging existing leadership moments through holding space for critical collaboration in the investigation of sites of education in (and then beyond) moments of precarity and flux.

Chapter 3: Flux Leadership

In this chapter Ravitch and Kannan offer the flux leadership framework for supporting flux pedagogy and enacting antiracist, humanizing leadership that is responsive to and grounded in the tenets of critical pedagogy and healing-centered engagement. The chapter outlines this robust educational leadership framework with corresponding tenets that provide guidance for leadership practices and data-driven decision-making. The chapter provides detailed examples of how to humanize leadership practices within a holistic model that is attentive to contextual factors. It describes how flux leaders can utilize rapid-cycle inquiry to capture and generate data in situations of crisis and rapid change for direct educational improvement.

Chapter 4: Hard Pivot: Compulsory Crisis Leadership Emerges From a Space of Doubt

Andrew Phillips, Kelly Grimmett, and Elizabeth Fernandez-Vina examine what happens amid crisis for educational leaders. They use narrative to understand how identities converge to create isolation and displacement in a moment of crisis. As the first year of their doctoral program begins, so too does COVID-19. A myriad of questions emerge for a cohort trying to make sense of the ways that COVID-19 will forever change U.S. education. Beginning to engage with flux pedagogy, cohort members reflect on their own self-care, specifically rituals and boundaries, during the emerging crisis as a way to conceptualize this moment. The narratives show how crisis continues to impact identity as educational leaders struggle with doubt. To move forward, authors encourage readers to lean into leadership as an inquiry stance. Their inquiry asks questions—*How do we communicate our thinking to our constituents? How do we keep track of everything? What operational systems remain in place?*—as a way to dismantle existing systems and frameworks. Though not without grief, authors encourage leaders to see the possibilities for a bolder, bigger, and more authentic world that this stance and moment creates.

Chapter 5: "And How Are the Children?"

Written by Rahshene Davis, Amelia Coleman-Brown, and Michael Farrell, three school district leaders, this chapter uses rapid-cycle inquiry to intentionally examine how twin pandemics—COVID-19 and racial—impact in/equity for students. Building on the previous chapter, authors fuse flux leadership to critical inquiry stance to center narratives of those most poignantly feeling the impacts of leadership decisions made amid COVID-19: children. Specifically, this chapter bravely seeks to understand how children's safety and well-being ebb and flow during a crisis. Surveying principals, the authors dig into racial trauma amid the pandemic to understand how leadership decisions collide with dynamics of structural, social, and organizational power. To understand how to move forward, the authors argue that we must critically interrogate the now. In doing so, the chapter details the important role that brave spaces play in rehumanizing the dissemination of knowledge. This type of leadership ultimately requires that we grow through grief and help children learn to do this as well.

Chapter 6: Real Talk: Teaching and Leading While BIPOC

In this chapter, Deirdre Johnson Burel, Felicia Owo-Grant, and Michael Tapscott, a group of educational leaders, take on a rapid-cycle inquiry that examines what it means to teach and lead while being Black, Indigenous, or a Person of Color (BIPOC) across educational contexts, including traditional public schools, charter schools, and independent schools. To conduct this work, the authors interview other leaders about their lived experiences, thereby centering the flux tenet of racial literacy. Navigating identity-based stress becomes a central focus for these educators within these moments of flux and paints the backdrop of how they navigate to support their students and stakeholders within their educational contexts successfully. This chapter ultimately reminds us that the flux tenet of a critical inquiry stance is fundamentally premised on one's ability to understand their own racial identity and its connection to the surrounding context in which they serve. The chapter provides a unique lens and perspective that can help readers better understand that leading while BIPOC in a crisis brings forth equity, deficit, and identity issues in both familiar and unfamiliar ways. The centrality of flux pedagogy to the future of U.S. education emerges.

Chapter 7: Systems of Emotional Support for Educators in Crisis

In this chapter, Carla Haith and Jeannine Minort-Kale use rapid-cycle inquiry to understand what was happening behind the scenes with educators navigating the COVID-19 pandemic. Using data through a research effort between Yale Center for Emotional Intelligence and the Collaborative for Social-Emotional and Academic Learning for over 5,000 educators, the authors found that the five most frequent words that teachers used to describe their feelings were "anxious," "fearful," "worried," "overwhelmed," and "sad." To story the gap, authors centralize these questions: *How were school systems working to support these educators' emotional well-being?*

How did educators feel about the impacts of these supports, or lack of, on their well-being and ability to do their jobs?

The chapter shares powerful vignettes that echo the importance of responsive and humanizing leadership to create the systems for educators to feel supported and sustained in these moments.

Chapter 8: Listening Leadership: The Student Voices Project

In this chapter, Manuela Adsuar-Pizzi discusses what it means to lead in crisis and where students factor into leadership decisions in moments of precarity. Centering the Student Voices Project, the author seeks to answer a single question: *Who was listening when students called for help?* The collaborative, informal storytelling initiative of this chapter allowed students to share their experiences unapologetically and reflects the ways that flux leadership embodies the tenet of distributive wisdom. Storytelling in this chapter represents a decolonized form of knowing; students convey their realities through videos, drawings, photos, and other media on social media platforms such as TikTok, Instagram, and Facebook. Through these stories, other questions emerge for the author: *How do students ask questions when confused? Could a series of videos ever replace in-person instruction?* Ultimately, this chapter understands stories as invaluable and humanizing data points. Key takeaways emerge such as understanding how student sense-making of crisis moments must be centered for us to navigate leadership when times are in radical flux.

Chapter 9: Global Engagement, Perspective Sharing, and Future Seeing in and Beyond Global Crisis

Moving outside of a U.S.-centered context, Drew Cortese, Kiet Hoang, and Clare Sisisky explore the fundamental importance of global experiences and transnational identities in shaping leader crisis agility. Amid COVID-19, these educational leaders reflect on the ways that education continues to develop amid an interconnected and globalized world. The authors shed light on how a global perspective can be an educational affordance. In this chapter, interviews from educational leaders across numerous countries—Australia, Brazil, Canada, China, Denmark, France, India, United Kingdom, United States, and Vietnam—provide compelling data to support the intercultural competencies necessary to shape leadership abilities that adapt to the current moment and build into the future. To do so, the authors ask questions that center ideas: *What might it mean to decolonize education? How do global perspectives shape who we are and our leadership decisions?* In this chapter, authors consider how the flux leadership tenet of distributive wisdom is reflected through reaching out to networks across borders and leaning on international partnerships.

Chapter 10: Teaching and Leading During COVID-19: Lessons From Lived Experiences

Karen D'Avino, Muronji C. Inman-McCraw, and Curtis A. Palmore use ethnographic-style, rapid-cycle inquiry to conceptualize what adaptive leadership looks like in the COVID-19 pandemic in three educational leaders' respective sites of practice. As noted in the tenet of critical inquiry stance within flux leadership, adaptive leadership requires a critical perspective when considering the intertwining impacts of the COVID-19 pandemic and racial injustice. Digging into what adaptive leadership looks like within their own context, the importance of responsive and humanizing leadership emerges. This chapter begins rapid-cycle inquiry with a vignette that provides an in-depth examination of what humanizing adaptive leadership moves looked like. The chapter pushes back against the idea that school improvement is all about data sets. The stories in this chapter show why leadership moves should not simply respond to numbers. Leaders should, instead, respond to the hearts of the community they serve.

Chapter 11: Crisis Leader Literacies in K–12 Independent Schools During COVID-19

Three educational leaders, Jessica Flaxman, Christopher J. Hancock, and David Weiner, use rapid-cycle to investigate what crisis leadership looks like within the K–12 independent school context. Through semi-structured interviews with heads of independent schools across the country, authors tease out crisis definitions and various leadership approaches. This chapter shows how various stakeholders complicate leader agility in charting a path forward for leaders. Seeking to answer the question of how crisis leadership is enacted within the context of independent schools, the authors highlight numerous strategies and approaches from all angles, including the emotions embedded within these leadership practices.

Rather than crisis leadership feeling abstract, authors show how independent heads of school make sense of their leadership practices in real time. This chapter centers the flux tenet of what it means to exemplify the characteristics of a reflexive visionary—evolving, emerging, and building through humanizing collective circumstances

Chapter 12: Rituals, Routines, and Relationships: High School Athletes and Coaches in Flux

This chapter, written by Steve A. Brown, generates student-athlete-centered conversations to understand better what it means to humanize learning spaces amid crisis. It reiterates how flux pedagogy enacts criticality to humanize spaces by creating schooling networks and communities that center students and their evolving needs. Specifically, this chapter takes a nuanced look at how athlete as identity both complicates and adds to the way educational leaders create humanizing learning spaces. Using interview data, the author seeks to understand how the support networks, specific to student-athletes, increased their motivation to improve in their sport during COVID-19. Thus, the chapter discusses how educators might leverage the community-cultivated resiliency mindset, emerging from athletics and fueled by athletics-based support structures, to contribute to stronger learning outcomes for student-athletes in times of crisis.

Chapter 13: Story-Based Frameworks and Practices for Educational Change

In the concluding chapter, Ravitch and Kannan take us back to the start of the journey, where 25 students in the mid-career doctoral program searched for frameworks and tools that could translate diversity, equity, and inclusion into action for their schools and districts, with a curated solution. Flux leadership, an educational leadership framework, guides leaders in making humanizing and culturally responsive decisions in times of rapid change. It serves as the final piece of the puzzle, bringing each chapter together to remind us how these doctoral students chapters became flux pedagogy—each critically critiquing existing frameworks to transform their leadership and pedagogical approaches. Again, Ravitch and Kannan bring together the pieces of flux leadership and rapid-cycle inquiry as tools that leaders can use to build the case for why storying the uncomfortable ambiguities in education, through brave-space leadership, is the way forward for a brighter educational future.

REFERENCES

Adichie, C. N. (2009). *The danger of a single story*. TedTalk.

Anderson, R. E., & Stevenson, H. C. (2019). RECASTing racial stress and trauma: Theorizing the healing potential of racial socialization in families. *American Psychologist, 74*(1), 63–75.

Arao, B., & Clemens, K. (2013). From safe spaces to brave spaces: A new way to frame dialogue around diversity and social justice. In L. M. Landreman (Ed.), *The art of effective facilitation: Reflections from social justice educators* (pp. 135–150). Stylus.

Bhabha, H. K. (2004). *The location of culture*. Routledge.

Brayboy, B. M. J. (2005). Toward a tribal Critical Race Theory in education. *Urban Review, 37*(5), 425–446.

Brayboy, B. M. J., Faircloth, S. C., Lee, T. S., Maaka, M. J., & Richardson, T. A. (2015). Sovereignty and education: An overview of the unique nature of Indigenous education. *Journal of American Indian Education, 54*(1), 18–36.

Brown, A. M. (2017). *Emergent strategy: Shaping change, shaping worlds.* AK Press.

Chilisa, B. (2020). *Indigenous research methodologies* (2nd ed.). Sage.

Cochran-Smith, M., & Lytle, S. L. (2009). *Inquiry as stance: Practitioner research for the next generation.* Teachers College Press.

Crenshaw, K. (2021). *On intersectionality: Essential writings.* The New Press.

Davis, W. (2020, August 6). The unraveling of America. *Rolling Stone.* www.rollingstone.com/politics/political-commentary/covid-19-end-of-american-era-wade-davis-1038206

Eikeland, O. (2012). Action research—Applied research, intervention research, collaborative research, practitioner research, or praxis research? *International Journal of Action Research, 8*(1), 9–44.

El Ashmawi, Y. P., Sanchez, M. E. H., & Carmona, J. F. (2018). Testimonialista pedagogues: Testimonio pedagogy in critical multicultural education. *International Journal of Multicultural Education, 20*(1), 67–85.

Erickson, F. (2004). Culture in society and in educational practices. In J. A. Banks & C. A. M. Banks (Eds.), *Multicultural education: Issues and perspectives* (pp. 31–60). Jossey-Bass.

Freire, P. (1973). *Education for critical consciousness.* Seabury Press.

Freire, P. (1985). *The politics of education: Culture, power, and liberation.* Bergin & Garvey.

Ginwright, S. A. (2016). *Hope and healing in urban education: How urban activists and teachers are reclaiming matters of the heart.* Routledge.

Ginwright, S. A. (2018). The future of healing: Shifting from trauma informed care to healing centered engagement. *Medium.* https://ginwright.medium.com/the-future-of-healing-shifting-from-trauma-informed-care-to-healing-centered-engagement-634f557ce69c

Giroux, H. A. (1988). Teachers as transformative intellectuals. In H. A. Giroux (Ed.), *Teachers as intellectuals: Toward a critical pedagogy of learning.* Bergin & Garvey.

González, N., Moll, L., & Amanti, C. (Eds.). (2005). *Funds of knowledge: Theorizing practices in households, communities and classrooms.* Erlbaum.

Hanisch, C. (1970). The personal is political. In S. Firestone & A. Koedt (Eds.), *Notes from the second year: Women's liberation: Major writings of the radical feminists* (pp. 76–78). Feminism.

Hochschild, A. R. (1983). *The managed heart: Commercialization of human feeling.* University of California Press.

hooks, b. (1994). *Teaching to transgress: Education as the practice of freedom.* Routledge.

Khalifa, M. (2018). *Culturally responsive school leadership.* Harvard Education Press.

Lorde, A. (1988). *A burst of light: Essays by Audre Lorde.* Firebrand Books.

Nakkula, M. J., & Ravitch, S. M. (1998). *Matters of interpretation: Reciprocal transformation in therapeutic and developmental relationships with youth.* Jossey-Bass.

Pak, K., & Ravitch, S. M. (2021). *Critical leadership praxis: Leading educational and social change.* Teachers College Press.

Paris, D., & Alim, H. S. (2017). *Culturally sustaining pedagogies: Teaching and learning for justice in a changing world.* Teachers College Press.

Pugach, M. C. (2001). The stories we choose to tell: Fulfilling the promise of qualitative research for special education. *Exceptional Children, 67*(4), 439–453.

Ravitch, S. M. (2020a). Why teaching through crisis requires a radical new mindset: Introducing flux pedagogy. *Harvard Business Publishing Education*. https://hbsp.harvard.edu/inspiring-minds/why-teaching-through-crisis-requires-a-radical-new-mindset

Ravitch, S. M. (2020b). Flux pedagogy: Transforming teaching and leading during coronavirus. *Perspectives on Urban Education, 17*(4), 18–32.

Ravitch, S. M., & Carl, N. M. (2021). *Qualitative research: Bridging the conceptual, theoretical, and methodological* (2nd ed.). Sage.

Ravitch, S. M., & Tillman, C. (2010). Collaboration as a site of personal and institutional transformation: Thoughts from inside a cross-national alliance. *Penn GSE Perspectives on Urban Education, 8*(1), 3–10. https://urbanedjournal.gse.upenn.edu/archive/volume-8-issue-1/collaboration-site-personal-and-institutional-transformation-thoughts-insid

Rosales Montes, I., & Peynado Castro, L. (2020). Finding hope, healing and liberation beyond COVID-19 within a context of captivity and carcerality. *Perspectives on Urban Education*. https://urbanedjournal.gse.upenn.edu/archive/volume-18-issue-1-fall-2020/finding-hope-healing-and-liberation-beyond-covid-19-within

Rushdie, S. (1991). Excerpts From Rushdie's Address: 1,000 Days 'Trapped Inside a Metaphor'. *New York Times*. https://archive.nytimes.com/www.nytimes.com/books/99/04/18/specials/rushdie-address.html

Schein, E. (2013). *Humble inquiry: The gentle art of asking instead of telling*. Berrett-Koehler Publishers.

Sen, A. (2004). *Rationality and freedom*. Harvard University Press.

Solórzano, D. G., & Yosso, T. J. (2002). Critical race methodology: Counter-storytelling as an analytical framework for education research. *Qualitative Inquiry, 8*(1), 23–44.

Stevenson, H. C. (2014). *Promoting racial literacy in schools: Differences that make a difference*. Teachers College Press.

Valencia, R. R. (2010). *Dismantling contemporary deficit thinking: Educational thought and practice*. Routledge.

CHAPTER 2

Flux Pedagogy

Sharon M. Ravitch and Chloe Alexandra Kannan

Everything is in a state of flux, including the status quo.

—Robert Byrne

EMERGING INTO FLUX PEDAGOGY

Flux pedagogy emerged as an equity-oriented pedagogical framework for crisis in March 2020, during the onset of the coronavirus pandemic, as the world, and our lives, drastically changed seemingly in an instant. Although COVID-19 disrupted schooling as we knew it, radical flux has been omnipresent in the educational landscape over the past few decades as issues of racial inequity have dominated the conversations in our strategic planning meetings, professional development, and teaching and learning seminars. In these times of rapid change, educators and educational leaders need tools and frameworks adaptable to crisis and evolving change in real time. What might happen if a pedagogical framework could make sense of this complexity in humane, ethical, culturally responsive, and multifaceted ways? Flux pedagogy promotes the conditions for educational change that uplifts stakeholders in a humanizing manner where their stories and identities matter within teaching, learning, and schooling.

Educational leaders are in an indefinite state of flux trying to navigate the landscape of teaching and learning. Students have unprecedented concerns about their academic lives and futures—what will happen next? How will the realities of today affect them tomorrow? Teachers are also concerned about these issues, suffering higher levels of burnout from the transition to hybrid learning environments, concerns about their well-being, ongoing struggles with managing the stress of child care and their families, and how to support their students in a variety of needs. These are embodied concerns in a time of radical flux—global displacement, racial unrest, schools facing budget cuts, people looking for jobs, juggling employment and family responsibilities, worried about and responsible for their health, family health, and public health. The lines between well and sick, healthy and unhealthy, have blurred, as have other suddenly irrelevant binaries like safe and unsafe, productive and unproductive, distance and connection. Shifting with and meeting the times requires a pedagogical approach that centers and engages this moment of relational and educational uncertainty, upheaval, and reverberation. In meeting this time and taking everything we do in person online, we are met with a dire need for an emergent, responsive, and humanizing education approach: *flux pedagogy.*

Flux pedagogy integrates relational and critical pedagogy frameworks into a transformative and humanizing teaching approach. It is constructivist, student-centered, relational, adaptive, and reflexive; it is an antiracist, humanizing pedagogy that examines the goals and processes of schooling, teaching, and learning through uncertainty with a goal of mutual, durable societal growth and transformation. Given that the main purposes of our courses have shifted seemingly overnight to meet the needs of our students— from specialized teaching and learning to more broadly solutionary and connective in both humanitarian and pedagogical ways—we must shift as well. Flux pedagogy supports an inquiry-based, emergent design teaching mindset that is adaptive, generative, responsive, and compassionate; it is a framework for balancing radical compassion for students with high-yet-humanely-calibrated expectations for their learning in our courses. This global moment requires us to learn new skill sets with a mindset for designing and enacting humanizing and transformative pedagogies with our students even as we teach them specific content areas.

Flux pedagogy integrates critical relational frameworks into a complex adaptive pedagogical approach that identifies and addresses lived problems as a form of radical learning toward informed action. For example, developing your class as a community of practice that can support students in identifying, naming, and pushing against real-time inequities broadly can be the beginning of an emergent critical literacy of educational transformation— an enacted extension of Appiah's (2006) cosmopolitanism as a literacy of human connection and interdependence. This is a universality of concern for all people coupled with the belief that people are entitled to live into their priorities and ideals without the imposition of what others would choose for them. Further, we can, and should, use current global, national, and local struggles—and the gross disparities so vivid across them—as texts in our courses. With these kinds of texts, we can teach literacies of critical inclusivity that support considerably more humanistic and equitable schooling, teaching, learning, and pedagogy development (Pak & Ravitch, 2021).

In being responsible for the education of 25 educational leaders on the front lines in crisis, Dr. Ravitch utilized this complex adaptive pedagogical approach and held space for students to collaboratively explore, process, and investigate their sites of practice that were in the midst of crisis. As a professor of qualitative methods (specifically practitioner research) utilizing flux pedagogy, she enacted a space where students could utilize their own lived experiences situated in current struggles that were layered with inequity to engage in qualitative methods in a critical way. Through a focus on human connection and interdependence, Dr. Ravitch could accomplish the goals of the course in a way that met the needs of the students (as leaders), the needs of worlds they were situated in, and the needs of the people for whom they were responsible.

TENETS OF FLUX PEDAGOGY

Figure 2.1 shows the central tenets of flux pedagogy, which are

1. Critical inquiry stance
2. Healing-centered, trauma-informed pedagogy
3. Radical compassion and radical self-care
4. Responsive and humanizing pedagogy
5. Critical pedagogy
6. Racial literacy
7. Brave-space pedagogy

Figure 2.1. Central Tenets of Flux Pedagogy

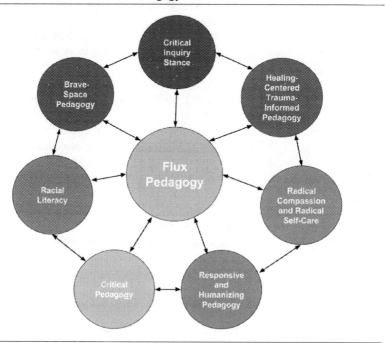

This chapter discusses each of these tenets and engages flux pedagogy as a framework for equitable, responsive, ethical pedagogies that can serve as a compass for educators in crisis.

These theories are not new. Healing-centered and trauma-informed pedagogy, responsive and humanizing pedagogy, critical inquiry stance, critical pedagogy, racial literacy, and brave-space pedagogy are existing frameworks that have proven generative to theory, research, policy, and practice in ways that support more equitable pedagogy than has been the norm. It is in their intentional integration toward antiracist teaching that these theories as frameworks constitute a necessary and useful pedagogical framework in this moment of global, national, state, and local crisis. Together, these frameworks help us to examine harmful social constructions, impositions of asymmetrical power, and hidden structural influences through multiple perspectives in terms of how they shape personal, communal, familial, and intra-psychic experiences ongoingly and during this time of crisis. In our work with superintendents, principals, heads of school, teachers, school counselors, school staff, and students, we've found that the flux pedagogy framework enables the co-creation of a decolonizing *third space* (Bhabha, 2004). Educators can take a reflexive step back, given that this relational space engenders active and empathetic creativity, thought hybridization, active compassion, care, and connection in teaching and learning.

Educational practitioners enact a flux pedagogy approach to help them learn how to push against inequitable norms and power dynamics that create powerlessness, staleness, and hopelessness in schools. Flux pedagogy generates a critical inquiry stance, and through rapid-cycle inquiry, practitioners can generate local data that speak back to the ways that schools and those working within them are pressured and constrained by the current tyranny of numbers. It is a tyranny because the current education system, in many ways, forces professionals to paint by numbers (gathered by others) rather than allowing for the freedom to be innovative place-based knowledge creators (Ravitch & Carl, 2019).

We seek to interrupt the current de-professionalization that pervades the educational system in the United States with a hopeful, critical, and substantive approach to more effective and equitable schooling practices. Flux pedagogy presents a realistic approach to education that can help shift the ethos in schools to more humanizing and equitable outcomes for all stakeholders. This equity-oriented pedagogical framework will help teacher leaders and other educators build more holistic understandings of the range and variation of lived experiences within learning spaces, fostering the conditions for teaching and learning to be more collaborative and community-informed.

CRITICAL INQUIRY STANCE

For apart from inquiry, apart from the praxis, individuals cannot be truly human. Knowledge emerges only through invention and re-invention, through the restless, impatient, continuing, hopeful inquiry human beings pursue in the world, with the world, and with each other.

—Paulo Freire

With all that's going on globally—and in students' and teachers' worlds—educators need frameworks and mindsets that help them identify, examine, and challenge their beliefs about who is knowledgeable and their assumptions about how learning best happens. Educators must learn how to critically examine their mindsets, tacit beliefs, and internalized knowledge hierarchies. Leading from an inquiry stance (Cochran-Smith & Lytle, 2009) means that educators show up—as their raison d'être—as reflective, curious, and engaged learners, not knowledge droppers or performative experts.

This shift in power dynamics, when everyone's wisdom is centralized to push into knowledge hierarchies, constitutes a *distributive wisdom approach*—in which all wisdoms are foregrounded, weighted equally in value, brought into the conversation and hybridized. Co-creating intentional practices and processes for shared knowledge generation elevates everyone and is central to an inquiry stance. In these ongoing fraught times wherein most students, teachers, families, and communities feel helpless, creating the conditions in which they feel agentic and authentic in sharing feelings, perspectives, experiences, ideas, and concerns without fear is vital for learning, positive development, and well-being in and beyond school.

It is vital as an educator to situate yourself as a learner, to examine your ideologies, tacit beliefs, and implicit biases, to work to ever more critically understand how these shape your ideas and professional practice. This effort requires critically reading self with disciplined, curious, and compassionate humility. Inquiry as stance, which is foundational to a flux pedagogy approach, requires that practitioners take a reflexive learning stance on self, professional practice, and the contexts—near and far, personal and societal—that shape their practice, their sites of practice, and understandings of that practice in and beyond the immediate setting. Through intentional, societally contextualized self-reflection that questions what they know and how they know it, practitioners create possibilities for authentic growth and durable learning. Inquiry as stance is a mindset that helps upset normative ideas and knowledge hierarchies to foster an equitable school ecosystem.

Working from an inquiry stance positions everyone as "legitimate knowers and knowledge generators, not just implementers of others' knowledge" (Cochran-Smith & Lytle, 2009, p. 18). A *critical inquiry stance* extends this further by questioning why, in many Western educational contexts, knowledge (epistemology) is valued over values (axiology) and ways of being (ontology) (Ravitch, 2020a). A critical inquiry stance upsets traditional notions of what constitutes valid knowledge and who is a knower by identifying and challenging ways that traditional learning practices, steeped in White Western values and norms, are imposed on everyone as universal. Further, it exposes the invisible yet pervasive imposition of Western hierarchical logics—including the devaluation of emotion, values, and Indigenous wisdoms (Chilisa, 2020). As Nobel Prize–winning economist Amartya Sen (2004) implores, "It is important to reclaim for humanity the ground that has been taken from it by various arbitrarily narrow formulations of the demands of rationality" (p. 51). The moment to reclaim this stolen ground is now. This moment requires us to stand together against current narrow formulations of the demands of rationality and their harmful reverberations in and across all of our systems.

The ability to identify and upset the tacit beliefs and value systems into which we have been socialized, which often undermine authentic connection and true collaboration, requires a willingness to question our own indoctrination into systems of performance and evaluation based on proscribed forms of social, cultural, and educational capital that reflect and perpetuate an imagined White male ideal. Questioning our socialization is what scholar-activist bell hooks (1994) refers to as *teaching to transgress*—going against the grain of imposed normative White Western value systems can be framed (and punished) as transgression. hooks, alongside other critical pedagogues, teaches us that, in reality, such "transgression" is vital to survival and well-being. This departure is liberation from the indoctrination that separates us from the sources of our own most imaginative and authentic learning, and from equitably supportive educational ecosystems and learning environments.

Critical thinking is an evergreen pedagogical value. In this fraught social moment, replete with necessary civil unrest that ebbs and flows in relation to anti-Black and anti-Asian violence, and that will likely continue to do so for some time, prioritizing relational authenticity by pushing into established hierarchical norms, foregrounding local wisdoms and kinds of expertise (e.g., activist expertise, community wisdom), and engaging multiple perspectives and funds of knowledge (González, Moll, & Amanti, 2005) within an ethic of interdependent care is vital for the well-being of everyone in learning communities. A critical inquiry stance foments humanizing and relational learning possibilities instead of sustaining useless, divisive (and even harmful) knowledge hierarchies and binaries that constrain equitable progress on humanizing education.

Binaries are reductive and generally false, and in education they do harm (e.g., gender binaries marginalize gender nonconforming students). Identity binaries preclude meaningful conversations about intersectionality, justice, and equity (Crenshaw, 2021). In shifting to a *distributive wisdom approach*, practitioners can build a more receptive sensibility, become a more responsive solutionary, and create possibilities for dialectics of mutual growth and reciprocal transformation (Nakkula & Ravitch, 1998). These new communication pathways, norms, and processes, and the meaning frameworks behind them, help to interrupt the transactionalism of schools and, in its place, offer transformative possibilities through collaborative and intentional action.

HEALING-CENTERED, TRAUMA-INFORMED PEDAGOGY

Liberated relationships are one of the ways we actually create abundant justice, the understanding that there is enough attention, care, resource, and connection for all of us to access belonging, to be in our dignity, and to be safe in community.

—Adrienne Maree Brown

In this moment of collective trauma, educators must be attuned to student trauma (past and present) as the necessary first step to co-creating an affirming learning community. Trauma-informed pedagogy foregrounds understanding trauma—personal, communal, and intergenerational—and its social and emotional reverberations as central to cultivating a learning environment that can be comfortable and affirming to those who have experienced trauma (Pak & Ravitch, 2021). Moreover, it recognizes the resilience and resources of individuals and communities who have experienced or are currently experiencing trauma. Trauma-informed researchers understand the need to attend to trauma in ways that help people create the conditions to feel agentic in relation to their own trauma. Further, they see the transformative possibilities that post-traumatic growth can generate (Eren & Ravitch, 2021).

Trauma-informed education must address students' lived realities both in and out of school within a healing-centered engagement framework (Ginwright, 2018). As Ginwright envisions it,

A healing-centered approach is holistic involving culture, spirituality, civic action and collective healing. A healing-centered approach views trauma not simply as an individual isolated experience, but rather highlights the ways in which trauma and healing are experienced collectively. The term *healing-centered engagement* expands how we think about responses to trauma and offers a more holistic approach to fostering wellbeing. (p. 2)

This reframe of trauma and trauma-informed care is much needed as the field has residue from a history steeped in eugenics and positivist psychology, with their attendant deficit-oriented and binaried systems of mis/understanding complex lived human identities and experiences (Rosales Montes, 2019).

Ginwright's healing-centered engagement framework invites critique of the deficit language, logics, and practices that can be sedimented yet invisible in trauma-informed approaches (even though they are intended to be person-centered). It has helped me to challenge my own internalized Western logic, which assumes trauma to be an individual experience rather than collective and contextualized. As Ginwright suggests, "By only treating the individual, we only address part of the equation leaving the toxic systems, policies, and practices neatly intact."

The realities on the ground could not be further from Ginwright's humanizing vision of resonant student healing in community. For example, schools and districts often utilize the Adverse Childhood Experiences (ACE) Score as reliable metrics to assess trauma. However, when the ACE was developed, childhood trauma that resulted from systems of oppression and inequity like racism and homophobia were unaddressed (Merrick, Ford, Ports, & Guinn, 2018) and further racial trauma is not addressed. Therefore, ACE falls short in situating a child's trauma within the systems of power and inequity both near and far (Gaffney, 2019). Thus, there is a gap within the metrics that schools utilize to assess student learning, evaluate students in a range of ways, and determine the best-contextualized supports for them. Storying these gaps requires attention to criticality in school processes, practices, and structures; it requires seeing beyond the current logics of schooling because they are not humanizing and are often dehumanizing.

We must situate healing-centered work in the lived realities of racism, homophobia, transphobia, and other systems of oppression that affect our students' lives. It is vital to consider the intersection of trauma with aspects of social identity and structural inequity including culture, gender, ethnic, race, social class and caste, religion, immigrant status, and so on within a framework of critical intersectional inclusivity (Pak & Ravitch, 2021). Without this awareness and intentionality, schools can retraumatize students. Schools must reflect deeply on their role in these inequities and how they play out in policies and other school structures. We must question our learning engagements, selection of readings, and assignments carefully in culturally responsive ways that acknowledge the inequalities within our society that cause harm to our students. When we are critical of school policies and practices that may be deeply implicated in these systems, we can work toward creating more humanizing and affirming spaces for students. In our work, we believe this is about leveraging healing-centered, trauma-informed pedagogies in classrooms.

Healing-centered, trauma-informed pedagogy offers a generative framework and language for responsive and humanizing trauma-informed approaches. Imagining a constructively critical leveling up of the field, Ginwright (2018) avers,

> What is needed is an approach that allows practitioners to approach trauma with a fresh lens that promotes a holistic view of healing from traumatic

experiences and environments. One approach is called *healing-centered*, as opposed to *trauma-informed*. A healing-centered approach is holistic involving culture, spirituality, civic action and collective healing. A healing-centered approach views trauma not simply as an individual isolated experience, but rather highlights the ways in which trauma and healing are experienced collectively. The term *healing-centered engagement* expands how we think about responses to trauma and offers a more holistic approach to fostering well-being. (p. 4)

In this time of collective social trauma—our own trauma and vicarious, secondary, and intergenerational trauma—educators must be attuned to the intersection of both trauma and healing as a necessary foundation for co-creating affirming communities. Healing-centered, trauma-informed pedagogy foregrounds understanding trauma—personal, familial, communal, intergenerational—and its socioemotional reverberations as central to cultivating environments that affirm, recognize, and lift up the resilience and resources of individuals and communities that have experienced/are experiencing trauma.

Healing-centered, trauma-informed practitioners understand the need to attend to trauma in ways that create the conditions for individuals and groups to build a sense of agency and set of stress-navigation skills in relation to their experiences. Further, they see the transformative possibilities that post-traumatic growth, which is "a positive psychological change experienced as a result of adversity and other challenges in order to rise to a higher level of functioning" (Tedeschi & Calhoun, 2004), can generate in groups, teams, and organizations.

Arguing for necessary shifts in the language currently used to conceptualize, discuss, and engage trauma, and for the need to interrupt deficit-based orientations to trauma and replace them with asset-focused and culturally relevant ones, Ginwright (2018) explains:

A shift from trauma informed care to healing centered engagement (HCE) is more than a semantic play with words, but rather a tectonic shift in how we view trauma, its causes and its intervention. HCE is strength based, advances a collective view of healing, and re-centers culture as a central feature in wellbeing. . . . A healing centered approach to addressing trauma requires a different question that moves beyond "what happened to you" to "what's right with you" and views those exposed to trauma as agents in the creation of their own wellbeing rather than victims of traumatic events. (p. 5)

Enacting a healing-centered, trauma-informed pedagogical approach means understanding the need to, and how to, foster conditions and processes that support organizational agility and responsiveness to the daily, lived effects of trauma as a central ethic of practice. It involves becoming knowledgeable about and building informed and compassionate attention toward the range of traumas people face and the effects and possible impacts of these traumas in work environments, including online. As well, it requires understanding how trauma shapes cognitive functioning, relational skills, and engagement styles. Broadly, this means building a concept of trauma as part of community life that can, and should, be seen and affirmed as a mission mode and central organizational stance.

RACIAL TRAUMA AND IDENTITY-BASED STRESS

Beyond simply rejecting deficit perspectives widely attributed to people who have experienced trauma, with a double bind on people of color who experience trauma given its intersection with structural racism, educators must understand racial trauma and identity-based stress as they manifest in teams and organizations. Racial trauma and identity-based stress grow from direct and vicarious discriminatory racial encounters that can impact individuals during and after a stressful event (Anderson & Stevenson, 2019). These discriminatory racial encounters can occur at interpersonal, institutional, and systemic levels (and sometimes occur simultaneously); they are triggered in environments with threats of harm or injury, where there are humiliating or shaming events, and where people observe or experience harm to other people of color due to both real and perceived racism and discrimination (Stevenson, 2014). Understanding the racial and identity-based dimensions of trauma matters, especially in racially fraught times when people feel victimized and vulnerable in a host of ways that relate to political trends, state-sanctioned racial violence, and a global health pandemic.

Healing-centered, trauma-informed pedagogy foregrounds storytelling and re-storying in ways that pay critical attention to contexts that shape and constrains people's lived experience of possibility. This pedagogical approach foments culturally responsive support systems and processes that are informed by an intersectional approach to identity and equity. Storytelling and re-storying processes help shift normativizing myths and social scripts that can keep people locked into patterns of thinking and behavior that are not in the service of their individual well-being or conducive to organizational health (Solórzano & Yosso, 2002). In order to work against the double-deficit discourse attributed to trauma survivors of color in ways that affirm intersectional identities, educators must normalize the reality that *no one is "normal."*

Jettisoning this deficit-generating language is a form of community inclusion, compassion, and care. Communities can choose language, ideas, metaphors, and shared processes that help them to re-story and re-humanize everyone as central, valuable, and worthy of support and respect. Working from and promoting an assets-based approach for each person and with the collective is a vital leader stance. Healing-centered, trauma-informed pedagogy benefits everyone in organizations and teams that impact teaching and learning for students.

With all that's happening in the world, people yearn for a place to name, understand, and process their stress and trauma in community—for their experiences to be seen, heard, and validated, to feel affirmed and connected, and to feel a sense of control over their lives while the world feels so fraught and coarse. People need to be actively supported as they learn to navigate the stress and trauma of the twin pandemics and their aftermath and build inner resources for calm in rolling conflict. Attention to this relational and reflexive aspect of well-being is a necessary foundation for all kinds of learning, collaboration, and development. As Ginwright (2018) offers,

> Healing centered engagement views trauma and well-being as [a] function of the environments where people live, work and play. When people advocate for policies and opportunities that address causes of trauma, such as lack of access to mental health, these activities contribute to a sense of purpose, power and control over life situations. All of these are ingredients necessary to restore well-being and healing. (p. 7)

Healing-centered, trauma-informed practitioners work to understand the emotional and relational dimensions of organizational life and actively consider how trauma histories play out in professional contexts. It is vital to understand that while we are all traumatized by the pandemic in a broad sense, all traumas are not the same. While the pandemic and civil unrest is a kind of shared trauma, it lands into the lives of already vulnerable populations in ways that can cause more severe diffusion effects. People already have trauma histories separate from COVID-19 that must be considered in relation to current stressors and challenges. Educators need to connect with people to ensure that they feel seen and heard, and that they have access to support based on what they share. Understanding the diverse and dynamic ways trauma is lived is vital to creating healing-centered, trauma-informed organizational processes and practices. Understanding the transcendent power of post-traumatic growth creates new individual and organizational possibilities that uplift everyone. Healing-centered, trauma-informed pedagogy is a defining leader mindset and stance in these trying times.

In "The Pandemic Is a Portal," Arundhati Roy (2020) criticizes the humanitarian failure to provide equal protection for all people during coronavirus. Roy contextualizes the COVID-19 pandemic within the long history of global pandemics that have radically altered the world. On this timeline of human suffering, Roy places the COVID-19 pandemic as a necessary portal—an opening that we ourselves can, and must, widen to collectively enact global political, economic, social, environmental, and spiritual change. Roy inspires us to strategically and reflexively unlearn in order to remake forward:

> Historically, pandemics have forced humans to break with the past and imagine their world anew. This one is no different. It is a portal, a gateway between one world and the next. We can choose to walk through it, dragging the carcasses of our prejudice and hatred, our avarice, our data banks, and dead ideas, our dead rivers, and smoky skies behind us. Or we can walk through lightly, with little luggage, ready to imagine another world. And ready to fight for it. (2020)

We must leave behind our dead ideas and prejudices by choosing to "walk through lightly, with little luggage, ready to imagine another world. And ready to fight for it." We must leave the luggage of misunderstanding, pathologizing, and invisibilizing trauma in schools behind us. An informed, imaginative healing is the path forward to collective dignity, belonging, and liberation.

In creating spaces for healing-centered, trauma-informed pedagogy to thrive, we must attune ourselves to trauma and its reverberations, for ourselves and school community. Trauma-informed educators grounded in healing-centered, trauma-informed pedagogy continuously work to understand the emotional dimensions of relational and organizational life and consider how trauma histories play out in learning situations, experiences, and various contexts. It's important to cultivate a critical understanding that all traumas are not the same. While the pandemic is shared trauma, it lands into the lives of already vulnerable populations in a myriad of ways. As well, many people already have trauma histories completely separate from COVID-19 that must be considered.

Given the complexity, simply rejecting deficit perspectives widely attributed to students of color and Indigenous students is insufficient. Educators must identify and acknowledge identity-based trauma and how it manifests in self and systems. For example, racial and identity-based stress grows from direct and vicarious discriminatory racial encounters that can impact individuals both during and after a stressful event (Anderson & Stevenson, 2019). These discriminatory racial encounters can occur at interpersonal, institutional, and systemic levels (and sometimes occur simultaneously); they are triggered in environments with threats of harm or injury, where there are humiliating or shaming events, and where students observe or experience harm to other people of color due to real or perceived discrimination (Stevenson, 2014). This ethic of leader compassion evinces Muriel Rukeyser's (1968) words, "My lifetime listens to yours" (p. 36).

Listening to another's lifetime requires that we gain critical distance from our own. Healing-centered, trauma-informed pedagogy is about making space for individual story and a multiplicity of stories. Enacting this approach requires understanding how we view and interpret trauma within the frames of our own cultures and belief systems. For example, one difference between justice-oriented frames and White Western frames on trauma is the foundational assumption of the latter that trauma recovery means the reclamation of safety. This is built on a problematic assumption that safety is a resource that is "out there" for the universal taking (Cheng Thom, 2020).

The implication of this false notion of safety is a limited perspective on trauma—that all people of color need to do to heal trauma, including racial and intergenerational trauma, is to work harder in therapy or engage in more positive self-talk or self-care irrespective of structural conditions. As Cheng Thom (2020) avers, people of color are not necessarily preparing their bodies to return to a general sense of safety that's widely available. Assuming this uncritically negates the traumatic lived realities of structural racism since people of color may feel they're preparing their bodies/their children's bodies for struggle—training for healthy survival and the ability to experience joy in the midst of threat (Cheng Thom, 2020). A critical understanding of trauma, and the diverse and dynamic ways trauma is lived and conceptualized, is necessary to create inclusive trauma-affirming educational spaces. Moreover, understanding the transcendent power of post-traumatic growth is a defining leader stance in this moment.

Healing-centered, trauma-informed pedagogy creates the conditions for a trauma-informed and humanizing pedagogy that is integrated in a productive manner. In the pandemic and its ensuing aftermath, students need a place to name and process their stress in community—to be seen, heard, and validated, to see that they matter, and to feel connected while the world feels fraught and coarse. Attention to this aspect of student development is a necessary foundation for all other kinds of learning right now—so it is important, for example, to greet each student by name as they come onto your screen, begin each class with warm and compassionate check-ins, and to explicitly discuss the importance of each person engaging in this community as a form of respect and self-care.

As educators, we must educate ourselves to build the skills that identify possible signs of trauma and to connect with our students to make sure they have access to a support system that is healing. As well, it is important to be intentional with our language when discussing topics that might trigger student trauma or distress, for example. Ideally, as educators, we read about ways that we can create the conditions for psychological safety so that we take up an actively supportive role with our students and colleagues.

RADICAL COMPASSION AND RADICAL SELF-CARE

Do you already know that your existence—who and how you are—is in and of itself a contribution to the people and place around you? Not after or because you do some particular thing, but simply the miracle of your life. And that the people around you, and the place(s), have contributions as well? Do you understand that your quality of life and your survival are tied to how authentic and generous the connections are between you and the people and place you live with and in? Are you actively practicing generosity and vulnerability in order to make the connections between you and others clear, open, available, durable? Generosity here means giving of what you have without strings or expectations attached. Vulnerability means showing your needs.

—Adrienne Maree Brown

Radical Compassion

Leaders, teachers, staff, students, parents, and communities are exhausted, working at a pace and intensity that is not sustainable without additional support. This twin-pandemic moment lands into preexisting identity-based privileges and oppressions in important ways. Teachers must take intentional care of themselves for many reasons, including so that they have the energy needed to support their students, teachers, families, and each other. To do this, they must understand how social identities, in terms of their proximity to structural power and resources, are central to student and community experiences of this racially fraught and socially divisive pandemic. The working ability to conceptualize and articulate how systems of domination and marginalization show up daily at the individual, group, and community levels is of utmost importance for justice and equity in schools.

Radical compassion is the internal imperative to understand reality in order to change it. It alleviates the distress, pain, and suffering of others, and views suffering within its macro sociopolitical and socioeconomic realities and contexts in equity-oriented and liberatory ways. The concept of radical compassion stems from criticism of U.S. schools as places that create, exacerbate, deny, and neglect student distress and struggle rather being places that help students achieve optimal development by supporting their struggles, resources. and needs through compassion as a mission mode (Lampert, 2003). When enacted as a pedagogical stance, radical compassion helps educators build connection between ourselves and our staff and students and, through this, to see and invent new possibilities for mutual growth and reciprocal transformation (Nakkula & Ravitch, 1998).

Radical Self-Care

Radical self-care is the practice of radical compassion toward self. Practicing self-care has never felt more urgent than in these socially, politically, economically, medically, environmentally, and spiritually troubling times. Self-care has become part of many people's lexicon. Yet, few consider its deeper vicissitudes, its relationship to social identities and issues of structural discrimination, and the promise it holds for transformative education that supports optimal development. Fewer yet consider self-care to be political. Radical self-care requires examining social and political powers and systems of dominance, grand societal narratives of deficit, and the cultivation of a radical growth mindset. This foundation is built on a critical examination of how the personal is political (Hanisch, 1970)—how structural racism and discrimination mediate people's lives during COVID-19 and the spiraling of the United States in its reckoning. Radical self-care bridges the political and personal in ways that create the conditions for individuals to see that much of what they judge or blame themselves for is systemic and socialized into them as fact.

Radical self-care transcends material pleasantries to focus on the cultivation of liberatory narratives and routines that help people to lovingly revise parts of themselves as a necessary dimension of our work to re-envision and reconstruct the world. As Audre Lorde makes visible through her activism, thought leadership, essays, and poetry—standing in and declaring her own power, speaking truth to unjust structural violence and discrimination and to those who uphold it, taking joyful care of her body, mind, soul, and love as a Black woman were acts of powerful resistance, radical healing, self- and social transformation in a harmful White system with exclusionary logics and dehumanizing policies. Lorde illuminates how in a racist society, replete with misogynoir and intersectional marginalization, self-care is a radical act—a revolution. Lorde (1988) wrote, "Caring for myself is not self-indulgence, it is self-preservation, and that is an act of political warfare" (p. 77). This ethic of identity-mediated radical self-care as a political stance illuminates current struggles for peace and justice in terms of how leaders of justice must be supported. The personal has always been, still is, and will always be—political. A powerful flux pedagogy practice can be found in Appendix E: Radical Student Check-Ins as a Form of Radical Self-Care, written by school leader William N. Thomas, IV.

In *Emergent Strategy: Shaping Change, Shaping Worlds*, Adrienne Maree Brown (2017) positions radical self-care as an emergent strategy for shaping individual and societal liberation through shared healing, interdependent future-imagining, and future-building. Brown's imaginative approach to life-learning evinces the value of living in relationally generative, ecological, authentic, and ethical ways that create the conditions for sustaining personal and collective healing, healthy interdependence, and transformation. Living in this way is as much about unlearning as learning, about imagining beyond the confines of our individual and collective indoctrination into inorganic and dominating values and belief systems that do not serve us well since we understand that everyone's well-being depends on everyone's well-being.

In these dark times, we are blessed by luminaries like Adrienne Maree Brown and Kai Cheng Thom who help us see liberated/ing ways of being. Brown refers to this as an emergent strategy of radical self-help, society-help, and planet-help in which individual liberation connects in ever-more widening circles of liberation in a diffusion effect—a blossoming of equity and transformation. Brown grows the concept that "the only way to deal with an unfree world is to become so absolutely free that your very existence is an act of rebellion" (2017) as an invitation to build our own responsive growth strategies and to integrate this into organizational functioning as a mission mode. These roadmaps for personal growth, relational healing, and societal transformation, built on the margins of an extractive and exclusionary White America, are necessary.

As an educator, encourage and support radical self-care, engage in and model this yourself, and introduce it as part of a classroom culture that invites everyone to take care of themselves. By advancing discussions of self-care during such pervasive suffering and dis-ease, and by engaging in these critical conversations in our own lives, leaders help teachers, staff, and students develop their identity- and pandemic-related stress-navigation skills, including racial literacy, radical self-care, and radical compassion. In turn, we enable the development of authentic communication pathways that sustain in these relentlessly trying times. Pedagogies of critical hope, love, and interdependent care (Freire, 1997; hooks, 2003) must be centralized. Further, across these growth processes, leaders can learn, model, and teach that, as Holocaust-surviving social psychologist Viktor Frankl wrote, humans can create an internal space of transcendent power even, and perhaps especially, amidst moments of intense suffering, stress, and powerlessness. Frankl (1946) teaches us how to cultivate a safe inner-world within threatening and unsafe external realities, he avers,

> Between stimulus and response there is a space. In that space is our power to choose our response. In our response lies our growth and our freedom. (p. 18)

Educators and students can cultivate this space as an inner-resource, an internal space of quiet curiosity they invoke in moments when calm feels inaccessible, when they experience physical and existential threats (Frankl, 1977). They must give themselves and those around them not only permission, but also an enthusiastic invitation to engage in learning the skills of humble inquiry—calm, nonjudgmental, authentic curiosity toward ourselves and each other. Educators must critically examine how we interpret, make meaning of, react to, and behave by working to notice and compassionately challenge our socialized knowledge, embedded cognitive distortions, and implicit biases—to see how they shape our values and approaches.

From this, we can work with communities to build bridges of capacity together. These bridges ensure that one is left behind so that the concepts of left and behind no longer even make sense. To build these inner resources practitioners use their *emotional imagination*, discussed in depth in the next chapter, to cultivate an inner *third space* (Bhabha, 2004). A third space is an intentional, creative, and reflexive dimension within us that enables the practice of meta-analytic self-reflection toward deeper self-knowing, internal calm, healing, relational compassion, and the cultivation of a *radical growth mindset*. Given that leader well-being is significantly tested by increased exposure to organizational turbulence, this intentional and creative (rather than habituated) meaning-making space is essential right now.

In these times, educators need opportunities to build inner resources as a central dimension of their strategy. While the world feels unsafe, teachers can model and teach that each person can—within self—create a reliable inner-space. They can do so by observing their own struggle and evaluate if their stress is a healthy kind that motivates or the unhealthy kind that immobilizes (Hanson, 2018). Leaders can build—and help teachers, students, staff, and communities to build—a shared ethic of interdependence, conflict resolution, relational self-trust and compassion, and self-care.

What's "radical" about radical compassion and radical self-care is their unwavering focus on political, embodied intersections between equity, identity, individual and social transformation. To discuss self-care without foregrounding the political nature of social identities as lived dimensions of structural discrimination that significantly stress our bodies and minds undermines efforts for equity. Without considering the political, we create false privilege and moral equivalencies that help people in power at all levels abnegate their responsibility in upholding White supremacy, White entitlement, and gaslighting people of color, people with disabilities, and other marginalized populations by acting as if they can herbal tea and bubble bath their way out of structural conditions that place undue stress, suffering, opportunity and trajectory costs, and disproportionate disease burden individually and as a group.

In the news every day is evidence of how the preexisting, chronic, systemic racism of the U.S. health care system already in motion before the pandemic creates a diffusion effect of racial suffering during COVID-19. Radical self-care can help educators and students feel calm within themselves while the world around them is chaotic. This includes identity and emotion affirmation, structures and processes of psychological support, storytelling, counter-storying, and re-storying processes (Khalifa, 2018; Stevenson, 2014), and cultivating racial mindfulness strategies that help students identify and skillfully manage identity-based stress (Anderson & Stevenson, 2019; Ravitch & Carl, 2019).

A powerful enactment of radical compassion and self-care is storytelling and re-storying, a process that can shift normativizing myths and socially constructed scripts that keep people locked into patterns not in the service of their well-being (Solórzano & Yosso, 2002). Generations, for example, have understood the concept of "normal"—a mythology steeped in White male heterosexual upper-class ableism—as a way to exclude, pathologize, and minoritize individuals and groups who "deviate" from a White dominant set of assumptions, values, and frames that undergird all facets of society and schooling (Annamma, Boelé, Moore, & Klingner 2013). U.S. history cannot be separated from racism, eugenics, and settler colonialism. It is time to do away with deficitizing impositions of "normal" altogether by supplanting reductive and hegemonic language and narratives with complex, layered stories of our own and each other's diversity, uniqueness, multiplicity, and complexity (Annamma, 2017; Rosales Montes, 2019). Educators must take a stance that *no one is normal*—jettison this deficit-generating language as a form of radical compassion and radical self-care, choose language and ideas that re-story and re-humanize everyone.

Communal re-storying enables individuals and groups to identify, reckon with, reframe, and move beyond the harmful myths and societal scripts that shape sense of self, hopes, and life choices (Stevenson, 2014). Re-storying helps people learn to review past experiences and renew their conceptualizations of self that no longer serve them well (and perhaps never did). Learning to re-index formative experiences that shape self-narratives is a powerful approach to building an authentic sense of self, healthy thinking, and liberating choice making (Anderson & Stevenson, 2019).

Importantly, re-storying helps people cultivate authentic and liberating stories, to hear their inner voices that have often, as they learn in talking them out in community, been ignored (even by them) because they were buried underneath internalized social scripts (Stevenson, 2014). Re-storying helps people to build counter-narratives to the grand narratives of deficit that they often turn on themselves and each other. Re-storying also actively cultivates inner voices that are increasingly liberated from harmful social constructions and cognitive distortions that rule people's inner lives and corrode healthy relationships (including with ourselves) if not identified, explored, and addressed. Radical self-care is the process of envisioning and enacting our bespoke-yet-relational paths forward into a healthier, less burdened, and more agentic vision of self in/and the world.

RESPONSIVE AND HUMANIZING PEDAGOGY

> We are socialized to see what is wrong, missing, off, to tear down the ideas of others and uplift our own. To a certain degree, our entire future may depend on learning to listen, listen without assumptions or defenses.
>
> —Adrienne Maree Brown

Learning happens best when it is active, responsive, and contextualized. In this moment of global, institutional, and personal flux-induced stress, educators must take pause to consider the ways this crisis lands into each student's life. Crisis lands differently given status and finances, whether or not students have family and community supports, and how students have unique coping mechanisms formed from past experiences that may or may not serve them well in the present moment. It is important that we focus on our students in these moments of crisis so that we can help them to face their realities calmly and with a sense of structure, agency, and support.

Learning experiences during and post-pandemic must approach emotional well-being as central, help students traverse complex systems during chaotic times, build relational trust, and view pedagogical flexibility as an ethical stance, wherein everyone's knowledges and insights are actively valued and called into play, thereby shaking hierarchical norms to become more of a learning collective in a time of chaos and shared vulnerability. This applies to changes in assignments, responsibilities, and presentations.

For our students' socioemotional health and well-being, we need to actively consider their levels of stress—including re-entry post-pandemic—as we plan each class and send communications about changes in assignments. Specifically, we must be aware of how a student's situation, as it changes over time, may influence their ability to engage or to collaborate on group projects. This awareness is about flexibility as an ethic of practice in times of chaos and flux, about being actively student-centered as we work to understand students' individualized experiences in the context of broader social and political forces so that we can actively support them.

For educators to be responsive to their constituencies and engage in humanizing pedagogy while the world feels so threatening requires educator responsiveness within teaching and learning. Creating this milieu around change is absolutely vital so that schools are in a position to respond to the array of demanding needs of urgent change for students and their families and communities. Leading through such extreme and continuously unfolding change requires a higher-than-the-usual-high tolerance for the unknown. Educators must demonstrate that they can respond quickly, calmly, and with clarity by making timely and culturally responsive decisions with a focus on the most vulnerable in the communities they serve, while being able to function not only the onset but the duration of the crisis at multiple levels (Darkow, 2018). This is ongoing, as new crises seem to erupt by the minute since March 2020.

In this moment of global, institutional, familial, and interpersonal stress, teachers must actively consider how this time lands into each student's life differently in relation to status and finances, whether or not students have family or community supports, and how people have unique coping mechanisms formed from past experiences that may or may not serve them well in the present moment. The realities of COVID-19 and ongoing civil unrest add urgency to the call for *critical intersectional inclusivity* in our schools. As Pak and Ravitch (2021) offer,

> Critical intersectional inclusivity adds additional layers of analysis to enactments of inclusivity in groups and organizations. A critical intersectional analysis

interrogates the ways in which traditionally inclusive policies and practices may disenfranchise, exclude, or repress some identities while privileging and advantaging others. A critically inclusive organizational environment or group ethos fosters the democratic participation, acceptance, and belonging of students and adults with a range of identities and continuously redistributes resources and opportunities until non-dominant identities are equally valued and foregrounded as dominant ones. Critical intersectional inclusivity recognizes and works to eliminate individuals' experiences with intersectional forms of marginalization within so-called inclusive organizations and groups. (p. 7)

This means considering representation in your learning spaces and addressing marginalization within and across identity dimensions within an ecosystem of interdependent care for teachers and students. While students must remain everyone's focus and priority, it's vitally important to pay attention to teacher well-being in these moments of crisis, to help teachers face challenging pedagogical realities with a sense of structure, agency, and with the needed support for all they are being asked to do. To actively engage students during and beyond class time, teachers must quickly become facile in synchronous online teaching and, further, proactively support their students in learning these technologies as well. It is important to work collaboratively with teachers and help them to create the conditions for seamless, calm, and highly engaging learning environments for and with students. This is vital to their sense of safety, engagement, and to their sense of belonging to a community of interdependent concern, justice, and care (hooks, 2003).

Teaching and learning must centralize emotional well-being, help teachers, students, and communities develop the skills they need to traverse complex systems in chaotic times. Teaching and learning must also build relational trust, and view pedagogical flexibility as an ethical stance, wherein everyone's wisdom and expertise are actively valued. Embracing this mindset requires us to shake hierarchical norms and become more of a learning collective in a time of chaos and shared vulnerability (Hanson, 2018). For the socioemotional health and well-being of students, teachers must actively engage in responsive and humanizing pedagogy. Engagement translates into a receptive sensibility in relation to their own emotions and stress levels during communication and conflict. This enables teachers to communicate more effectively in fraught moments—for example, when communicating sudden changes in plans given how overwhelmed everyone feels right now.

Specifically, teachers must be aware of how people's situations change throughout the pandemic and influence their ability to engage and collaborate in various ways. This awareness is about flexibility as an ethic of teaching and learning in a time of radical flux, being actively student-centered by working to understand individualized experiences in the context of broader sociopolitical forces and actively supporting students through this time.

Now more than ever, students need help navigating the complexities of the world and their lives. Issues emerge by the day, and students struggle to figure out their feelings about Black Lives Matter, #SayHerName, and #MeToo. Entangled in the coarseness of social media, youth tend to have less relational outlets than when school was physically in session. Young people are struggling against the backdrop of a pandemic that's changed their lives in every way; they are struggling to make sense of and navigate a social media landscape rife with bullying, misinformation, and stressful information related to their own struggles and fears.

CRITICAL PEDAGOGY

The world as it was, is, or will be, is beyond common sense, beyond natural understanding: it must be taught.

—Masood Ashraf Raja

Critical pedagogy situates and engages students as agentic knowers who investigate, question, and critique social and educational norms in relation to their own experiences; it is a framework in which students learn to challenge traditional educational practices that reinforce inequitable arrangements of schooling—students viewed as passive recipients of teacher knowledge transmission; it can also locate teachers as transformative intellectuals in systems that often deprofessionalize them (Giroux, 1988). Critical pedagogy positions students as critical citizens who have the will and skill to act as agents of change. Cultivating students' *critical consciousness* is part of a process of building education as an antiracist practice of freedom (Freire, 1970, 1973; hooks, 1994). It helps students work together to create the conditions in which they can cultivate a sense of agency in relation to what many experience right now as helplessness, confusion, and hopelessness.

In a Freirean conceptualization of critical literacy, real-life struggles are texts to read and decode as/in a process of building new, liberating literacies that interrupt and supplant Western hegemonic ones and that help educators build culturally responsive teaching (Freire, 1970, 1997; hooks, 1994). The pandemic and movement for racial justice offer wide-ranging opportunities for constructing new critical literacies—opportunities to re-read, re-write, and re-enact education as an agentic project of freedom-building and to reject oppressive structural constraints sedimented into the education system long before coronavirus. The texts of pandemic life offer wide-ranging opportunities for developing critical literacies that can evince informed action amidst chaos and upset. Reading inequities as texts of liberation means that leaders enact a mindset of critical intersectional inclusivity, a term that speaks to the need for recognizing and eliminating traditional structures, policies, and practices that disenfranchise, exclude, and repress intersectional identities while privileging others, which truly is the goal of critical leadership practice (Pak & Ravitch, 2021).

Education for critical consciousness refers to the development of critical understandings that enable reflection on social and political contradictions as grounding for action to improve living conditions as they are illuminated by emergent learning (Freire, 1973). As it pertains to teaching and leading during crisis, this creates openings for cultivating critical understandings of the arrangements and limitations of our own educational experiences by transforming them into educational movements of disruption and reinvention. This requires that we move into our most flexible and humanizing pedagogies, the pedagogies of critical hope and love (Freire, 1997; hooks, 2003), as we work to minimize opportunity costs by supporting abundance rather than scarcity in learning. Abundance-oriented mindset is the heart of critical pedagogy, and it is vital to engage with our students as active meaning and changemakers (Love, 2019; Santamaría & Santamaría, 2013).

All educators can learn a great deal from this crisis by reading it as a living text that offers opportunities to foreground, hybridize, and engage local literacies, values, and ways of being rather than relying on media and government to tell us what we value and need. Re-storying crisis is necessary so that all educators stop deferring to a mythological, hegemonic center that reproduces White male dominance and pushes all "others," along with their values, logics, resources, and needs, to the margins (Love, 2019; Tuck & Yang, 2012). As we construct critical literacies for this moment, we rebuild education differently, but only if we reject the continued conferral of dominance onto people, structures, and processes that have corroded possibilities for true educational equity from the beginning of the United States. To do this, we need to understand racial literacy within an intersectional framework (Crenshaw, 2021). We can't forget for a moment that preexisting life conditions shape each person's experience of the pandemic. Do not assume your experience is similar to staff or students, or that their experiences are similar to each other. Examining your implicit biases in this is vital.

Storytelling and re-storying are forms of critical pedagogy, intentional approaches to cultivating intra- and interpersonal awareness. Storytelling is powerful for all students. It engages them in inquiry, reflection, and meaning-making by creating portals into their own interpretive processes and the experiences and perspectives of others. While in some educational circles storytelling is considered new, educators must be aware of the long oral traditions, including storytelling, of many peoples, communities, tribes, and cultures. Storytelling is increasingly centralized in the education of traditionally minoritized communities to center their wisdoms, affirm and contest false narratives of their histories, and ground and foment critical consciousness, civic engagement, and political resistance (Khalifa, 2018). As Brayboy (2005) shares, "many Indigenous people have strong oral traditions . . . stories remind us of our origins and serve as lessons for the younger members of our communities; they have a place in our communities and in our lives" (p. 439).

Concerning societal narratives of deficit, counter-storytelling serves as an analytical tool for challenging dominant narratives and dominating stories by foregrounding the stories and storytelling of marginalized people and communities (Solórzano & Yosso, 2002). Similarly, testimonios are first-person accounts, a form of narrative inquiry used by Latinx communities to center their knowledges, insights, and histories, to share and affirm collective, group, and individual experiences. Rosales Montes and Peynado Castro (2020) draw on El Ashmawi, Sanchez, and Carmona (2018) as they explain: "Through our *testimonios*, we explore our lived experiences and bear witness to advance our own liberation, build bridges to reclaim and produce a collective account that is told by us and that is centered on our agency to overcome oppressive barriers" (p. 36). Storytelling is a deeply generative approach to learning, providing powerful embodied opportunities to build decolonizing third spaces (Bhabha, 2004) of identity expression, affirmation, and preservation for all learners. It is particularly powerful when focused on re-storying, counter-storytelling, and counter-narratives in BIPOC (Black, Indigenous, People of Color), LGBTQ, disability, and healing-centered communities given the powerful need to push back on dehumanizing grand narratives and the harmful policies, programs, and pedagogies they generate and uphold.

Critical pedagogy cultivates students' sense of agency and possibility in relation to what's happening globally and in their lives (Santamaría & Santamaría, 2013). A powerful approach to social justice work in schools is Participatory Action Research (PAR). PAR is an action research process in which leaders, teachers, and/or students work together as applied research teams. A generative approach to critical pedagogy and youth leadership cultivation is YPAR (Youth Participatory Action Research), which "is an innovative approach to positive youth and community development based in social justice principles in which young people are trained to conduct systematic research to improve their lives, their communities, and the institutions intended to serve them" (YPAR Hub, n.d.). YPAR can help students:

Redefine expertise—youth produce knowledge about their own lives.
Develop inquiry, evidence, and communication skills important to being agents of change in their schools and communities.
Generate findings to illuminate issues and generate resources for solving those issues.
Promote sociopolitical development and psychological empowerment to understand roots of problems facing their communities; build skills and motivation to take action.
Evaluate programs, policies, and practices that affect them (adapted, YPAR Hub, n.d.).

YPAR can be a transformational experience for youth and everyone around them because it enables critical engagement with local data gathered by those living the realities they seek to understand and transform. YPAR helps youth learn research, leadership, collaborative data collection and analysis, and how findings can inform school policy, practice, and pedagogy.

RACIAL LITERACY

you are a story. do not become a word. one word. because you want to be loved. love does not ask you to be nothing for something.

—Nayyirah Waheed

Racial literacy is the ability to read, recast, and resolve racially stressful encounters and navigate identity-related stress. In Stevenson's racial mindfulness and socialization framework, "Read" means the ability to decode racial subtexts, subcodes, and scripts, to accurately interpret the meaning-making of actors and actions in racially stressful encounters that arise in relation to written materials, social discourse/media, and social interactions. "Recast" means the ability to reduce stress in racially stressful encounters using racial mindfulness and racial socialization practices which reduce, recast, and reframe racial stress in racially stressful encounters and helps people to build racial self-efficacy and confidence (Stevenson, 2014). This practice relies on telling, sharing, and taking in people's stories of race, including our own.

Racial literacy includes reading race through the lens of intersectionality. As Crenshaw (2017) describes it,

> Intersectionality is a lens through which you can see where power comes and collides, where it interlocks and intersects. It's not simply that there's a race problem here, a gender problem here, and a class or LBGTQ problem there. Many times that framework erases what happens to people who are subject to [some or] all of these things.

Racial literacy requires a critical understanding of intersectionality and structural systems of power and domination. This is important to understand because it relates to how people locate ourselves in conversations about race, identity, and equity. In the United States, people tend to understand and discuss race in Black and White binary terms, as we see all too often in group discussions on identity. Racial literacy requires understanding intersectional identities (i.e., being a Black woman means facing gendered racism, being Asian and transgender means multiple axes of oppression). As Dr. Howard Stevenson shares in racial literacy sessions, "*Everyone* has a powerful and important racial story," meaning that we are all racialized beings living within a racialized system. We all have racial identities and racial experiences whether we've been socialized to see and understand this or not. Therefore, and importantly, we all need racial mindfulness, and we all configure into racial literacy, racial stress, and navigating identity-related stress. Educators must read themselves into racial literacy and push back against identity tropes and binaries because they reduce people and are false.

It is crucial for teachers to stand up for intersectional racial justice. As representatives of a system that imposes racial and identity-based stress on BIPOC students and communities, all school leaders and practitioners must take an active stand against school and district cultures and policies that engender or allow microaggressions, the imposition of White fragility, the masking of racial bullying and toxic positivity under the guise of safe spaces (Chiu, 2020). These classes or meetings, as the teachers, staff, and students from marginalized identities in them know, are often White-dominating spaces that create racially stressful encounters for people of color (Anderson & Stevenson, 2019). The Black Lives Matter movement is not just about racial terror outside the walls of schools, but also inside schools and classrooms, as the Black@Movement shows so clearly.

Understanding where you are on the continuum of racial literacy happens through continued practice of "courageous noticing and admitting" to self (Edwards, 2016)—about your own patterns of tension, conflict, and struggle. Dr. Howard Stevenson's work on racial literacy and navigating identity-related stress situates racial mindfulness as a central node of school leadership, focusing on the professional development and support of teachers, students, parents, and school communities as a whole right now. It's useful in these learning moments to remind people that (1) racial stress matters and it is distinct from general stress and therefore requires specific skills; (2) racial encounters matter and must be attended to for healthy resolve; (3) it is vital to approach racial literacy as a practice of racial competence, not as an issue of flawed character; (4) organizational contexts broadly, and educational contexts specifically, are socialization hubs of avoidant and dysfunctional racial coping; and (5) people can resolve racial stress in everyday life, which leads to better learning experiences, life experiences, and health outcomes (Stevenson, 2014).

Racial Encounter Coping Appraisal and Socialization Theory (RECAST) is an approach to developing racial literacy and learning to navigate racial and identity-based stress through the intra- and interpersonal process of recasting imposed stories or versions of self. RECAST is a framework for understanding how people "anticipate, process, and respond when confronted by racially stressful encounters" (Anderson & Stevenson, 2019, p. 66). The resolve part means navigating racially stressful encounters toward a healthy conclusion through communicating affection, protection, correction, and connection during racially stressful encounters, which requires preparation and practice. By identifying and naming racially stressful situations and creating curious and compassionate awareness of our affective and cognitive responses in these moments, we can re-story ourselves more agentic ways that make room for healthier experiences. Storytelling is a powerful practice for recasting and resolving racially stressful and traumatizing experiences in groups since it allows for neural coupling and empathy, leading to deeper understanding and authentic connection (Stevenson, 2014).

Being a racially literate educator means creating the conditions in which everyone in the organization practices racial literacy and mindfulness so that they can experience interaction through an active racial empowerment framework (Stevenson, 2014). In this case, this enables people—teachers, staff, students, and families—to cultivate identity-focused tools and coping strategies that they can immediately employ when stressed or tense during conversations about identity and equity or in racialized communication. A racially literate educator understands there are always varying (and conflicting) levels of racial literacy and identity-related self-awareness as well as tolerance for tension and disagreement within groups and organizations (Stevenson, 2014). Educators need new skills to read a room (or screen) to gain a sense of where people are in their racial identity development and with respect to their identity-based coping skills. We must be able to feel into people's discomfort, frustration, and seek out feedback on how to best respond to what's shared and presented with a clear and steadfast vision of equity.

There's no panacea for engaging racial and identity-based stress—your own and others'—that emerges during conversations about race, identity, and justice. However, building your reflective capacity and skills in this area through creating your individualized education plan for racial literacy is the first step. Once you've taken up this work as an ethic of practice, design and steward generative discussions in ways that contribute to

1. a more authentically engaged milieu;
2. less cognitive dissonance and increased capacity to cultivate and maintain equitable systems, norms, and processes;
3. a sense of community, compassion, connection, and belonging; and
4. the prevention and de-escalation of tensions and disagreements.

Cultivating your own racial literacy is necessary to support colleagues and students to do the same. Racial literacy helps practitioners build and sustain a learning culture ready to deeply examine issues of inequity, social identity, racial literacy, and identity-based stress, and that can do so critically, supportively, and productively (Stevenson, 2014).

Developing racial literacy and racial mindfulness through storytelling is "a means of learning, confirming reality, preserving community, and conveying knowledge" (Khalifa, 2018) that allows educators to "ease into self-reflection and become self-critical without public scrutiny" (Stevenson, 2014). In this crisis, wherein social identity directly shapes people's lives broadly and their everyday pandemic experiences, racial storytelling is an important, powerful, vital tool for building an understanding of identity-based stress and trauma; it helps people to co-create the conditions for teachers, students, staff, and community members to engage in healing conversations about what's happening in their lives in relation to the pandemic and current racial strife. Storytelling helps people feel into each other's racialized experiences and share resources, challenges, and ideas; it helps people feel connected and valued, and over time, to understand the impacts of social, cultural, and political forces on individual and collective experiences. Further, it shows the generative value of equitable and authentic dialogue about racial inequality in schools (Melanated Educators Collective & the Racial Justice Organizing Committee, 2020).

Consider Stevenson's (2014) CLCBE Racial Stress and Mindfulness and Management Model—Calculate, Locate, Communicate, Breathe, and Exhale. *Calculate* it (on a scale of 1 to 10, how stressful was the racially stressful encounter? Did it shift, spike?), *Locate* it (find in your body where you feel the stress; be detailed.), *Communicate* it (tell yourself, "I'm feeling stressed at the level of 9 and I feel it in my left leg, which is twitching"; tell a trusted peer or disclose within the dynamics of your work), and *Breathe* and *Exhale*. This is a powerful approach to individual and group processing of racial and identity-based stress. For yourself, and then with staff and students, develop new routines and rituals that help build a positive relationship with thoughts and feelings about race and equity. And, further, to foster understanding of the mind–body connection in racial stress by seeing firsthand how emotions speak through our bodies, engage in racial literacy strategies such as storytelling, journaling, debating, and role-playing.

Model and facilitate racial literacy and racial mindfulness in your classrooms and teacher leadership teams. As part of this, attune yourself to the norm that people of color are often expected to do emotional labor (Hochschild, 1983) in relation to White people, in the ways that White fragility is imposed on staff and students of color, and in the ways that microaggressions happen without being named. Speak—and think—in terms of people's complex lived experiences in and beyond the organization. Racial literacy requires and promotes critical intersectional inclusivity (Pak & Ravitch, 2021). For example, understand that the Black Lives Matter movement is a humanitarian movement that should not be suppressed, and also that it may feel marginalizing to some LGBTQ students, so ensure there are spaces in which they can feel seen and affirmed (Reid, 2020). Relatedly, work on nonbinary gender language and the language you use to refer to all minoritized populations. Finally, to model a radical growth mindset, invite staff and students to offer observations and suggestions to you relative to specific topics and language choices on your verbal and written communication.

BRAVE-SPACE PEDAGOGY

If the structure does not permit dialogue, the structure must be changed.

—Paulo Freire

Within a school, learning experiences and well-being are always an educator's responsibility, but that responsibility has gotten exponentially broader and deeper since March 2020. It's vital to (1) approach colleagues and students' emotional well-being as central to learning; (2) support staff, students, and families traverse inequitable and complex systems and stressful relational moments within those systems; (3) build relational trust with and between students, staff, and leaders; and (4) view pedagogical flexibility as an ethical stance, wherein everyone's insights are actively called into play in a time of chaos and collective vulnerability (Melanated Educators Collective & the Racial Justice Organizing Committee, 2020). This vulnerability, if harnessed collectively with clarity and vision, can help move individuals and groups into their most resonant, uplifting, and humanizing pedagogies—the pedagogies of hope and love (Freire, 1997; hooks, 2003)—which is needed now more than ever.

Brave spaces refer to a set of communication and process norms that invite, create, and uphold the conditions for authentic, equitable, and critical dialogic engagement in groups, teams, classrooms, and organizations (Arao & Clemens, 2013). Brave spaces directly contrast to so-called "safe spaces," which serve to uphold White male middle-class heterosexual norms of communication (see Table 2.1). The cultivation of brave spaces requires leader and group bravery as well as ongoing leader modeling and engagement so that people feel comfortable enough to discuss educational, social, and group dynamic issues in ways that go deeper than what is typically discussed given identity-privilege-based norms that tend to marginalize people of color and undermine equality in groups (Ravitch & Carl, 2019).

All educational practitioners must develop competencies and norms for enacting assets-based pedagogies and rejecting deficit-based ones to foster the conditions for authentic brave spaces rather than false "safe" spaces (Arao & Clemens, 2013). Importantly, the promise of safe spaces sets up expectations that can ultimately create unsafe realities that are harmful and even re-traumatizing, particularly with respect to racial trauma for people of color (Baker, 2020). As Colón (2016, p. 1) avers, "There is no space in the real world where harm can be prevented 100% of the time, and while we can collectively struggle for physical and emotional safety, the revolution lives in handling conflicts, even and perhaps especially violent conflicts, lovingly and bravely." Brave spaces take a radical growth mindset to the relational realm vis-à-vis understanding individual roles in group communication norms.

Table 2.1. Characteristics of Safe and Brave Spaces

Safe Spaces	Brave Spaces
Prioritize notions of politeness of some	Prioritize honesty and authenticity for all
Primacy on socially constructed idea of comfort when discussing difficult issues; comes with invisible rules	Acknowledge discomfort is inevitable in discussing difficult issues and invite it as a constructive process/experience
Can lead to defensiveness, lack of authenticity and reflexivity, deflection	Value risk taking, vulnerability, learning, and being challenged to reflect
Narrowly define safety, usually stemming from a dominant White male middle-class ableist perspective imposed as norm	Safety means different things across people, attend to how individuals experience it to reach group understanding and norms
Tend not to prepare participants to engage in difficult conversations; reinforce "taboo topics" and marginalization of POC	Prepare groups for difficult conversations; develop understandings of critical dialogic engagement as professional development

Importantly, the very act of inviting the concept of a brave space is a departure from current practices that do not support BIPOC students, teachers, and communities. This can mark the beginning of new group dynamics and accountability in organizations and classrooms because it acknowledges what anyone who is marginalized in the room already knows: Those with social and institutional power (or proximity to that power) get to decide and reinforce what constitutes appropriate communication (Arao & Clemens, 2013; Ravitch & Carl, 2019). Educators must ensure that brave-space processes are brought to fruition in direct relation to the practices of racial literacy and racial mindfulness and that they are enacted with fidelity to antiracism and critical intersectional inclusivity (Pak & Ravitch, 2021).

Engaging in intentional processes of developing brave-space norms is critically important; a single conversation does not create brave-space accountability. Leaders can use this for teams. Teachers can facilitate the development of brave-space norms in classrooms. It is important that brave-space norms be developed through a collaborative face-to-face (even if virtual) group process. As an example, the Anti-Defamation League (2020) offers these norms for moving to a brave-space classroom:

1. Be open to different and multiple viewpoints and perspectives, especially those that differ from yours.
2. If people share experiences and feelings that are different or unfamiliar to you, show respect by taking them seriously and understand the impact of your response.

3. Explore, recognize, and acknowledge your privilege.
4. Even if you are uncomfortable or unsure, contribute and take risks.
5. Make space by sharing speaking time; try to speak after others who have not spoken.
6. Listen actively, even and especially when people say things that are difficult to hear.
7. View the candor of others as a gift.
8. Find ways to challenge others with respect and care, and be open to challenging your own points of view.
9. Work hard not to be defensive when people challenge what you say or the impact of your words.
10. Commit to confidentiality and not disclosing what people say; at the same time, take responsibility for sharing important messages and themes outside the group/class. Remember that "stories stay, lessons leave." (Anti-Defamation League, 2020)

Developing brave-space norms that foreground collective accountability, authenticity, radical compassion, and radical self-care moves teams, classrooms, and schools forward. To take a brave-space leadership stance, begin by building your understanding and explicating your rejection of the problematic false construct of safe spaces. Share the need for re-norming and describe how re-norming requires seeing, naming, and examining problematic and hurtful norms in groups. Leaders must build a focused understanding of norms that serve to protect BIPOC students and teachers and to name White fragility and White entitlements to people of color's emotional labor. Do, model, and facilitate "emotional labor scans" (Ravitch, 2021) and pay attention to emergent patterns. Then make deep and wide changes in these workplace dynamics.

MOVING INTO FLUX PEDAGOGY

Contemplating these emerging realities, the words of bell hooks (1994) speak to critically hopeful presence in education and offer a way to imagine and build forward:

> The academy is not paradise. But learning is a place where paradise can be created. . . . with all its limitations, [it] remains a location of possibility. In that field of possibility we have the opportunity to labor for freedom, to demand of ourselves and our comrades, an openness of mind and heart that allows us to face reality even as we collectively imagine ways to move beyond boundaries, to transgress. This is education as the practice of freedom. (p. 52)

Like hooks, we believe that education is a location of immense possibility even with its limitations and constraints, especially right now in the world. The possibility we need right now lies precisely in finding, creating, and re-creating the desire and will to view working toward freedom as an opportunity. The work of demanding of ourselves, our students, and our colleagues an openness of mind and heart can help us face the realities of the less than ideal society in which we live as we strive to move beyond the borders that confine our lives and our work. While the work of socially transformative teaching requires considerable focus and energy, our freedom and our individual and collective growth and survival are at stake. To see what these processes look like in practice, see this book's final chapter.

REFERENCES

Annamma, S. A. (2017). The pedagogy of pathologization: Dis/abled girls of color in the school-prison Nexus. Routledge.

Annamma, S. A., Boelé, A. L., Moore, B. A., & Klingner, K. (2013). Challenging the ideology of normal in schools. *International Journal of Inclusive Education*, 17(12), 1278–1294.

Anderson, R. E., & Stevenson, H. C. (2019). RECASTing racial stress and trauma: Theorizing the healing potential of racial socialization in families. *American Psychologist*, 74(1), 63–75.

Anti-Defamation League (2020). *Moving from safe classrooms to brave classrooms*. Anti-Defamation League.

Appiah, K. A. (2006). *Cosmopolitanism: Ethics in a world of strangers*. W. W. Norton.

Arao, B., & Clemens, K. (2013). From safe spaces to brave spaces: A new way to frame dialogue around diversity and social justice. In Lisa M. Landreman (Ed.), *The art of effective facilitation: Reflections from social justice educators* (pp. 135–150). Stylus.

Baker, A. (2020). An activist-therapist's 15 affirmations for hope amidst COVID-19. *Medium*. https://themighty.com/2020/04/hope-affirmations-coronavirus-covid-19

Bhabha, H. K. (2004). *The location of culture*. Routledge.

Brayboy, B. M. J. (2005). Toward a tribal Critical Race Theory in education. *The Urban Review*, 37(5), 425–446.

Brown, A. M. (2017). *Emergent strategy: Shaping change, shaping worlds*. AK Press.

Cheng Thom, K. (2020). Ask Kai: Advice for the apocalypse. https://kaichengthom.com

Chilisa, B. (2020). *Indigenous research methodologies* (2nd ed.). Sage.

Chiu, A. (2020). Time to ditch "toxic positivity," experts say: "It's okay not to be okay." *The Washington Post*. www.washingtonpost.com/lifestyle/wellness/toxic-positivity-mental-health-covid/2020/08/19/5dff8d16-e0c8-11ea-8181-606e603bb1c4_story.html

Cochran-Smith, M., & Lytle, S. L. (2009). *Inquiry as stance: Practitioner research for the next generation*. Teachers College Press.

Colón, K. R. (2016, August 7). At Freedom Square, the revolution lives in brave relationships. *Truthout*. https://truthout.org/articles/at-freedom-square-the-revolution-lives-in-brave-relationships

Crenshaw, K. (2021). *On intersectionality: Essential writings*. The New Press.

Crenshaw, K. (2017). Kimberlé Crenshaw on intersectionality, more than two decades later. Interview. Columbia Law School.

Darkow, P. M. (2018). Beyond "bouncing back": Towards an integral, capability-based understanding of organizational resilience. *Journal of Contingencies & Crisis Management*, (14), 1–12.

Edwards, J. (2016). Personal communication with Dr. Howard Stevenson.

El Ashmawi, Y. P., Sanchez, M. E. H., & Carmona, J. F. (2018). Testimonialista pedagogues: testimonio pedagogy in critical multicultural education. *International Journal of Multicultural Education*, *20*(1), 67–85.

Eren, N. S., & Ravitch, S. M. (2021). Trauma-informed leadership: Balancing love and accountability. In K. Pak & S. M. Ravitch, *Critical leadership praxis: Leading educational and social change* (pp. 187–200). Teachers College Press.

Frankl, V. E. (1946). *Ein psycholog erlebt das konzentrationslager*. Verlag für Jugend und Volk. (In German)

Frankl, V. E. (1977). *Trotzdem ja zum leben sagen: Ein psychologe erlebt das konzentrationslage*. Kösel. (In German)

Freire, P. (1970). *Pedagogy of the oppressed*. Continuum.

Freire, P. (1973). *Education for critical consciousness*. Seabury Press.

Freire, P. (1997). *Pedagogy of the heart*. Continuum.

Gaffney, C. (2019, Summer). When schools cause trauma. *Learning for Justice* (62) .62. https://www.learningforjustice.org/magazine/summer-2019/when-schools -cause-trauma

Giroux, H. A. (1988). Teachers as transformative intellectuals. *Teachers as intellectuals: Toward a critical pedagogy of learning* (pp. 121–128). Bergin & Garvey.

González, N., Moll, L., & Amanti, C. (Eds.). (2005). *Funds of knowledge: Theorizing practices in households, communities and classrooms*. Erlbaum.

Hanisch, C. (1970). The personal is political. In S. Firestone & A. Koedt (Eds.), *Notes from the second year: Women's liberation: Major writings of the radical feminists* (pp. 76–78). Radical Feminism.

Hanson, R. (2018). *Resilient: How to grow an unshakable core of calm, strength, and happiness*. Crown.

Held Evans, R. (2018). *Inspired: Slaying giants, walking on water, and loving the Bible again*. Thomas Nelson.

Hochschild, A. R. (1983). *The managed heart: Commercialization of human feeling*. University of California Press.

hooks, b. (1994). *Teaching to transgress: Education as the practice of freedom*. Routledge.

hooks, b. (2003). *Teaching community: A pedagogy of hope*. Routledge.

Ginwright, S. (2018). The future of healing: Shifting from trauma-informed care to healing-centered engagement. *Medium*. https://ginwright.medium.com/the -future-of-healing-shifting-from-trauma-informed-care-to-healing-centered-enga gement-634f557ce69c

Khalifa, M. (2018). *Culturally responsive school leadership*. Harvard Education Press.

Lampert, K. (2003). *Compassionate education: Prolegomena for radical schooling.* University Press of America.

Lorde, A. (1988). *A burst of light: Essays by Audre Lorde.* Firebrand Books.

Love, B. L. (2019). *We want to do more than survive: Abolitionist teaching and the pursuit of educational freedom.* Beacon Press.

Melanated Educators Collective & the Racial Justice Organizing Committee (2020). *10 demands for radical education transformation.* Melanated Educators Collective & the Racial Justice Organizing Committee.

Merrick, M. T., Ford, D. C., Ports, K. A., & Guinn, A. S. (2018). Prevalence of adverse childhood experiences from the 2011–2014 behavioral risk factor surveillance system in 23 states. *JAMA Pediatrics, 172*(11), 1038–1044.

Nakkula, M. J., & Ravitch, S. M. (1998). Matters of interpretation: Reciprocal transformation in therapeutic and developmental relationships with youth. Jossey-Bass.

Pak, K., & Ravitch, S. M. (2021). *Critical leadership praxis: Leading educational and social change.* Teachers College Press.

Ravitch, S. M. (2020a). Flux pedagogy: Transforming teaching and leading during Coronavirus. *Perspectives on Urban Education, 17*(4), 18–32.

Ravitch, S. M. (2020b). Why teaching through crisis requires a radical new mindset: Introducing flux pedagogy. *Harvard Business Publishing Education.* https://hbsp.harvard.edu/inspiring-minds/why-teaching-through-crisis-requires-a-radical-new-mindset

Ravitch, S. M. (2021). *Equitable teaching takes time and practice here are strategies to help: How to prepare yourself—and your students—to discuss race, identity, and equity.* Harvard Business Publishing: Education.

Ravitch, S. M., & Carl, M. N. (2019). *Applied research for sustainable change: A guide for education leaders.* Harvard Education Press.

Rosales Montes, I. (2019). "I feel like I'm the same as the other students": Negotiating language policy used to identify students as English learners and disabled. Dissertation on ProQuest. https://repository.upenn.edu/dissertations/AAI13857108

Rosales Montes, I., & Peynado Castro, L. (2020) Finding hope, healing and liberation beyond COVID-19 within a context of captivity and carcerality. *Perspectives on Urban Education, 18*(1). https://urbanedjournal.gse.upenn.edu/archive/volume-18-issue-1-fall-2020

Roy, A. (2020). The pandemic is a portal. *Financial Times, 3*(4). https://www.ft.com/content/10d8f5e8-74eb-11ea-95fe-fcd274e920ca

Rukeyser, M. (1968). Käthe Kollwitz. *The speed of darkness.* Random House.

Russo, A. (2018). *Feminist accountability: Disrupting violence and transforming power.* New York University Press.

Santamaría, L. J., & Santamaría, A. P. (2013). *Applied critical leadership in education: Choosing change.* Routledge.

Sen, A. (2004). *Rationality and freedom.* Harvard University Press.

Solórzano, D. G., & Yosso, T. J. (2002). Critical race methodology: Counter-storytelling as an analytical framework for education research. *Qualitative Inquiry, 8*(1), 23–44.

Stevenson, H. C. (2014). *Promoting racial literacy in schools: Differences that make a difference.* Teachers College Press.

Tedeschi, R. G., & Calhoun, L. G. (2004). Posttraumatic growth: Conceptual foundations and empirical evidence. *Psychological Inquiry, 15*(1), 1–18.

Tuck, E., & Yang, K. W. (2012). Decolonization is not a metaphor. *Decolonization: Indigeneity, Education & Society, 1*(1), 1–40.

Waheed, N. (2013). *Salt.* Nayyirah Waheed.

YPAR Hub. (n.d.) http://yparhub.berkeley.edu/

CHAPTER 3

Flux Leadership

Sharon M. Ravitch and Chloe Alexandra Kannan

As the demographics of the nation rapidly change, Black female school
superintendents continue to persevere and keep the commitments they
have made to the children, the families, and the communities they serve.
The lived leadership experiences of Black female leaders in the 21st century
can facilitate a new look at the principles of leadership in education. The
question remains: Are our research communities in educational leadership
ready, "in the thick of battle," to fill the gap?

—Judy Alston, 2005

THIS LEADERSHIP MOMENT

Even before the pandemic crisis of COVID-19, educational leaders were
constantly forced to reckon with change. Judy Alston, a preeminent educational leadership scholar, reminds us that the ever-evolving changes and
rapid flux that our educational leaders must contend with are situated
within larger sociopolitical forces around race, class, gender, and injustice.
Before the pandemic, our demographics were evolving rapidly, our budgets
were being slashed, our communities were caught in the middle of polarizing views on education, and our world had penetrated our board meetings
and classroom walls.

While COVID-19 was a moment of entry for these conversations, our
25 students in the Mid-Career doctoral program were clamoring for frameworks and tools that could translate diversity, equity, and inclusion into
action for their schools. To embark on this call for action, flux pedagogy
creates humanizing and equitable learning conditions that support educational leaders. In turn, flux leadership, an educational leadership framework, was born. Flux leadership, a framework that guides our educational
leadership students to write the rest of the chapters for this book, provides
a multifaceted framework to guide leaders in making more humane, ethical,
and culturally responsive decisions in times of rapid change.

As an educational leadership framework, flux leadership acknowledges that stories and narratives matter when making decisions in times of rapid change. Judy Alston avers that the "lived experiences of Black female leaders" allow for new understanding within the educational leadership field. From Alston's perspective, the research in educational leadership has gaps, and these voices are often lost. We could not agree more and ask what other gaps have we not reckoned with yet? *Whose voices are missing? What identities and complexities are under-represented? What tools do we not yet have?*

We feel that the educational leadership research field is missing crucial stories from and narratives of educational leaders, teachers, students, community members, and other stakeholders, which have deep ramifications— not only for research but for practice. To set the stage for flux leadership, we provide context on how we fostered these learning conditions for our educational leadership students to engage in flux leadership.

During the onset of the COVID-19 pandemic in March 2020, teachers were at a loss of how to respond in a moment that was ever-changing. In a matter of days, everyone recognized that "education as the great equalizer," already a contested phrase, was being replaced with, "how do educators and students survive in this moment?" Teachers needed to adjust to online instruction, students needed to help younger siblings with online learning, and parents were forced to become teachers overnight. These sudden changes become compounded with tech issues, loss of community connection, and grieving the lost routines of our lives: high school sports, the middle school spring play, PTA meetings, faculty collaboration time, and graduation. The inequality is made worse when families are made up of front-line workers at grocery stores and medical facilities. Then add the economic devastation to the pandemic: the threat of eviction and lost income. In these moments, flux pedagogy was created to support our educational leadership students, and provide a model for teaching and learning, which fostered the learning conditions needed for this moment and beyond (Ravitch, 2020a).

Flux pedagogy is a mindset and a corresponding set of practices for enacting critical and humanizing pedagogy in a moment of radical flux. While this framework for teaching and learning was conceived during COVID-19, it is grounded within something more timeless: It is a mindset grounded in an adaptive and compassionate pedagogical approach that views classrooms as complex adaptive systems of care (Ravitch, 2020a). Flux pedagogy responds to context and social issues as they manifest in real time. For example, over the past year, we have seen racial turmoil come to a breaking point: social response has erupted to speak out against state-sanctioned police brutality, racialized carcerality, and anti-Asian hate crimes. These realities influence the learning environments within our schools and communities, and flux pedagogy provides a pathway for responsive teaching when educators and students have unprecedented concerns about their lives.

Given that all stakeholders are concerned about their communities and their lives being disrupted in ways that affect daily experiences, livelihoods, and well-being, it is essential that both pedagogical choices and leadership decisions must be grounded in this contextualized reality. In the context of COVID-19, educational leadership was being forced to reckon with some difficult challenges: strategic plans were no longer relevant, teachers unions stated publicly they did not feel safe to go back to in-person teaching, and standardized tests were no longer possible. What does leadership mean when a leader must respond to so much inequity while navigating ongoing change and crisis management? What do these leadership practices look like? How can educational leaders navigate times of radical flux in a manner that can promote sustainability while also being able to adapt in ways that are data-driven?

FLUX LEADERSHIP FOR CHANGE

In this time of radical flux, flux leadership offers a set of mindsets, frames, and practices for being responsive to emergent school and community needs that humanizes every aspect of school. Flux leadership is premised on the idea that researchers and practitioners are "in the thick of battle" (Alston, 2005). In turn, a flux leadership mindset and corresponding tools provide an approach to capture data in ways that promote the conditions for educational change. The approach includes tenets that uplift stakeholders and generate contextualized data amid crisis and rapid change. While our educational leaders at the heart of this book were relatively new students in an executive doctoral research seminar when COVID-19 hit, they were in desperate need of a way to gather and make sense of data relevant to their practice, for humanizing schooling in crisis, and to leverage authentic collaboration.

While COVID-19 has brought unprecedented challenges into education, educational leaders have been forced to navigate and make decisions in contexts that have been plagued by rapid changes and deep-seated inequities. Thus, our leadership framework strives to be comprehensive and inclusive in the ways that it approaches decision-making within leadership. First, navigating ongoing change within schooling and education is stressful. We believe that employing a flux leadership mindset in response to change provides an unprecedented opportunity: to disrupt and reinvent schooling, teaching, and the field of education, and to embrace the socially transformational. In addition to crisis management, on a broader level, educational leaders must listen to, engage with, lift up, and advocate for marginalized voices and silenced concerns (including their own for leaders of color) as a mission mode.

To do this, educational leaders need frames, approaches, and supports to make sense of these new realities and their implications for their leadership, teachers, staff, communities, and colleagues, and for the field of education. The deep structural inequity, hyper-individualism, greed, and neoliberal transactionalism of the United States education system—with its sidestepping of racial equality and systematic marginalization and dehumanization of Black, Brown, Indigenous, and Asian students and communities—must be countered by constructively critical, transformational leadership and pedagogical approaches that this moment of radical flux makes room for, and that our collective humanity demands. In these moments, we need a model that is willing to think about and approach these complexities in new ways and provide leaders with an alternative in how to think about their own leadership in both crisis and times of rapid change.

INTRODUCING FLUX LEADERSHIP

This moment of social and educational rupture, upheaval, struggle, advocacy, and hope, of taking much of what we do in person online, of re/evaluating the "hidden curriculum of schooling" that marginalizes, oppresses, and deficitizes people of color and Indigenous communities (Santamaría & Santamaría, 2013) provokes, as it underlines, the dire need for humanizing, equity-focused leadership and pedagogy. *Flux leadership* is a framework that supports leader learning agility, self-awareness, and cultivation of important mindsets—to support flux pedagogy. As a framework for teaching and learning, flux pedagogy brings together and integrates critical practice frameworks—critical inquiry stance; healing-centered, trauma-informed care; radical compassion and radical self-care; critical pedagogy; racial literacy; and brave-space pedagogy (Arao & Clemens, 2013)—as the foundation on which leaders develop, enact, and support assets-based and antiracist organizational norms, processes, and structures.

Flux leadership, like flux pedagogy, integrates relational and critical pedagogy frameworks into a humanizing and contextualized leadership approach. It is constructivist, adaptive, and reflexive; it is a humanizing framework that helps leaders examine the systems and processes of schooling toward the goal of fomenting transformative teaching and learning. Flux leaders support their teachers in enacting flux pedagogy—teacher pedagogy cultivated in and for an adaptive, responsive, racially literate, critical inquiry mindset and ecosystem. Flux pedagogy supports healing-centered, trauma-informed pedagogy and balancing radical compassion for students (and teachers) with high-yet-humanely-calibrated expectations for learning, engagement, and performance (Eren & Ravitch, 2021; Russo, 2018). This multifaceted moment—and all the ones to come—necessitate that leaders build new mindsets and skills for inspiring transformative pedagogy and the co-construction of dialogic spaces to make sense of crisis leadership moments and foment equitable organizational development.

Equally important to creating the conditions for flux pedagogy to flourish within classrooms and learning spaces, flux leadership brings humanizing and contextualized decision-making to the forefront of its model. In doing so, the leadership model acknowledges an urgency and necessity for educational leaders to utilize everything in their toolbox in times of radical flux to make data-driven decisions that are best for their school community. The distinction in our model is that we argue that meeting the moment might require looking at what we already have in a fundamentally different manner.

The flux leadership model is grounded in the idea that "it takes a village," and those community stories are often missing or marginalized as crucial data points in both the literature and educational leadership practice. As educational leaders, it is our responsibility to "story the gaps" with contextualized information to make the best decisions for our school community in these times of rapid change and stark inequality. In March 2020, our educational leadership doctoral students needed both support and a way to answer critical questions emerging in real time: *How are the children, what are the leadership challenges for our BIPOC leaders, or what should systems of emotional support look like for our teachers?* In response to the urgency of surfacing these narratives, these students pivoted from their traditional, individual qualitative pilot studies to investigate more pressing issues as a collaborative team. Within their educational leadership seminar, our educational leadership doctoral students engaged in a flux leadership practice called *rapid-cycle inquiry* to investigate these types of questions through a story-based inquiry model. As a collaborative data process, rapid-cycle inquiries are an ethical and applied mechanism to gather and analyze data through the centering of stories; the rest of this book sheds light on what this applied work can look like for your school's most pressing concerns.

To gather data for a rapid-cycle inquiry, flux leadership as a model centers the concept of brave spaces. While brave spaces in flux pedagogy serve as an important mechanism for thinking through problems of practice, immediate goals, and emerging concerns to investigate further, brave spaces as the focal point of the flux leadership model symbolize the place where the narratives and stories of our schools and communities live and breathe. Within schools, educational leaders and stakeholders must mobilize in a way where everyone can come together to share their experiences around a particular concern. The utilization of these spaces to surface these narratives are essential to help schools move forward in times of rapid change or crisis. Power and identity must be engaged as central to designing and enacting these conversations and storytelling processes. Appendixes A–D offer process considerations and templates to start your own rapid-cycle inquiry processes.

Flux leadership is a model guided by the belief that stories are an under-utilized and vitally important data point to guide school improvement, whether in moments of change or crisis. While school improvement has often been guided by the stringent demands imposed on educational leaders as a result of No Child Left Behind and Race to the Top, flux leaders ask whether there are other data points to guide schools forward during times of imminent change and through crisis. What insights can be gained from the long-standing members of our communities healing from decades of racial injustice in their neighborhoods? How are students experiencing this moment? What is happening that no survey or standardized test can tell us? Utilizing insights from stories is not a novel concept. Indigenous communities already center stories in their approaches to making decisions. But in these communities, sharing stories is a safe practice amongst a trusting collective. In schools, there is a difference. Educational leaders must create the groundwork to build spaces where stakeholders feel compelled and safe to share their stories, given the diversity of experiences that constitute a school community.

We also argue that centering a flux leadership mindset can create the conditions for flux pedagogy to flourish through an equity-focused leadership approach. To center flux pedagogy, we foreground its primary tenets here since flux leadership creates the conditions for flux pedagogy to grow, thrive, and be sustained in organizational culture, strategy, and functioning. As presented earlier, the central tenets of flux pedagogy are

1. Critical inquiry stance
2. Healing-centered, trauma-informed engagement
3. Radical compassion and radical self-care
4. Responsive and humanizing pedagogy
5. Critical pedagogy
6. Racial literacy
7. Brave-space pedagogy

The groundwork to create these spaces for stories to be shared, data to be humanized, and communities to heal and thrive can be found within the other tenets of flux leadership shown in Figure 3.1: Critical Inquiry Stance, Racial Literacy, Crisis Agility and Reflexive Visionary, Radical Growth Mindset and the Emotional Imagination, Distributive Wisdom Approach, Inner Resource Cultivation, and Responsive and Humanizing Leadership.

As mentioned, brave-space leadership falls into the center of this model because we believe that a leader must engage in the other tenets thoughtfully

Figure 3.1. Central Tenets of Flux Leadership

in order to create the conditions for brave spaces to thrive as a space of school improvement and healing. While these seven tenets of flux leadership are essential to creating brave spaces in schools, there is a crucial emphasis on leaders being willing to develop a mindset of *leader learning agility* to engage in this framework. Leader learning agility is the ability to actively learn and enact crisis leadership skills in periods of radical change. When leaders situate themselves as intentional learners in unfamiliar, challenging, and even threatening (in the identity sense) experiences, they are better able to apply emergent lessons in real time. For example, when specific policies or understandings of equity-oriented topics such as structural racism or intersectional identities are challenged, leaders must be able to respond in informed ways that connect, not deflect, and that are justice focused and supportive. Leading with a *radical growth mindset* means engaging with colleagues, students, teams, parents, and community members as active thought and action partners. This helps leaders foster the conditions for people to come together to identify and address current struggles—and the racial and socioeconomic disparities across them—as living texts that advocate for critical intersectional inclusivity and racial justice in schools (Pak & Ravitch, 2021).

Flux leadership is a model for equitable, responsive, and agile leadership. This chapter explains each of these central tenets in depth and sheds light on the importance of incorporating these processes into school culture. This chapter provides essential insight into how a flux leadership mindset works on the ground and how leaders must make urgent decisions regarding how systems of power and oppression impact our school communities. The central tenets of flux leadership are built upon the foundation that leaders must identity and examine their views and choices through the prism of antiracist curriculum, teaching, and schooling. Reflecting and challenging ourselves in this way happens through collective reckoning—learning from multiple perspectives on personal, communal, and familial educational experiences and how these are mediated by intersectional identities and systemic forces (Pak & Ravitch, 2021). These professional practices constitute core competencies leaders must have (and build) now. A flux leadership mindset enables leaders to understand the impacts of structural racism on schooling and how their social identities show up and shape what they offer—and do not offer—their school communities. In times of radical flux, *No Justice, No Peace* must be the underfloor of schooling, not the ceiling.

CRITICAL INQUIRY STANCE

Not everything that counts can be counted and not everything that can be counted counts.

—Albert Einstein

As mentioned in the critical inquiry stance section of flux pedagogy in Chapter 2, both teachers and educational leaders need frameworks and mindsets that help them identify, examine, and challenge their beliefs about who is knowledgeable and their assumptions about how learning best happens. Within educational leadership, this idea around an inquiry stance could not be more vital.

An inquiry stance aligns with the thinking around Heifetz and Linsky's oft-cited (2002) work on the "adaptive leadership" model that differentiates between technical and adaptive challenges. This work highlights that complex problems in schools require a more nuanced approach to addressing the root issues (Lytle, Lytle, Johanek, & Rho, 2018). Adaptive leaders can take moments of crisis and reflect on the current moment while also adapting their organization for the future (Heifetz, Grashow, & Linsky, 2009a). In moments of precarity, adaptive leaders "change key rules of the game, reshape parts of the organization and redefine the work people do" (p. 64). We believe that an adaptive approach, like an inquiry stance, is an essential component of leadership effectiveness. A flux leader, specifically, must exercise adaptive leadership in a manner that is predicated upon a critical understanding of race as the defining feature of American life, shaping the societal and educational realities for students of color (Bell, 2018; Ladson-Billings & Tate, 2006; Pak & Ravitch, 2021).

At this moment, faculty, staff, students, parents, and community members deserve for educational leaders to engage not only an inquiry stance, but a *critical inquiry stance*—an inquiry stance that is intentionally antiracist and intersectional. A critical inquiry stance engages critical social theories like Critical Race Theory and Decolonial Theory, which help practitioners identify and interrogate structural power and its lived vicissitudes in the life of schools. This includes a direct focus on how knowledge and learning reflect broader issues of hegemony and social inequity.

A critical inquiry stance iterates the concept of an inquiry stance—positioning it as more of a radical process through which leaders actively question their belief systems, mindsets, and biases about what constitutes valid knowledge. This process is mediated by social identity, structural discrimination, and power. A critical inquiry stance critiques traditional notions of knowledge as largely byproducts of Western ideologies and questions why knowledge is placed in hierarchy—both by social identity and in terms of the presumed hierarchy of traditional knowledge over emotion and wisdom. Central to this critique is the intersectional analysis of axes of oppression within systems and sites of domination with a focus on structural oppression.

As we write this, students struggle in classrooms trying to make sense of what happened at our nation's capital on January 6, 2021. Hundreds had incited a violent riot and domestic terror attack on the Capitol building with an intent to overturn the 2020 election results. Five people died, police officers were seriously injured, and our democracy was under threat. At the same time, congressional aides scrambled to keep the electoral college votes safe as our public servants were hiding in fear for their lives. On various social media platforms, teachers, students, activists, and community members are trying to make sense of how their Black friends and colleagues can be tear-gassed and arrested at peaceful Black Lives Matter protests that took place over the summer after George Floyd's murder. At the same time, White Americans can show up to the nation's capital with guns and violently take over the Capitol building during a transfer of power without immediate consequence. In this moment, schools must grapple with how to respond to this act of White supremacy and how it influences the sociopolitical moment and its vicissitudes. On a broader scale, school communities must also reckon with how this event is emblematic of the ripple effect that race and other intersections of power exert on our students' lives.

Within educational leadership, Critical Race Theory has been underutilized (Amiot, Mayer-Glenn, & Parker, 2020). However, the emergence of scholars within the field have pushed to make the field more critical while exploring elements of power within leadership practices (Alston, 2005; Dantley, 2009; Liang & Peters-Hawkins, 2017; Martinez, Rivera, & Marquez, 2020; Rivera-McCutchen, 2020; Tillman, 2004). These scholars value centering the narratives and experiences of educational leaders of color. We look to these leaders of thought and action as a reminder that the educational leadership field must continue to provide educational leaders with guidance—guidance on navigating research and practice in a manner that acknowledges the roles that race has in how we manage, lead, and execute the teaching and learning of schools on behalf of students. White supremacy must be dismantled as our approach to leading at this moment—with an understanding that there is a nuanced complexity when thinking about the implications and lived realities around race in American life. By ensuring criticality in research and practice, educational leadership can better determine how to move forward in this moment.

A *critical inquiry stance* provides educational leaders with a framework for considering how our leadership decisions are positioned and enacted within the nexus of structural, social, and organizational power. This leader stance is deeply informed by an approach called *critical intersectional inclusivity*, which adds additional layers of analysis to enactments of inclusivity in groups and organizations (Pak & Ravitch, 2021). A critical intersectional analysis can interrogate ways in which traditional inclusive policies and practices may work to disenfranchise or exclude particular identities while advantaging others. In schools, an environment that is critically inclusive works to foster acceptance, participation, and belonging of stakeholders with a diverse range of identities. Additionally, these environments also continuously redistribute resources and opportunities until nondominant identities are equally valued within the community and beyond.

Leaders who work from an inquiry stance position everyone as "legitimate knowers and knowledge generators, not just implementers of others' knowledge" (Cochran-Smith & Lytle, 2009, p. 18). As mentioned in flux pedagogy, a *critical inquiry stance* extends this further by questioning why, in many Western educational contexts, knowledge (epistemology) is valued over values (axiology) and ways of being (ontology) (Ravitch, 2020b). A critical inquiry stance upsets traditional notions of what constitutes valid knowledge and who is a knower by identifying and challenging ways traditional learning practices are imposed on everyone as universal. Further, it exposes the invisible yet pervasive imposition of Western hierarchical logics that erase and devalue emotion, values, and Indigenous wisdoms (Chilisa, 2020). The ability to identify and upset the tacit beliefs and value systems into which we have been socialized, which when steeped in Whiteness undermine authentic connection and collaboration in schools, requires a willingness to question our indoctrination into systems of performance and evaluation.

Additionally, a critical inquiry stance requires a shift in power dynamics as it pertains to thinking about the centralized knowledge within decision-making. Leaders must co-create intentional practices and processes for shared knowledge generation that works to elevate everyone and push into knowledge hierarchies. Bringing this knowledge to the forefront can allow it to be hybridized and situated within the larger sociopolitical context. In this fraught moment—wherein most students, teachers, families, and communities feel helpless—creating the conditions in which they can feel agentic and authentic in sharing feelings, perspectives, experiences, ideas, and concerns without fear is vital for learning, positive development, and well-being in and beyond school (Eren & Ravitch, 2021).

It's vital to situate yourself as a learner by examining your ideologies, tacit beliefs, and implicit biases, and working to ever more critically understand how these shape your ideas and professional practice. This reorientation requires critically reading self with disciplined, curious, and compassionate humility. A critical inquiry stance requires that leaders take a reflexive learning stance on self, professional practice, and the contexts—near and far, personal and societal—that shape their practice, their sites of practice, and understandings of that practice in and beyond the immediate setting. Leaders open possibilities for authentic learning and growth through intentional, societally contextualized self-reflection, which questions what they know and how they know it. By exercising this stance grounded in criticality, a leader can work to upset normative ideas and knowledge hierarchies to foster an equitable school ecosystem.

Binaries are reductive and generally false, and in education, they can do harm. For example, Black and White binaries in conversations about racism oversimplify what is lived in complex and intersectional ways (Crenshaw, 2021). Relatedly, educational leaders must work to disrupt the "expert-learner binary" that confers dominance on a narrow knowledge hierarchy and marginalizes the experiences and knowledges of people and groups farthest from dominant power (Ravitch & Tillman, 2010). These new communication pathways, norms, and processes, and the meaning frameworks behind them, help leaders to interrupt the depersonalizing transactionalism of schools and, in its place, to offer transformative possibilities through collaborative action. A critical inquiry stance requires racial literacy—one simply cannot read the world accurately without it.

RACIAL LITERACY

The lion's story will never be told as long as the hunter is the one to tell it.

—African Proverb

As described in flux pedagogy, racial literacy—which is undoubtedly needed to read the world authentically—is the ability to read, recast, and resolve racially stressful encounters and navigate identity-related stress (Stevenson,

2014). This dimension of flux leadership serves as a crucial prerequisite and baseline for a critical inquiry stance to be embodied. It must, furthermore, remain a priority when there are times of rapid change transpiring with an educational context. Within this moment, we must intentionally build efficacy in these skills around racial literacy, recognizing that it is a collaborative project (Crary, 2017). Crary highlights the importance of showing awareness around White privilege, developing "rules of thumb" for engaging in race-related interactions, and those organizational resources support this work. Some of this work might include incorporating role models among peers and leaders, developing organizational norms that support learning and development around constructive race work, and providing opportunities in diverse work settings around diversity education.

Our educational contexts need this work to help build capacity for critical inquiry stance and to create inclusive and safe learning environments for all stakeholders. There is necessary skill building required, skills that are crucial to start building and refining. For example, as explored in flux pedagogy, Dr. Howard Stevenson's work around racial mindfulness is a way to reflect upon the necessary skills and mindsets that are required for individuals to acquire in educational contexts. Leaders need to build spaces in schools to practice telling and sharing stories consistently. When we do this, we hear people's racial stories in order to ensure that everyone is immersed in the same language. Centering racial literacy in school communities can combat deficit frames and mindsets in important ways that often hinder our minoritized teachers, students, and families.

It is crucial for educational leaders to stand up for intersectional racial justice. It is crucial that they understand how intersectionality is central to conversations about structural racism, racial identity and racial socialization (Crenshaw, 2021; Stevenson, 2014), and racial stress. As representatives of a system that imposes racial and identity-based stress on BIPOC students and communities, all school leaders and practitioners must take an active stance against school and district cultures and policies that allow microaggressions, the imposition of White fragility, and the masking of racial bullying and toxic positivity under the guise of safe spaces (Chiu, 2020). School leaders should instead centralize a racial literacy framework within an equity framework of critical intersectional inclusivity (Crenshaw, 2021; Pak & Ravitch, 2021).

Understanding where you are on the continuum of racial literacy happens through continued practice of "courageous noticing and admitting" to self (Edwards, 2016)—a hallmark of a critical inquiry stance—becoming increasingly facile at understanding your patterns of tension, conflict, and struggle. Stevenson's work on racial literacy and navigating identity-related stress situates racial mindfulness as a central node of school leadership, focusing on the professional development and support of teachers, students, parents, and school communities as a whole right now. It's useful in these learning moments to remind people that (1) racial stress requires specific skills; (2) racial encounters need to be attended to for healthy resolve; (3) it is vital to approach racial literacy as a practice of racial competence, not as an issue of morality or flawed character; (4) organizational contexts broadly, and educational contexts specifically, are socialization hubs of avoidant and dysfunctional racial coping; and (5) people can resolve racial stress in everyday life which leads to better learning experiences, life experiences, and health outcomes (Stevenson, 2014). Storytelling is a powerful practice for recasting and resolving racially stressful and traumatizing experiences in groups. It allows for neural coupling and empathy, while leading to a deeper understanding and authentic connection building (Stevenson, 2014).

Being a racially literate leader means creating the conditions in which everyone in the organization practices racial literacy and mindfulness so that they can experience interaction through an active racial empowerment framework (Stevenson, 2014). These conditions enable people—teachers, staff, students, and families—to cultivate identity-focused tools and coping strategies that they can immediately employ when stressed or tense during conversations about identity and equity or in racialized communication. A racially literate leader understands there are always varying (and conflicting) levels of racial literacy and identity-related self-awareness as well as tolerance for tension and disagreement within groups and organizations (Stevenson, 2014). Leaders need new skills to read a room (or screen) to gain a sense of where people are in their racial identity development and with respect to their identity-based coping skills. Leaders must be able to feel into people's discomfort and frustration, while also seeking out feedback on how to best respond to what's shared and presented with a clear and steadfast vision of equity.

For transformative leaders whose preexisting experiences and racial literacy have been confirmed in these times, racial mindfulness is vital to ground yourselves in healthy rather than unhealthy stress that may lead to burnout. In this self-reflexive context, racial literacy is not just the ability to decode racial subtexts and understand how racism is inextricably linked to inequities in the United States. For BIPOC leaders, this requires recasting and resolving a relentless barrage of racially stressful encounters and microaggressions. For White leaders, it means being mindful and humble in interactions with students, staff, and families of color, and in racially stressful moments, seeing, taking responsibility for, and stopping our own and other people's White fragility (DiAngelo, 2018). For all leaders, it means examining where and how your privileges (i.e., race, social class, gender, ability, language, citizenship status) leave you missing or misunderstanding others' experience of marginalization and struggle in ways that hurt them and opportunity-cost them out of being seen, engaged, and affirmed.

RESPONSIVE AND HUMANIZING LEADERSHIP

No one can be authentically human while he prevents others from being so.

—Paulo Freire, *Pedagogy of the Oppressed*

Even before COVID-19 and the killing of George Floyd, our society was working in various ways to systematically dehumanize students, teachers, and schooling. Standardized testing, top-down leadership decisions, budget cuts, pension shortfalls, deficit labels increasingly attached to students, and lack of culturally responsive resources fueled the fire in chipping away at the heart of our school community. The demands and systemic pressures felt never-ending and endless initiatives flooded into our schools without much change. One question prevails: *Where is the humanity and responsiveness in these leadership decisions?*

In these moments, responsive and humanizing leadership is necessary for fighting ongoing crises in schools and constitutes a crucial tenet of flux leadership. At the core of this tenet, responsiveness is fueled by a deeper humanity for ourselves and stakeholders rather than a leadership stance grounded in fear. In a stressful system, educational leaders must be in a position to respond to the array of demanding needs and urgent change for students, families, and communities; but equally important, these decisions must acknowledge and respond to the full humanity and complexity of people and circumstances within this system.

In *Pedagogy of the Oppressed*, Paulo Freire defines praxis as "reflection and action directed at the structures to be transformed" (1996, p. 127). This definition also situates praxis as a deeply humanizing act that strives toward transformative outcomes (Blackburn, 2014; Paris & Winn, 2013). For school leaders, praxis becomes a necessary tenet within a humane and responsive leadership mindset. It requires deep awareness of the conditions and realities that stakeholders are situated within, accompanied by action that humanizes school improvement processes.

A commitment to praxis allows for school change to move forward in more humanizing and responsive ways for all stakeholders. As a guiding example, Giancola and Hutchinson, two practitioner-scholars, studied a school for many years examining the *humane dimension* at work. They define this dimension as "a place in an organization where personal transformation is allowed to occur in a culture of compassion, trust, empowering relationships, and common purposes" (2005, p. xv). Their work suggests that schools can transform with this dimension of culture. Without it, long-lasting school change is not possible.

Leading before the pandemic was not easy and guiding a school during the pandemic is even more challenging. While there are no easy answers to navigating sickness and instability, there are numerous obstacles to face. These obstacles include but are not limited to: the abrupt halt of in-person collaboration time in faculty meetings, informal instructional walk-throughs, and in-person student and family check-ins. The sudden halt to these activities and the sheer complexity of how this might affect an organization and community shed light on the importance of one guiding principle: being humane is the best route to take.

Leaders cannot press on with their initiatives ignoring the disproportionate impact that COVID-19 has had on Black and Latino families (Stokes, Zambrano, Anderson, Marder, Raz, Felix, Tie, & Fullerton, 2020) or expect everyone to somehow rise to the occasion without the ability to do so. We must recalibrate expectations that can allow for the prioritization of kindness, the support of each other as human beings, solutions that make the most sense for most, the sharing of resources generously, and clear communication norms. We cannot expect the same outcomes in department meetings, and we cannot spearhead new initiatives with the same fortitude. Some initiatives are no longer possible, some teacher expectations are no longer reasonable, and some teaching and learning task forces are no longer valuable. Educational leaders need to root their decision-making in care. We also argue that rooting decision-making in equity inherently goes hand and hand with a commitment to responsiveness. A commitment to equity is equally grounded in humanizing stakeholders and how we make and follow through on decisions.

When it comes to galvanizing communities and drafting priorities, educational leaders must ground these decision-making processes within the ever-evolving context of their school. Instead of a narrow focus on something like growth and results, there should be a focus on intellectual nourishment, social connection, and flexible adjustment in pursuit of moving forward. Given that no one knows where things are going given the rapid, unprecedented, and evolving changes to teaching and learning, budgets, and learning environments, leaders will have to constantly adapt and adjust to the new situation, which is mentally draining for all stakeholders. This adaptation means they need to encourage time investment in the humane pathways that will allow people to be sustained, connected, and feel supported in their educational journeys during times of rapid change. For example, it may be time to re-examine evaluation systems such as classwork, homework, and assessment. Leaders can explore more responsive and humane ways to achieve equally valuable learning outcomes given current challenges. What assessment frameworks might make better sense in a particular moment? A school leader can examine old lesson plans with teachers as an artifact of a pre-pandemic mindset and chart what has shifted and what implications are for their pedagogy and expectations in a new academic year.

Creating an organizational culture rooted in humane responsiveness is vital. The entire organization must be able to respond to the array of demanding needs or urgent changes for students and their families. Ultimately, we must create this culture for our faculty and staff so that they can create this for our students and their families. Teaching through such extreme and continuously unfolding changes requires a higher than usual tolerance for the unknown. Leaders must demonstrate that they can respond quickly, calmly, and with clarity, to make timely and culturally responsive decisions with a focus on the most vulnerable in the communities they serve. For example, a school leader might plan a listening and discovery session with different groups (teachers by grade level, parents, affinity groups, grade level of students) to hear about how a racial incident in the community has affected stakeholders. Leaders can model active listening and structured perspective-taking processing. We recommend being thoughtful about groupings with respect to issues of hierarchy, power, and confidentiality. It is also essential to have an inquiry group or thought partner to debrief these sessions and plan forward in ways that affirm people's experiences by responding to their concerns (see Chapter 2's discussion of brave-space pedagogy).

As described above, when a leader employs a humane and responsive approach, they are attuned to the power dimensions that manifest across various contexts and situations. As mentioned in the previous tenet, a *critical intersectional inclusivity* (Pak & Ravitch, 2021) is necessary when making leadership and instructional decisions in this moment of radical flux. It requires grounding in being equally humane and responsive. For example, it is important to remember that we cannot abdicate our responsibilities to families in moments of hardship and change. New responsibilities might require reprioritization or releasing some asks of teachers and staff so they have space both emotionally and physically to meet new demands, such as helping ensure students can stay connected to the school and have sufficient food. This example highlights an important point: in moments of global, institutional, familial, and interpersonal stress, leaders must actively consider how circumstances lands into each person's life differently in relation to status and finances, whether or not students have family or community supports, and how people have unique coping mechanisms formed from past experiences that may or may not serve them well in the present moment.

Additionally, this means considering representation in your organization and addressing marginalization within and across identity dimensions. These considerations are done within an ecosystem of interdependent care for teachers, students, and families. While students must remain everyone's focus and priority, it's vitally important for educational leaders to pay attention to teacher well-being in these moments of crisis. Further, we must help teachers face challenging pedagogical realities with a sense of structure, agency, and with the needed support for all they are being asked to do. This is vital to their sense of safety, engagement, and to their sense of belonging to a community of interdependent concern, justice, and care (hooks, 2003).

Learning during moments of radical flux must centralize emotional well-being for both adult-centered and student-centered learning spaces.

Teaching and learning initiatives must help teachers, students, and communities develop the skills they need to traverse complex systems in chaotic times, build relational trust, and view pedagogical flexibility as an ethical stance. Here, everyone's wisdom and expertise are actively valued, shaking hierarchical norms and becoming more of a learning collective in a time of chaos and shared vulnerability (Hanson, 2018). Leaders must also actively engage in responsive and humanizing pedagogy for the socioemotional health and well-being of teachers, staff, students, and communities. Engagement in this way translates into a receptive sensibility in relation to their own emotions and stress levels during communication and conflict. It enables leaders to communicate more effectively in fraught moments. For example, considering communication strategies and sensitivities about sudden changes in plans given how overwhelmed and stressed everyone is in schools.

An empathic and responsive teaching and leadership approach is essential right now; it's a form of radical compassion and self-care as well as a humanizing education stance. To cultivate that teaching approach, flux leadership requires a responsive and humanizing approach to all stakeholders responsible for the care of our children.

INNER-RESOURCE CULTIVATION

Self-care and healing and attention to the body and the spiritual dimension—all of this is now a part of radical social justice struggles.

—Angela Davis

So, what helps you enact a critical inquiry stance and responsive and humanizing leadership approach? How do you support yourself to learn and practice the needful? This tenet offers a guide of how educational leaders can approach the ongoing project of inner-resource cultivation that rests on radical compassion and radical self-care practices.

District leaders, school administrators, teachers, staff, students, parents, and community members are exhausted. Educational leaders are consistently overworked—at a pace and intensity that is not sustainable without additional support given the emerging challenges within the educational landscape. COVID-19 and racial unrest have only further illuminated the stark inequality and increasing political polarization that face our school communities. Additionally, COVID-19 exacerbates the distress on public school district finances, with revenue and student enrollment dramatically impacting school budgets (Hubler, Taylor, & Nierenberg, 2020). According to Pew Charitable Trust, an analysis shows that education has been one of the worst impacted in terms of economic devastation, with state and local education employment down 8.8% in October from the year earlier. As many educational leaders understand firsthand, the economic impacts will have devastating implications for critical resources such as staffing. Equally important, as a result of the stresses of COVID-19, the effect of teacher burnout is causing educators to leave the profession, which will leave our most vulnerable students without educators in their classrooms.

Issues around the teacher shortage, however, existed before COVID-19. There was a shortage of 110,000 teachers in the 2017–2018 school year, when before 2013 there was no teacher shortage (Sutcher, Darling-Hammond, & Carver-Thomas, 2016). Teacher shortages exert an incredible impact on schools exacerbating the stresses of school staffing and compounding issues around teacher effectiveness (García & Weiss, 2019). While states and districts are doing their best to hold onto funding and manage the moment, these structural impacts trickle down to educational leaders at the local level in pernicious ways. On top of the budgetary stress and teacher shortage that already existed, educational leaders must reckon with how emerging challenges land into preexisting identity-based privileges and systems of oppression on a diverse group of stakeholders. It is evident that at the heart of educational leadership, leaders must mobilize the resources within themselves to cultivate systems of care. To make this journey sustainable for themselves and others, leaders must make time to take care of themselves and create space for others to do so. Within the flux leadership model, we call this work *inner-resource cultivation* and argue that it is a crucial component of leading within schools. For without inner-resource cultivation, educational leaders do not have the strength to live into their visions and inspire others to do the same as challenges become increasingly more nuanced and challenging.

While the field of education desperately needs more attention and investment in terms of funding, resources, and support in the current moment, we believe that by leaders taking intentional care of themselves both within school and outside of it, they can have the energy needed to support their students, teachers, families, and each other as these crises continue to unfold. It allows for sustainability and recharge that is desperately needed to embark upon this work. By reframing restoration as part of the job for leaders, they are more likely to care and sustain their best selves (Su, 2019). To do this in schools, leaders need to think about how to recharge, sustain, and show up for their communities' situating crisis within larger sociopolitical power dynamics. Leaders must work to understand how social identities, in terms of their proximity to structural power and resources, are central to student and community experiences of this racially fraught and socially divisive pandemic. The working ability to conceptualize and articulate how systems of domination and marginalization show up every day at the individual, group, and community levels is of utmost importance for leaders. These underpinnings can be embedded within two essential aspects of inner resource cultivation: *radical compassion* and *radical self-care*.

One component of inner-resource cultivation is radical compassion. As mentioned in Chapter 2, radical compassion is the internal imperative to understand reality in order to change it to alleviate the distress, pain, and suffering of others. Suffering is viewed within its macro-sociopolitical contexts in ways grounded in equity and more liberatory natures. In practice, a leader committed to radical compassion understands the need to push against asymmetrical power relations that cause "toxic positivity" (Chiu, 2020). This toxicity represents a kind of performative positivity in the face of challenges that deny a person's lived experience of discrimination or microaggressions in organizations. Being told to have a "good vibes" approach will not be effective, for instance, if an Indigenous teacher keeps being told by her White colleagues that she "doesn't look Native enough." These patterns of microaggressions can calcify racial tensions and even retraumatize BIPOC teachers, staff, and students. Instead, educational leaders must cultivate critical understanding—their own and others—to engage in the ethical use of a pedagogy of discomfort (Boler & Zembylas, 2003) for students and staff, a teaching and learning approach attuned committed to the disruption of power asymmetries as a central dimension of the pedagogical process. This helps practitioners examine and change problematic behaviors and assumptions genuinely.

An educational leader can ensure that teaching and learning priorities are guided by the importance of incorporating authentic discussion and exploration of people's lived minoritization broadly and specifically in school communities, teams, and classrooms. In this example, the intentional act of incorporating a pedagogy of discomfort into teaching and learning makes a difference to people's lived experiences. For instance, it leads to an Indigenous teacher feeling genuinely supported by her school leader's acts of radical compassion integrated seamlessly into school culture and climate.

By enacting radical compassion in our micro and macro interactions at the school level, educational leaders can respond to crises in a more responsive and sustainable approach. In "The New Leadership Literacy of Creating and Sustaining Positive Energy," Bob Johansen states, "If leaders are going to thrive in a future of extreme disruption, they must not only manage their energy, they must encourage, model, and reward positive energy in others" (2018, p. 31). We believe that radical compassion brings forth a "love ethic" that is rooted in "showing care, respect, knowledge, and the will to cooperate" (hooks, 2001). By cultivating radical compassion as a leader within the community, others are inspired to show up for themselves and others.

These tenets help sustain communities as circumstances ebb and flow outside of people's control. They help leaders provide a loving commitment to working together to find ways to navigate difficult situations. As illustrated above, radical compassion can lead to the generation of new frameworks that shift the way we approach essential school leadership practices like strategic planning. Radical compassion embedded into the vision for strategic planning can help create more humanizing alternatives for how students can approach their individualized learning in the classroom. Radical compassion provides an interdependent strength and community lens to combat individualistic measures of success for teaching, learning, and leading.

To be able to embark upon a path of radical compassion, school leaders must be willing to engage in radical self-care. Radical self-care is the practice of radical compassion toward self. Practicing self-care has never felt more urgent than in these socially, politically, economically, medically, environmentally, and spiritually troubling times. It has become part of many people's lexicon. Few consider its deeper implications, its relationship to social identities and issues of structural discrimination, and the promise it holds for transformative education that supports optimal development. A commitment to optimal development allows us to honor ourselves in important ways: reflect upon our energy cycles in relation to stress, create rituals to build into our workday, and teach ourselves to build internal barometers to know "what's enough" (Nakkula & Schneider-Muñoz, 2018; Su, 2019). In centering this commitment to optimal development as a part of radical self-care, educational leaders can ensure that ongoing stress and crises do not determine the norms and set the stage for school culture and climate. Instead, leaders are choosing their best selves to lead.

Radical self-care is a political act. The political dimension of a radical growth mindset situates how structural racism, inequality, and discrimination mediate people's lives within a particular context (more information on a radical growth mindset can be found later in this chapter). Radical self-care bridges the political and personal in ways that create the conditions for individuals to see that much of what they judge or blame themselves for is systemic and socialized into them as fact. As Brown (2017) states, "We need to learn how to practice love such that care—for ourselves and others—is understood as political resistance and cultivating resilience."

As an important example, we look to Audre Lorde's leadership. Lorde makes visible through her activism, thought leadership, essays, and poetry that she can stand and declare her power while speaking truth to unjust structural discrimination. She speaks these truths to those who uphold these inequities while taking joyful care of her body, mind, soul, and love as a Black woman. Educational leaders should view this example as an important model to help reorient the scope and purpose of radical self-care: Instead of conceptualizing inner-resource cultivation as solely something outside of their job, educational leaders should view it as something necessary to ignite desperately needed changes for our students and our future world. In her work, Lorde continually illuminates how in a racist society, self-care is a radical act—a revolution.

In practice, Lorde's wisdom translates into ensuring that educational leaders are nourishing and affirming themselves daily: listen to soulful music, sit in silence at the end of a long workday, read things that inspire you, or create something that makes you happy. Build time to unplug and unwire each day and build a structure that would allow school to run while attending to your psychological and emotional well-being. It is also important when you feel stressed to consider engaging in an activity like reflective writing to explore what you are carrying into the school year or how you are feeling. By engaging in these acts, an educational leader is much more able to show up, be present, and display radical compassion for their school community. We must understand that *everyone's well-being depends on everyone's well-being.*

In schools, leaders must do this radical self-care for themselves, and create structures so that faculty, staff, and stakeholders can engage in this work. In practice, educational leaders need to voice the importance of prioritizing radical self-care as a vital act for sustaining energy and wellness. Leaders can encourage their faculty and staff to write self-care plans to consider what supports they need to face current stressors. Encouragement in this way includes identifying inner resources they wish to cultivate (i.e., wellness practices like meditating or mindfulness) and how these inner resources relate to a broader self-care plan (i.e., plan for how to integrate healthy mind-body-spirit practices that support them through ongoing heightened stress). These memos can be a start-activity for radical self-care groups. We also encourage finding ways to integrate self-care ideas into school professional development. That said, school leadership teams should invest in radical self-care structures that can allow for flexibility and individualization for inner-resource cultivation: for example, create the structures that would grant teachers the flexibility to ensure work is completed while centering radical self-care.

For example, a female teacher comes to her urban-school principal with her radical self-care plan. She shares that it is dark when school is released each day, and her passion is running. She states that she would like to use her Friday planning block to go for an outdoor run to let off steam given the stresses of the hybrid learning model and continue improving her physical health. She has informed her department of this plan, and they are supportive—they also want to join. The principal enthusiastically supports this choice, feels that it is reasonable, and asks that as a part of the self-care plan memo, her department make a note of when they will complete the work they were supposed to do in the Friday meeting and how they feel this plan will contribute to their long-term self-care.

We should find ways to grant flexibility in how teachers utilize their day while being attentive to dimensions of power when encouraging these plans. Suppose a teacher can maintain her responsibilities at a high level and wants to be able to take a run during a planning block one day a week. In that case, leaders should find ways to make this happen, which can help prevent teacher burnout and loss of teacher talent in the profession for the long term. In this context, the self-care plan is radical because it shifts educational structures to accommodate both the concepts of self-care. Further, this plan combats the deprofessionalization of teachers within a system that does not allow for flexibility, including when women can run in terms of their safety.

Although "casual Friday," the day that we often see teachers wearing jeans to school, might be seen as a start to humanizing the idea of self-care, schools must be doing much more to think about what teachers need to sustain themselves in the profession for the long term. Leaders must understand one size does not fit all, and issues of equity are at play. Brown makes evident that creating these conditions becomes essential for ourselves and for fostering the conditions that lead to the equitable, healthy, and happy schools that our students deserve. It can lead to the transformation that all stakeholders are fighting for. Leaders should encourage and support radical self-care, engage in and model this yourself, and introduce it as part of an organizational culture that invites everyone to take care of themselves.

Radical self-care can help people feel calm within themselves while the world around them is chaotic. This includes identity and emotion affirmation, structures and processes of psychological support, storytelling, counter-storying, and re-storying processes (Khalifa, 2018; Stevenson, 2014), and cultivating racial mindfulness strategies that help students identify and skillfully manage identity-based stress (Anderson & Stevenson, 2019). While radical self-care looks different across people, places, and time, it must include processes that help people identify, name, and compassionately attend to the ways that external, systemic pressures, structures, and constraints—in their presence and absence—shape narratives of everyday life, self, and possibility (Lorde, 1988).

CRISIS AGILITY AND REFLEXIVE VISIONARY

I think it is healing behavior, to look at something so broken and see the possibility and wholeness in it.

—Adrienne Maree Brown

Even before the onset of COVID-19, educational leaders were barraged with crises. Structural inequality has severely impacted our school communities: More than 11 million children in the United States live in "food insecure homes" (USDA Economic Research Service, 2019), nearly 11 million children live in poverty (Center for American Progress, 2021), more than one in five students show signs of a mental, behavior, or developmental disorder (CDC, 2021), and nearly 80% of students who need mental health services will not receive them (Kataoka, Zhang, & Wells, 2002). Given the economic and structural impacts of COVID-19, these numbers will only increase. These crises and rapidly evolving circumstances have led to an onslaught of systemic inequities impacting our schools; in turn, there has been a manifestation of increasingly complex issues for school leadership to tackle.

After the 2008 financial crisis, business leaders were encouraged to use crisis as an opportunity to strengthen their organizations for the long term (George, 2009). Leaders in various fields must make sense of the crisis quickly to determine the current moment and how to adapt moving forward. As George states, "Denying reality destroys more careers and organizations than incompetence ever did" (2009, p. 25). While business leadership also understands the gravity of crisis leadership, we argue that schools are often in a state of emergence flux, with or without the events like the 2008 financial crisis, COVID-19, or racial turmoil in communities. Given the state of inequality in this country and political polarization, school leaders often navigate a state of disruption for longer periods of time without the necessary support. We believe that flux leaders must have a capacity for developing *crisis agility* to live into becoming a *reflexive visionary* to lead schools and communities. Schools must learn to exist within evolving change. Existing in this way starts with leadership developing capacity on this front.

A leader's learning agility in crisis or *crisis agility* mediates the impact of the crisis on everyone in the organization, both during and after a crisis ends. Educational leaders need tools and frames to balance the professional, psychological, and emotional dimensions of their work throughout this crisis and beyond. Balance can be difficult in any crisis, and it's especially challenging to keep it in a global pandemic with virulent racial inequalities and tensions. If emotions aren't attended to with intention and skill, the current moment that flux leaders face can create imbalances that tip the emotional scale (understandable but avoidable). As discussed earlier in the "Inner-Resource Cultivation" section, leaders need inner resources they can rely on as they enact consistently practical, relational, compassionate crisis leadership. Attending to leader psychology and emotions is the piece that brings together the flux leadership framework. Merging happens because leaders are the primary instrument of change. As James and Wooten (2011) assert:

> We refer to the capability to lead under extreme pressure as crisis leadership. Crisis leadership matters, because despite the damage that is caused by a crisis, effective leadership is the one factor that creates the potential for [an organization] to be better off following the crisis than it was before. . . . Crisis leadership is a continuous process that involves developing a mindset for reflecting, adapting and learning from the crisis situation and its aftermath. This requires the ability to strategically scan the environment for knowledge. . . . In a crisis situation, the individual leader's learning should happen in tandem with the organization's learning. (p. 61)

Flux leadership supports centering the cultivation of learning agility in and beyond crisis. A leader must constantly home in on skills to actively learn, grow, and build new skills through periods of radical flux. To do this, a leader will engage a *radical growth mindset* wherein "failures" and "mistakes"—their own and those of their teams, stakeholders, and constituencies—are re/positioned as portals for focused growth, powerful learning, and transformation. Importantly, a leader's learning agility is not an intensive academic pursuit; it's a set of inner resources and inner-management skills that leaders can experientially cultivate (i.e., build on the job) through practice.

We believe that a radical growth mindset, cultivated through this set of skills, can develop in tandem with a concept called the *emotional imagination*, which is an important part of the flux leadership model found in the next section. Given that flux leadership is a framework and mindset, leaders who engage in this model must seek out, develop, utilize, and enact new knowledge and strategies for rapidly emerging problems as they position schools as complex adaptive systems of care. Over time, leaders will learn from unfamiliar, challenging, and even threatening experiences, applying emergent lessons in real time, mastering learning agility.

An *agile crisis leader* or a leader who demonstrates *crisis agility* effectively reads and responds in a crisis. We believe that an agile crisis leader is a prerequisite in becoming a leader who can help organizations adjust when a school vision is forced to evolve and adapt. Educational leaders who can seamlessly utilize their leader learning agility toward organizational capacity building around school vision during radical flux are called *reflexive visionaries*.

A *reflexive visionary* is a leader who allows organizational vision to evolve, emerge, and build through humanizing collective circumstances and situations in crisis. This concept builds upon the thinking of Gianpiero Petriglieri:

> When a leader's appeal rests on a vision alone, leadership is not whole. And the limitations of such visionary leadership become painfully obvious in times of crisis, uncertainty, or radical change. Take the coronavirus pandemic. No one had anything like it in their "Vision 2020." Crises always test visions, and most don't survive. (2020, para. 3)

Integral to flux leadership is the following principle: While visionary leaders might be seen as transformative leaders, this work is too exhausting on both the educational leader and its stakeholders to be sustainable for the long term. This is particularly true given the evolving educational landscape and context. Visionaries work themselves to the point of exhaustion often carrying themselves and others to the breaking point. Petriglieri asserts: "Visions work the same way whether mystics or leaders have them: They promise a future and demand our life. In some cases, that sacrifice is worth it. In others, it is not. Just as it can ignite us, a vision can burn us out" (2020, para. 2).

Visionary leadership can no longer sustain educational systems at this moment, and we need an alternative that can sustain leaders and the people who carry the torch alongside them. We need educational leaders, teachers, support staff, parents, community members, and students to be invested in a vision for the long haul that can sustain the collective and not exhaust stakeholders to the point of no return. Instead, we argue for the merits of developing *reflexive visionaries* to build more sustainable school visions for collective social and educational change.

Within this moment in education, both the complexity and ongoing nature of crisis moments that transpire within schools force a reckoning within leadership. A different leadership mentality must be exercised to sustain the collective for the long term. Although crisis leadership typically situates crisis into an emergency phase that requires stabilization of a situation and an adaptive phase that helps organizations build capacity (Heifetz et al., 2009b), educational systems do not operate the same way and are distinct from other organizations. Schools, in contrast to other organizations, are a collective nexus of interdependence and care with the primary goal of helping children learn and thrive in the world. In a state of radical flux and chaos, educational leaders must utilize notions of intentional care of themselves and others in how they think about building vision and capacity in these moments.

We believe that Petriglieri's (2020) concept of "institutional holding" is an important lens for understanding the role of intentional care in building school vision for a reflexive visionary. Institutional holding is a concept built on the work of Donald Winnicott, a psychoanalyst who argues that children being held well promotes development that allows children to thrive into becoming healthy adults. A "holding environment" encourages children to make sense of themselves in the world around them in ways that are curious and that encourage cultivating resilience through hardships, which leads to creating more independent adults.

Petriglieri argues that adults need holding too—from leaders and organizations—to face difficult situations and adapt to the ever-changing world around us. Institutional holding, by comparison, works to "strengthen the structure and culture of an organization or group" through various adaptive mechanisms. Leaders, for example, should promote systems of dialogue that allow for a diversity of people to participate in decisions around ongoing situations and opportunities. By putting in policies that promote transparency in crisis, people are reassured on important issues like job security. Once a leader can provide institutional holding, they can turn to something called interpersonal holding, which requires being in the present moment. It is not only expressing support for someone in the moment, but it is also a demonstrated willingness to witness the experiences of ourselves and others as it may be. Ultimately, "the core of holding is acknowledging distress and difficulty without giving in to powerlessness" (Petriglieri, 2020, para. 15).

A reflexive visionary places unique emphasis on institutional holding—the intentional process of engaging in holding difficult emotions and tensions in constructive ways—as a core component of building an educational vision. In a time of budget cuts and hybrid learning environments, teachers need reassurance, transparency, and the safety to name what they are feeling in times of loss and grief. Reflexive visionaries understand that there is considerable loss in these moments. It is a time to reflect on how we determine and rethink district and school priorities. To embark on institutional holding as a district or school team, leadership must bring people together to discuss exactly what is happening with the school, what changes are happening to teaching and learning, and who is responsible for certain tasks.

Reflexive visionaries constantly think about what is reasonable and make informed decisions with often partial and emerging data points. This decision-making process must be rooted in sensible humanity given the current conditions and explain with clarity why this is the strategic route pursued. A reflexive visionary is constantly asking: *How are we supporting all stakeholders in crisis?* We need leadership to hold us with care and create spaces where leaders promote dialogue, actively combat rumors that emerge, and find the delicate balance of bringing everyone to the table while also protecting their time. They hold meetings where leadership feels transparent and humanizing while answering questions and concerns that need to be addressed. Most importantly, stakeholders feel leaders are present. Institutional holding provides an impactful approach that will lead to stakeholders feeling heard and supported even when circumstances are increasingly demanding.

Where does vision come into this? Reflexive visionaries are leaders who assemble stakeholders together in times of radical flux to bring their concerns and hopes around their children's education. Togetherness includes acknowledging that everyone is experiencing loss in different ways and from various vantage points. This work becomes a counter-space against traditional hierarchies to hold each other and name these realities. Additionally, reflexive visionaries mobilize and surface community strengths and stories for healing and collective action (see "Brave-Space Leadership" later in the chapter). In these moments, reflexive visionaries mobilize community strengths and build vision as a collective.

Ultimately, reflexive visionaries know that vision naturally emerges from these conversations and interactions. A reflexive vision comes to fruition through the mixture of intentionality, love, and care for others and the larger community. This interdependence of intention and love supports stakeholder mobilization toward a vision that everyone is invested in. Over time, this holding will continue through the continued disruption and developing changes in the school landscape. By grounding vision building as an emergent and collective action in a crisis, leadership can become sustaining soul and healing work. As a shared endeavor, reflexive visionaries understand that we are building capacity through our collective humanity of each other. In the flux leadership model, a reflexive visionary can navigate a crisis to help the community now which will sustainably transpire into the educational promise of tomorrow.

RADICAL GROWTH MINDSET AND THE EMOTIONAL IMAGINATION

We live inside an unfinished story.

—Rachel Held Evans

As discussed in the previous section, an agile crisis leader effectively reads and responds in crisis while moving the organization toward a vision that emerges from the collective's narratives, concerns, and hopes. These leaders are engaging people through crises in ways that uplift everyone. Further, that creates a collective sense of responsibility for the current conditions unfolding and how that will impact the future. By creating a resonant vision of the future and investing yourself and others in working toward it amidst the tyranny of the urgent, leaders inspire and hold up the people around them, which has a significant impact on organizational ethos in and beyond crisis (Hanson, 2018). Further, a leader's ability to read self and emotion in crisis as a reflexive mission mode supports being their most relational, creative, focused, and resilient.

Even beyond crisis, an educational leader must be aware of the role of emotions in professional life and possess skills to foreground this awareness regularly, especially in stressful moments—their own, ones they observe, ones they mediate. A flux leader engages their own emotions with compassion as part of their radical self-care and leads an organizational culture of relational trust, compassion, and well-being. This also translates into a leader's ability to resist feeling compelled by pressure to accommodate a person, political body, or external idea that's not in the best interest of their school community; they trust they can manage any blowback or strong emotions that arise from living their values as humanizing leaders grounded in the collective. Even when not in the midst of a crisis, this type of leader learning is often unfamiliar and challenging and becomes increasingly difficult when applying emergent lessons as situations unfold. For this reason, we argue that cultivating a *radical growth mindset* and the *emotional imagination* are necessary leadership mindsets that are required to engage in flux leadership, whether one is navigating a crisis or not.

Without a doubt, school leaders have walked by classroom lessons where teachers encourage students to exhibit behaviors aligned with a growth mindset, working toward supporting student emotional growth. We believe that having a growth mindset is important to flux leadership. In a growth mindset, "the hand you're dealt is just the starting point for development.

Growth mindset is based on the belief that your basic qualities are things you can cultivate through your efforts" (Dweck, n.d.). Given the generalized popularity of growth mindset, however, leaders tend to forget that even if they like the idea of growth mindset, "It's still not easy to attain a growth mindset. One reason why is we all have our own fixed-mindset triggers. When we face challenges, receive criticism, or fare poorly compared with others, we can easily fall into insecurity or defensiveness, a response that inhibits growth" (Dweck, 2016). Addressing these fixed-mindset triggers is vital to flux leadership because they can derail even the best-laid leader plans. In the flux leadership model, we also argue that a growth mindset must be rooted in an astute attentiveness to how power, identity, equity, and justice manifest in the self and one's leadership decisions.

In addition to physically transforming the structure and process of schools in this time of radical flux, educational leaders face increasing pressure to assume a transformative leadership stance committed to racial justice. Here, curriculum, pedagogy, policies, norms, and mindsets are critically appraised and transformed into a new normative state of antiracism (Love, 2019) in response to the surging centrality of the Black Lives Matter movement and continued public outcry for racial justice. Thus, leaders must be able to assess and build their racial literacy and identity-based stress navigation skills. Building these capacities requires that educational leaders understand the weaponized social construction of race (Omi & Winant, 2014) and how it is differentially used to re/produce the marginalization of students of color and Indigenous students in schools (Horsford, 2014). Understanding with this lens of criticality is vital to justice-focused school functioning in and beyond the current chaos, and it requires critical leader learning and a *radical growth mindset.*

A radical growth mindset is an active growth orientation to self-learning enacted through self-reflection and relational inquiry that centralizes critical literacy in its orientation. Critical literacy allows leaders an important lens that can work to "question power relations, discourses, and identities in a world not yet finished, just, or humane" (Shor, 1999, p. 1). A critical approach allows leaders to situate their leadership approach in the sociopolitical and think intentionally about how issues of power manifest into their daily work. Given the complexity of this leadership moment, leaders must be equipped to uncover implicit biases and deficit-based beliefs and how they shape leadership moves specifically. Without this criticality, leaders are reproducing social inequities that do not lead to the outcomes that our children deserve.

Educational leaders with a developed radical growth mindset can acknowledge the role that race, class, and other power differentials have played in determining the educational outcomes for children and be able to articulate how it impacts strategic decisions in their own context. A radical growth mindset is self-reinforcing—growth happens by seeking out and reckoning with challenging ideas and perspectives within dialectics of mutual influence (Nakkula & Ravitch, 1998). This work is a leadership process that supports leader mindsets in building the necessary racial literacy and identity-based stress navigation skills required at this moment. It will support them in facing professional struggles and mistakes with an understanding that learning includes vulnerability, being challenged, and engaging with a range of critiques in healthy ways. In leadership development, this is no longer an add-on luxury; it's a pedagogical imperative to develop this mindset, a leader's ethical responsibility.

A mindset is a self-perception or theory of self. People with a growth mindset (Dweck, 2016) understand that they get smarter as they learn through challenges, struggles, and mistakes; that they must learn directly in relation to problems as they emerge in real time, and further, that meaningful learning happens through dialogic engagement (intentional dialogue processes) and through seeking out opportunities to be challenged on biases and assumptions (Ravitch & Carl, 2019). Most important, this work is seen as a self-reflection that is growth oriented rather than self-blaming or ego-protecting. In a radical growth mindset, we must lean into a pedagogy of discomfort (Boler & Zembylas, 2003) and work to counteract the damage done when educational systems choose to ignore race, culture, and power pertaining to children's lives.

Leaders with a growth mindset view mistakes and struggles as opportunities for learning. They see themselves and others as a work in progress rather than viewing mistakes as weaknesses or fixed characteristics. This positioning of the dynamic (rather than fixed) nature of self—as always unfolding—distinguishes a growth from a fixed mindset, which views negative characteristics as unchanging. A radical growth mindset enables us to see past what we said or did in any given moment because we are committed to focused processes of self-development around elements of power for educational justice.

Additionally, building and sharpening a radical growth mindset will support the efficacy and power of a leader's ability to navigate the complexity of a crisis with diverse stakeholders. Enacting flux leadership requires leader learning agility—the ability to actively learn and enact crisis leadership skills in periods of radical change. When leaders situate themselves as intentional learners in unfamiliar, challenging, and even threatening (in the identity sense) experiences, they are better able to apply emergent lessons in real time. For example, when specific policies or understandings of equity-oriented topics such as structural racism or intersectional identities are challenged, leaders must be able to respond in informed ways that connect, not deflect, and that are justice-focused and supportive.

Leading with a *radical growth mindset* means engaging with colleagues, students, teams, parents, and community members as active thought and action partners. This mindset helps leaders foster the conditions for people to come together to identify and address current struggles—and the racial and socioeconomic disparities across them—as living texts that advocate for critical intersectional inclusivity and racial justice in schools (Pak & Ravitch, 2021). As noted, embodying a radical growth mindset requires leadership development across two sets of approaches. It is both a relational approach that leaders must cultivate through a *distributive wisdom approach* (please see the next section) and self-work that must be built through focusing on the *emotional imagination*.

The *emotional imagination* constitutes an inner space that needs much more attention in leadership development. Being in touch with this part of our mind can allow educational leaders to develop the skills to be deeply in touch with the span of their emotions to strengthen their radical growth mindset. Capacity building in this way thinks about increasingly difficult complex situations as they emerge from their contexts.

To understand the importance of the emotional imagination for educational leaders, it becomes important to think about what is required to be an effective, ethical, and accountable leader in these increasingly difficult contexts. First and foremost, an individual must be aware of what affects them emotionally. Understanding the ways that cognitive and overall neural functioning mediate emotions and interpersonal and organizational communication is essential to effectively navigate racial and identity-related stress and supporting others to do the same. Cognitive neuroscience helps us understand the continuum of physiological responses to daily emotional experience, including the science behind the popularized yet oft-misused and confused term "triggered." A trigger is a moment or event that prompts strong feelings in sudden ways that can feel out of or beyond our control in the moment; one feels besieged by emotion, often unable to react in ways more befitting to our ideas in our calmer moments.

Understanding how to navigate moments of intense emotion—for self and as an expected part of organizational life—is a vital leadership skill. It is even more urgent right now as people return to school exhausted and with fraught emotions given everything happening to and around them. Importantly, and this one really takes time to notice, process, and live into—our triggered reactions involve *projection*—we see unconscious aspects of ourselves in other people. Still, we believe the emotion we feel is entirely about them and their actions, not at all about us. Our reaction to projections is somatic—we feel it physically even though it lays outside of our conscious awareness. Seeing and feeling into our projections takes practice. Learning to identify these processes within yourself is life changing.

As leaders, moments that trigger us are significant and useful. Trigger moments (really, it is the unresolved pain underneath the moments) relate to when early needs—attention, acceptance, appreciation, affection, and allowing—remain unresolved from our past and therefore surface in the present (Richo, 2019). These moments of departure from our more practiced ways of being are our most powerful teachers when we position them as such. Disturbing trigger moments are a portal to new self-awareness, the resolve of hurt and healing, and intra-psychic and relational honesty when engaged with a radical growth mindset. Leaders support this through the practice of consciously reflecting on, and inviting dialogic engagement in relation to, our most intense emotional responses. This work is a central leadership cultivation practice since it creates increased capacity for leader presence and responsiveness (Ravitch & Carl, 2019). It's useful for leaders to know that there are shared trigger archetypes, which include (1) feeling self-conscious, (2) feeling discounted, (3) feeling controlled, (4) feeling taken advantage of, (5) feeling vulnerable, (6) relationship experiences, (7) boundary concerns, (8) feeling uncomfortable about what's happening, and (9) fearing what might happen (Richo, 2019). Understanding that these span personality types and social identities can help leaders identify them in problematic interactions.

Importantly, through practice, leaders can slow down our knee-jerk emotional reactions so that events that were once emotionally laden no longer automatically lead to overpowering reactions. Instead, we meet them with a reflective pause and then an intentional response of space building (rather than an automatic reaction). When we create an inner space between a stimulus and our response to that stimulus (ala Viktor Frankl), we use the space to identify our beliefs about, and explore the meaning of, the original experience. We can also begin to give the original hurt our compassionate attention while affirming and healing the feelings we felt as younger versions of ourselves to resolve and unproblematic new stressors in the present. When we do this, we see changes in our once-troubling and confusing behaviors in highly stressful leadership situations (common ones include observing a felt need to "retaliate" when feeling ego-injured or realizing that intense anger is eclipsing a more useful—though perhaps more uncomfortable—emotion such as sadness or grief, which we must allow ourselves to feel in order to resolve intense emotional experiences and the thought and behavior patterns that ensue/d from them). ·

We activate our inner resources in response to upsetting stimuli, and in doing so we quiet the emotional part of our brain (the adrenal system) and can access the calm reasoning part of our brain (the limbic system) (Richo, 2019). By engaging this process within the emotional imagination, we develop trust in ourselves—faith in our ability to build and access inner resources to respond intentionally and with calm no matter the stimulus. Over time, we become so practiced at creating this inner-space that it becomes automatic, even in times of acute stress.

In practice, the emotional imagination is intensive internal work, but dialogic engagement is necessary to unpack our own partial and sometimes distorted interpretations. Dialogic engagement around these issues that pertain to the emotional imagination is great to do in a critical friend's group.

In these types of environments, presenting a case study or utilizing a group protocol can help an individual unpack a situation with a trusted group in a solution-oriented setting. Group norms can guide this process in a productive manner.

It is essential to build space to engage in work around the emotional imagination with others. Like fish in the water, we do not recognize our own beliefs as subjective, and we often cannot see how pervasive they are in our thinking. As American education icon Mr. Rogers offered us many years ago, "Anything that's human is mentionable, and anything that is mentionable can be more manageable. When we can talk about our feelings, they become less overwhelming, less upsetting, and less scary. The people we trust with that important talk can help us know that we are not alone." This is an important component of self-growth, which involves identifying, naming, sharing our distress so that others can attune to us and help us to see differently from other viewpoints and socialization experiences other than our own.

Group processes like a critical friends group can help leaders cultivate the inner resources they need to fully live into a radical growth mindset. Leaders no longer fear what intense or upsetting moments will surface in their leadership. They can welcome the learning even with its pains and discomforts because they understand it is a portal to their necessary healing and growth. This is crisis agility at its best—building in the here and now and toward the future with equal parts tenacity, humility, awareness, and insight.

As we grow up, our socialization—at home and school—conditions us to believe in storied versions of ourselves, each other, and the way the world works. It's vital to engage our creative minds in unlearning the damaging parts of these storied versions of us in pursuit of our healing and growth as leaders. In the increasingly complex world we live in, educational leaders need the concept of the *emotional imagination*—the meeting place of the cognitive, creative, and reflexive dimensions of the human psyche—to honestly and humanely reflect on how various storied versions of ourselves contribute to our leadership decisions in these moments. It is an educational leader's duty to embark upon this work with humility, engaging with this process and the feelings it can surface thoughtfully. Imagination as a cognitive process involves how people conceptualize, take in, create, and envision reality and possibilities. Emotional imagination shapes how people feel, visualize, make meaning of, and understand ourselves *and* the world and ourselves *in* the world—through a nexus of emotions and experiences that shape our thinking, often without notice or conscious processing.

This work of cultivating a leader presence helps leaders develop liberating learning and inquiry processes, which can help facilitate the building blocks that collectively carry out a transformative school vision. When leaders understand themselves better, they are more skilled at identifying and attending to the ways that social identities play out in group dynamics and organizational norms, processes, and structures—for and beyond ourselves. This includes imposter syndrome and how it surfaces in groups, the imposition of White fragility and entitled expectations of emotional labor (Hochschild, 1983) from people of color, and the ways intersectionality plays out in group dynamics given that people have multiple, intersecting social identities.

Through active reflection and dialogic engagement, educational leaders can learn to see the degree to which we inadvertently project our versions of the world outward and onto the people around us (Ravitch & Carl, 2019). Clearing this very old but familiar noise in one's head enables a leader to be more present and, therefore, more accurately interpret and make decisions about situations at hand. It's powerful for leaders to come into a clearer understanding of the social constructions, thought patterns and paradigms, and socialization processes that shape how we view ourselves and our leadership. The key here is to learn to more critically interpret what was messaged, implicitly and explicitly, as we were schooled and how these experiences and other people's perspectives of us shape our decision-making and relational style (Ravitch & Carl, 2019). Also, this is vital to a leader's ability to build racial literacy and engage in radical compassion and self-care as a part of flux leadership.

A radical growth mindset enables leaders to challenge past experiences, storied selves, and false beliefs (e.g., "Dissent is disrespect" or "I don't cry" or "Needing help shows weakness") formed through messaging and life experience. These beliefs are embedded, often through the veil of transference and projection, in the human psyche as fact and filter during our developmental years when we have little say in how meaning and memory are laid down. Leaders can then begin to see our cognitive distortions and thought patterns, as well as those of the people around us. People's filters are reused over the course of our lives through continued unconscious projection and transference, and this continues ad infinitum unless interrupted and engaged with through a process of conscious reckoning and *undoctrination*. Leaders must *un*doctrinate ourselves—attend to our deflections, misunderstandings, cognitive distortions, and unexamined-yet-enacted biases as real-time openings to see ourselves more clearly. We must also *un*doctrinate ourselves to understand where we still must work to heal, grow, and move beyond our indoctrinated beliefs of self, people, and world. Decentralizing (and doing away with) logics that harm is the heart of a flux leadership.

Painful emotions are living large in our subconscious—and we let them stay rent-free to our detriment. These emotions surface in our conscious mind when we have a triggered response to a new experience that reverberates old difficult feelings (i.e., being helpless, feeling invisible or unheard). We feel distress—and possibly confusion—in the moment when our reaction is disproportionate to an event (which is a good indication that it's a trigger moment). We ideally approach these moments as gifts of transcendent possibility. Without the conscious intrusion of painful feelings, they remain dissonant—estranged parts of us stuck in the realm of assumptions, implicit biases, and tacit beliefs that shape how we view, interpret, and experience the world and how we view and treat everyone around us.

The powerful growth work is to make the subconscious ever more conscious in the moment of strong emergent feelings so that we can use them as tools—barometer, compass, failsafe cooling system, chisel—to change our relationship to our own and others' emotions and build our own bespoke approaches to stress management. Growth work is the power of what the emotional imagination can do for our ability to become flux leaders. It means learning to show up for ourselves, learning to give ourselves the 5As—attention, acceptance, appreciation, affection, and allowing—rather than expecting or demanding others to do this for us (Richo, 2019). Centering our well-being is empowering—we are no longer unknowingly controlled by past hurts and unmet needs—we have released them precisely by acknowledging and feeling them (rather than avoiding them). Leaders become more liberated *and liberating* when we engage emotions as helpful messages and opportunities for our own necessary growth work.

Schools are collection sites for people's emotional imaginations—for better and worse (i.e., some are disciplined, and liberated through intentional practice and others are still unconscious and constrained, waiting for freedom). Developing these inner resources foments internal freedom, which builds through an ever-widening practice of compassion for self, other people, and the world. Internal freedom gives us the ability to harness, rather than be controlled by, one's own emotional imagination—to use it toward self-development, collective equity, and healing. Engaging in generative reflection and developing a critical understanding of our socialized beliefs and triggers is generated by storytelling, which can help leaders re-story themselves in liberating ways that are generative to liberatory pedagogy. People's emotional imaginations are at play whether there is awareness of this or not. Flux leadership necessitates becoming critically conscious—"still in the midst of activity and to be vibrantly alive in repose"—ever reflexive and engaged with our emotional imaginations as a form of radical self-care that supports us to enact "education as the practice of freedom" (hooks, 1994).

DISTRIBUTIVE WISDOM APPROACH

> If you have come here to help me, you are wasting your time. But if you
> have come because your liberation is bound up with mine, then let us work
> together.
>
> —Elder Lilla Watson

In 21st-century leadership, educational leaders have often turned to leadership models that could support them in sharing responsibility around execution of school vision. Specifically, educational leaders turned to the work of distributed leadership, which supports the idea that multiple people were needed to lead, not just the school leader (Spillane, 2012). Lave and Wenger's (1991) conceptualization of communities of practice also contributed to the way these models were taken up within school leadership, which focuses on the social interactions among individuals.

Over time, this arrangement of leadership became more than a heuristic in the literature; in fact, it became a common language among district leaders, school leaders, and teacher leaders. People rallied around the concepts behind distributed leadership at staff professional development and championed the idea that leadership was a distributed practice. In the building, there was an increased focus on individuals taking responsibility for leadership in various ways. These arrangements of leadership were important in ensuring that children were the focus in working toward school improvement. It led to more professional learning communities and task forces in schools pushing various initiatives forward through multiple and diverse stakeholders. Professional learning communities push against the formal roles of leadership. They lead to initiatives like cycles of feedback and reflection, departmental collaboration time, and monitoring student assessment data (Gates Foundation, 2017). In this model, there is a strong emphasis on the formal and informal organizational roles and how this shapes leadership practices. Ultimately, no matter where individuals are situated within the leadership hierarchy, a distributed perspective could shape organizational structures to allow for the capacity to actively facilitate supporting others in their own leadership pathways (Harris, 2013b). These theoretical frames shaped investment into the type of professional development, school culture, and hiring practices that permeated in school buildings and at the district level.

While distributed leadership dominated much of the thinking around educational leadership practice, asymmetrical power relations are still evident within our school infrastructure and must be accounted for. Within school buildings, the opportunities to contribute and shape long-lasting leadership decisions are not equal, and there often exists an earth-shattering silence when it comes to structural barriers (Lumby, 2013). While leadership encourages everyone to be a leader, dialogue can become stifled when it comes to larger issues of who holds power and why and where issues of race and class fall into these conversations. In situations where asymmetrical power relations are not accounted for in leadership decisions, there also exists an unwillingness for the status quo to be questioned.

In these situations, distributive leadership becomes a way to create an illusion toward educational progress without an ability to disrupt the mechanisms that allowed inequity in the first place. As Lumby argues, there is still an "unequal inclusion in leadership" and an unwillingness to "trouble the underlying power structures" (2013, pp. 582, 592). Engaging in leadership work that might shed light on these structural issues is not an option. While social interaction is a core component of the leadership process (Harris, 2013a), school strategic planning as a social process often ignores what undergirds this reality to maintain the status quo.

Within an unequal system of education, educational leadership frameworks must consider how structures are building leadership capacity and dismantling the oppressive structures of marginalization that persist in our whole-staff meetings. Without recognition of these power inequities, these structures are modest at best and damaging at worst. For example, a school building leader encouraging the few people of color on school staff to take on the burden of educating all the White staff on antiracist teaching practices might be seen as an act of distributed leadership. In actuality, it is also an act of a school unwilling to force a school to confront the asymmetrical power dynamics and the inevitable harm that wrecks on people of color in their own building. Instead, we need models for leaders that are willing to actively engage in critical leadership frames that can work to "address the power inherent and generated in society, with the goal of building as complex, contextualized, and equitable a system as possible" (Pak & Ravitch, 2021, p. 7).

In this respect, we propose a *distributive wisdom* approach as an alternative for schools to build stronger knowledge and leadership capacities in their building. A *distributive wisdom* approach decentralizes pervasive knowledge hierarchies—in all of their epistemological violence—to create openings for marginalized knowledges and silenced values to emerge and be centered as critique and guide for leadership decisions. The shift from *distributed* to *distributive* is an intentional choice; given the evolving nature of contexts, distributive wisdom allows for a more active process targeted toward influencing the social dimensions of leadership around issues of equity and justice. This paradigmatic shift is necessary to lead and teach responsively in (and beyond) this moment as we work toward justice and peace. A distributive wisdom approach to learning broadly, to uncovering implicit biases and deficit-based beliefs and how they shape leadership specifically, is crucial for the work of educational leaders.

Seeking out the tenets of distributive wisdom becomes important on the pathway toward cultivating the emotional imagination and building a radical growth mindset. Seeking is a relational approach that helps elevate important self-work with the understanding that it is important to seek out thought-partners in continuous self-improvement. In seeking out dialogic engagement, leadership can uncover leader blind spots around structural issues of power. At the beginning, it becomes important to name and live out the culture of affirmed vulnerability in establishing these organizational shifts. Naming requires building a mutual and relational trust with stakeholders and situating your decision-making around disrupting systems of inequity and power in the pursuit of equity and justice. Building trust within this model focuses on leading and teaching in a way that places reciprocity, mutual love and respect, and understanding at the forefront of knowledge generation and practitioner decision-making (Kannan, 2021).

By centering these tenets, we can elevate the collective wisdom of our stakeholders, which helps to cultivate leadership within our community that can systematically disrupt harmful power dynamics. It also helps the ongoing development of our school leaders, creating the conditions for leaders to become more skilled in their decision-making and cultivating the ability for them to harness the power of a myriad of rich perspectives. Distributive wisdom elevates leadership conversations through authentic leadership frames, which promote dialogue to become more progressive, equitable, and brave in nature. Authentic leadership frames pave the way to acknowledging and reorienting systems of power in productive ways for school communities. Building and sustaining trust is paramount for the effective distribution of leadership, and without this, it is difficult to elevate organizational performance (Day, Sammons, Leithwood, Harris, & Hopkins, 2009; Harris, 2013a).

Flux leaders exhibit a radical transformative leadership style that requires and relies on distributive wisdom to shape fundamental school improvement decisions. The collective and relational approach is generative as it pertains to organizational learning. It works to centralize shared wisdom to support leaders and organizations in enacting culturally responsive schooling structures and processes, emergent design class structures and curricula, resonant communication structures for meetings and learning spaces, and maximally supportive professional development sessions. Inquiry-based learning is encouraged to take center stage, which allows for a range of knowledges and kinds of expertise to be uplifted. Through inquiry-based learning in school contexts such as professional development and family engagement, the approach can combat top-down hierarchies of leadership roles regarding decisions around teaching and learning.

In practice, professional development that integrates a distributive wisdom approach might create communities of practice that support racial literacy and identity-based stress navigation skills. These communities would foster the conditions for effectively identifying, naming, and pushing against real-time inequities within and beyond teams, classrooms, schools, and organizations. Creating these conditions should be navigated with humility. Educational leaders need to help everyone in the organization learn this by providing the necessary structures and supports. It cannot be a one-off initiative. Within family engagement, an inquiry-based learning approach at a family learning night might create richer opportunities to learn how families want to be involved and what they can contribute to the teaching and learning in the school. Community-based projects and project-based learning should be generated alongside the voices and perspectives of members in the community. Families have gifts of knowledge they want to share, and we should bring a critical inquiry stance to these conversations in brainstorming the best ways to partner that feel reciprocal.

When thinking deeper about the role of families in distributive wisdom, educational leaders must place the role within the context of their school community. Educational leaders must ask: *What power dynamics have been at place in the school history and what role has family and community played in decision-making?* Centralizing shared wisdom requires centering the experiential knowledge and experiences of a diverse group of stakeholders and groups that are often silenced in these decisions. School leaders must be willing to go beyond the traditional parent and family surveys to solicit the opinions and voices of community members to shape school policies leveraging the intergenerational voices of the communities they serve (Campano et al., 2016).

It becomes critical that family members are invited to these conversations in meaningful ways and are seen for the knowledge and wisdom that can shape our schools in important ways. Our families have funds of knowledge (González, Moll, & Amanti, 2005) which can create the sustainable, reciprocal, and robust networks that our school communities have always been striving for. They have networks, resources, and valuable insight, and long-lasting institutional history to share. Suppose educational leaders can acknowledge families' "cultural wealth" as a necessary cultural capital required in shaping school improvement. In that case, knowledge can be generated and centered to lead to sustainability and quality. Ultimately, we must be willing to ground the knowledge of our families beyond transactional checkboxes of traditional parental engagement practices. If we can uplift our families, we can uplift our children; this tenet becomes critical in how flux leadership can lean into and learn from the collective.

By focusing on the intentions of how leadership is exercised through a focus on criticality, distributive wisdom can foster collective knowledge generation that can ground leadership decisions in equity. For instance, we call upon school leaders to think more deeply about how we bring diverse stakeholders together to think about school improvement: Who is at the table? What structures are guiding the conversation? How are we ensuring that these voices are equitable? How are we going to follow through on these conversations to enact decisions? Flux leadership foregrounds the stance that thriving is necessarily interdependent. To live out this stance, educational leaders enact an approach that works to level up their organizations in foregrounding shared vulnerability, disruptive innovation, and challenging assumed knowledge hierarchies, mindsets, policies, and practices.

BRAVE-SPACE LEADERSHIP AND A CALL TO ACTION

I have been criticized throughout the course of my career for placing too much faith in the reliability of children's narratives; but I have almost always found that children are a great deal more reliable in telling us what actually

goes on in public school than many of the adult experts who develop policies
that shape their destinies.

—Jonathan Kozol, *The Shame of the Nation:*
The Restoration of Apartheid Schooling in America

Jonathan Kozol, an educator and progressive activist, reminds us of the
importance of surfacing youth narratives in the path toward educational
justice. In an educational landscape where school leaders are often being
bombarded with so-called experts who dictate school improvement priorities, the voices of children and other important stakeholders are often silenced or missing from school strategic priorities that shape teaching and
learning. In times of both crisis and ever-evolving change, we assert that
leaders must elevate these voices in a manner where they are centered for
data-driven school improvement. The act of utilizing story as a crucial data
point for strategic initiatives works to humanize data and provides the pathway for leaders to make data-driven decisions rooted in context. Within flux
leadership, we argue for the importance of *brave-space leadership*, a critical
space where leaders can mobilize stakeholders in sharing their perspectives,
narratives, and stories around a central question in real time.

Brave-space leadership is ostensibly the most important driver within
flux leadership because it supports leaders in gathering and immediately analyzing data in moments of crisis and change from their stakeholders. That
being said, leaders must exercise the other seven tenets of the flux leadership
model regularly to create the conditions for this space to operate and flourish. As mentioned in Chapter 2, brave spaces refer to a set of communication
and process norms that invite, create, and uphold the conditions for authentic, equitable, and critical dialogic engagement in groups, teams, classrooms,
and organizations (Arao & Clemens, 2013). Brave spaces directly contrast
so-called "safe spaces," which often do not acknowledge the sociopolitical
power dynamics around race, class, gender, and other axes of oppression.
The cultivation of brave spaces requires leader and group bravery (Arao &
Clemens, 2013). It also requires ongoing leader modeling and engagement
for people to feel comfortable enough to discuss educational, social, and
group dynamic issues in ways that go deeper than what is typically discussed.
At present, identity privilege–based norms marginalize people of color and
undermine equality in groups (Ravitch & Carl, 2019). Within *brave-space
leadership*, leaders are utilizing these spaces for the purposes of gathering
data in the forms of stories for school improvement and decision-making.

The data collection and subsequent analysis processes within brave-
space leadership are guided by the principles within *story-based inquiry*,
a crucial practitioner research methodology rooted in equity. Within flux
leadership, story-based inquiry is an essential driver in leaders embodying

the tenets of flux to engage in collaborative processes designed to engage in more equitable decision-making. In *Matters of Interpretation: Reciprocal Transformation in Therapeutic and Developmental Relationships with Youth*, Nakkula and Ravitch (1998) discuss the significance of data that is often silenced, missing, or erased from contexts such as schools. In the context of school improvement, when the tides are shifting and changes are transpiring in real time, there are windows into these experiences that leaders must consider to make decisions. Without these stories, our leadership choices and data-driven decisions are missing the rich complexity that can lead to initiatives lacking in effectiveness. At worst, stakeholders feel caught in a top-down system that does not include their perspectives. A story-based inquiry research methodology centers the importance of these stories and values the myriad of insights generated from this approach.

We argue that *storying the gap* on the ground requires research methods rooted in the practitioner context—attentive to educational leaders who are on the frontlines doing this work alongside their communities. In real time, data-driven school improvement must have tools and methods that leaders can utilize quickly and humanely. This toolbox must also be attentive to the dimensions of power that circulate within a school setting and braid the sociopolitical in a manner that feels ethical. In story-based inquiry, *rapid-cycle inquiry* is a research method that can support educational leaders in their quest to story the gap.

Rapid-cycle inquiry is a research method that is collaborative in nature. We argue that this inquiry approach becomes generative when individuals from various stakeholder positions engage in this data-driven work—from generating questions, collecting stories within brave spaces, and engaging in collaborative data analysis. This method acknowledges that time is a constraining factor for practitioners on the ground—especially in times of rapid change. Rapid-cycle inquiry leverages the power of stories as a dataset by creating a stronger sense of the moment for how to move forward. Forward-thinking in this way can help leaders engage in collaborative decision-making that can be more contextualized to the moment. In practice, rapid-cycle inquiry can be utilized in a method on taskforces as a way to gauge the temperature for a roll-out of a new initiative: *How is standards-based grading impacting our highest-tier students* all the way to how a crisis situation is unfolding: *How are families navigating online learning in April 2020?*

For our Mid-Career doctoral students who were simultaneously navigating the front lines of leading schools at the start of the COVID-19 pandemic and taking a research methods course in educational leadership, they knew there were essential voices that needed to be heard for the purposes of creating new initiatives and policies in real time. Conducting these inquiries seemed overwhelming emotionally and logistically. By utilizing rapid-cycle inquiry, our students were able to assets-based thinking to unearth the emerging questions that were popping up in their contexts in a manner that felt collaborative from start to finish. They could create brave spaces for their stakeholders to share their stories in ways that felt brave and humane through different mediums. Then, our teams could re-convene and feel supported to engage with these stories, honor their stakeholders, and engage in a rapid-cycle analysis to help generate ideas and themes with a richness that could help them decide how to move forward in real time. While rapid-cycle inquiries are by no means a replacement for other data collective methods in schools, this approach to data works to combat deficit perspectives by surfacing the complexity in people's lives, which can shape school initiatives for the better. It is time for us to offer up alternatives and other options to think about data in school improvement. Are standard metrics always the answer? Is there another way to make decisions based on data? What can stories provide us in times of rapid flux?

Flux leadership works to center the humanity of leaders and the people they lead in school ecosystems. In the chapters that follow, readers will see the results of the rapid-cycle inquiries conducted by mid-career educational leaders across various contexts from March–May 2020. Readers will also see what kinds of rapid-cycle inquiry methods were utilized in each inquiry. We hope this will prompt educational leaders to think about how you can utilize these methods within your own sites of practice. Appendixes A–D present process considerations and templates to begin your own rapid-cycle inquiry processes.

Our leaders engaged in flux leadership from start to finish allowing their stakeholders to restore and share their experiences in generative and affirming ways to sustainably, productively, and humanely work through crises. Through this work, we have learned that brave-space leadership is not the end of school improvement. On the contrary, it is only the beginning of shifting and creating the dynamic structures that our schools need for a more equitable tomorrow. In times of radical flux, brave-space leadership and flux leadership more broadly foster the conditions for the humanizing change to flourish—something all schools deserve.

REFERENCES

Alston, J. A. (2005). Tempered radicals and servant leaders: Black females persevering in the superintendency. *Educational Administration Quarterly, 41*(4), 675–688.

Amiot, M., Mayer-Glenn, J., & Parker, L. (2020). Applied critical race theory: Educational leadership actions for student equity. *Race Ethnicity and Education, 23*(2), 200–220.

Anderson, R. E., & Stevenson, H. C. (2019). RECASTing racial stress and trauma: Theorizing the healing potential of racial socialization in families. *American Psychologist, 74*(1), 63–75.

Arao, B., & Clemens, K. (2013). From safe spaces to brave spaces: A new way to frame dialogue around diversity and social justice. In L. M. Landreman (Ed.), *The art of effective facilitation: Reflections from social justice educators* (pp. 135–150). Stylus.

Bell, D. (2018). *Faces at the bottom of the well: The permanence of racism.* Hachette UK.

Blackburn, M. (2014). Humanizing research with LGBTQ youth through dialogic communication, consciousness raising, and action. In D. Paris & M. T. Winn (Eds.), *Humanizing research: Decolonizing qualitative inquiry with youth and communities* (pp. 63–80). Sage.

Boler, M., & Zembylas, M. (2003). Discomforting truths: The emotional terrain of understanding difference. *Pedagogies of Difference: Rethinking Education for Social Change, 110,* 135.

Brown, A. M. (2017). *Emergent strategy: Shaping change, shaping worlds.* AK Press.

Campano, G., Ghiso, M. P., & Welch, B. J. (2016). *Partnering with immigrant communities: Action through literacy.* Teachers College Press.

CDC. (2021). Data and statistics on children's mental health. www.cdc.gov/childrens mentalhealth/data.html

Center for American Progress. (2021). The basic facts about children in poverty. www.americanprogress.org/issues/poverty/reports/2021/01/12/494506/basic-facts-children-poverty

Chilisa, B. (2020). *Indigenous research methodologies* (2nd ed.). Sage.

Chiu, A. (2020). Time to ditch "toxic positivity," experts say: "It's okay not to be okay." *The Washington Post.* www.washingtonpost.com/lifestyle/wellness/toxic-positivity-mental-health-covid/2020/08/19/5dff8d16-e0c8-11ea-8181-606e603bb1c4_story.html

Cochran-Smith, M., & Lytle, S. L. (2009). *Inquiry as stance: Practitioner research for the next generation.* Teachers College Press.

Crary, M. (2017). Working from dominant identity positions: Reflections from "diversity-aware" White people about their cross-race work relationships. *Journal of Applied Behavioral Science, 53*(2), 290–316.

Crenshaw, K. (2021). *On intersectionality: Essential writings.* The New Press.

Dantley, M. E. (2009). African American educational leadership: Critical, purposive, and spiritual. In L. Foster & L. C. Tillman (Eds.), *African American perspectives on leadership in schools: Building a culture of empowerment* (pp. 39–56). Routledge.

Day, C., Sammons. P., Leithwood, K., Harris, A. & Hopkins, D. (2009) *The impact of leadership on pupil outcomes.* Final report. DCSF.

DiAngelo, R. (2018). *White fragility: Why it's so hard for White people to talk about racism.* Beacon Press.

Dweck, C. (2016). What having a "growth mindset" actually means. *Harvard Business Review Online.*

Dweck, C. (n.d.). A summary of growth and fixed mindsets. *Fs blog.* https://fs.blog/2015/03/carol-dweck-mindset

Edwards, J. (2016). Personal Communication with Dr. Howard Stevenson.

Eren, N. S., & Ravitch, S. M. (2021). Trauma-informed leadership: Balancing love and accountability. In K. Pak & S. M. Ravitch, *Critical leadership praxis: Leading educational and social change* (pp. 187–200), Teachers College Press.

Freire, P. (1996). *Pedagogy of the oppressed* (Revised Ed.). Continuum.

García, E., & Weiss, E. (2019). The teacher shortage is real, large and growing, and worse than we thought. The first report in "The Perfect Storm in the Teacher Labor Market" series. *Economic Policy Institute.*

Gates Foundation. (2017). 4 key things to know about distributed leadership. https://usprogram.gatesfoundation.org/News-and-Insights/Articles/4-Key -Things-to-Know-About-Distributed-Leadership

George, B. (2009). *Seven lessons for leading in crisis* (Vol. 166). John Wiley & Sons.

Giancola, J. M., & Hutchison, J. K. (2005). *Transforming the culture of school leadership: Humanizing our practice.* Corwin Press.

González, N., Moll, L., & Amanti, C. (Eds.). (2005). *Funds of knowledge: Theorizing practices in households, communities and classrooms.* Erlbaum.

Hanson, R. (2018). *Resilient: How to grow an unshakable core of calm, strength, and happiness.* Crown.

Harris, A. (2013a) Distributed leadership: Friend or foe? *Educational Management Administration & Leadership, 41*(5), 545–554.

Harris A. (2013b) *Distributed leadership matters: Potential, practicalities and possibilities.* Corwin Press.

Heifetz, R. A., & Linsky, M. (2002). A survival guide for leaders. *Harvard Business Review, 80*(6), 65–74.

Heifetz, R. A., Grashow, A., & Linsky, M. (2009a). Leadership in a (permanent) crisis. *Harvard Business Review, 87*(7/8), 62–69.

Heifetz, R. A., Grashow, A., & Linsky, M. (2009b). *The theory behind the practice.* Harvard Business Press.

Hochschild, A. R. (1983). *The managed heart: Commercialization of human feeling.* University of California Press.

hooks, b. (1994). *Teaching to transgress: Education as the practice of freedom.* Routledge.

hooks, b. (2001). *All about love: New Visions.* William Morrow.

hooks, b. (2003). *Teaching community: A pedagogy of hope.* Routledge.

Horsford, S. D. (2014). When race enters the room: Improving leadership and learning through racial literacy. *Theory into Practice, 53*(2), 123–130.

Hubler, S., Taylor, K., & Nierenberg, A. (2020, December 24) Public schools face funding "death spiral" as enrollment drops. *The New York Times.* www.nytimes .com/2020/12/22/us/public-schools-enrollment-stimulus.html

James, E. H., & Wooten, L. P. (2011). Crisis leadership and why it matters. *The European Financial Review, 81*(7), 77–82. December–January 2011.

Johansen, B. (2018). The new leadership literacy of creating and sustaining positive energy. *Leader to Leader, 88*, 30–37.

Kannan, C. A. (2021). A critical inquiry into college: Critical literacy in a college readiness program for first-generation students of color. Unpublished doctoral dissertation, University of Pennsylvania.

Kataoka, S. H., Zhang, L., & Wells, K. B. (2002). Unmet need for mental health care among US children: Variation by ethnicity and insurance status. *American Journal of Psychiatry, 159*(9), 1548–1555.

Khalifa, M. (2018). *Culturally responsive school leadership.* Harvard Education Press.

Ladson-Billings, G., & Tate, W. F. (2006). Toward a critical race theory of education. In A. D. Dixon (Ed.). *Critical Race Theory in education: All God's children got a song* (pp. 11–30). Routledge.

Lampert, K. (2003). *Compassionate education: Prolegomena for radical schooling.* University Press of America.

Lave, J., & Wenger, E. (1991). *Situated learning: Legitimate peripheral participation.* Cambridge University Press.

Liang, J. G., & Peters-Hawkins, A. L. (2017). "I am more than what I look alike": Asian American women in public school administration. *Educational Administration Quarterly, 53*(1), 40–69.

Lorde, A. (1988). *A burst of light: Essays by Audre Lorde.* Firebrand Books.

Love, B. L. (2019). *We want to do more than survive: Abolitionist teaching and the pursuit of educational freedom.* Beacon Press.

Lumby, J. (2013). Distributed leadership: The uses and abuses of power. *Educational Management Administration & Leadership, 41*(5), 581–597.

Lytle, J. H., Lytle, S. L., Johanek, M. C., & Rho, K. J. (Eds.). (2018). *Repositioning educational leadership: Practitioners leading from an inquiry stance.* Teachers College Press.

Martinez, M. A., Rivera, M., & Marquez, J. (2020). Learning from the experiences and development of Latina school leaders. *Educational Administration Quarterly, 56*(3), 472–498.

Nakkula, M. J., & Ravitch, S. M. (1998). *Matters of interpretation: Reciprocal transformation in therapeutic and developmental relationships with youth.* Jossey-Bass.

Nakkula, M. J., & Schneider-Muñoz, A. J. (2018). *The United States: Possibility development in the land of opportunity gaps. Adolescent psychology in today's world: Global perspectives on risk, relationships, and development* (3 vols.). Praeger.

Omi, M., & Winant, H. (2014). *Racial formation in the United States.* Routledge.

Pak, K., & Ravitch, S. M. (2021). *Critical leadership praxis: Leading educational and social change.* Teachers College Press.

Paris, D., & Winn, M. T. (Eds.). (2013). *Humanizing research: Decolonizing qualitative inquiry with youth and communities.* Sage.

Petriglieri, G. (2020). The psychology behind effective crisis leadership. *Harvard Business Review Online.*

Ravitch, S. M. (2020a). Why teaching through crisis requires a radical new mindset: Introducing flux pedagogy. *Harvard Business Publishing Education.* https://hbsp.harvard.edu/inspiring-minds/why-teaching-through-crisis-requires-a-radical-new-mindset

Ravitch, S. M. (2020b). Flux pedagogy: Transforming teaching and leading during coronavirus. *Perspectives on Urban Education, 17*(4), 18–32.

Ravitch, S. M., & Carl, M. N. (2019). *Applied research for sustainable change: A guide for education leaders.* Harvard Education Press.

Ravitch, S. M., & Tillman, C. (2010). Collaboration as a site of personal and institutional transformation: Thoughts from inside a cross-national alliance. *Penn GSE Perspectives on Urban Education, 8*(1), 3–10.

Richo, D. (2019). *Triggers: How we can stop reacting and start healing.* Shambhala.

Rivera-McCutchen, R. L. (2020). "We don't got time for grumbling": Toward an ethic of radical care in urban school leadership. *Educational Administration Quarterly*. https://journals.sagepub.com/doi/10.1177/0013161X20925892

Russo, A. (2018). *Feminist accountability: Disrupting violence and transforming power*. New York University Press.

Santamaría, L. J., & Santamaría, A. P. (2013). *Applied critical leadership in education: Choosing change*. Routledge.

Shor, I. (1999). What is critical literacy? *Journal of Pedagogy, Pluralism, and Practice, 1*(4), 2.

Spillane, J. P. (2012). *Distributed leadership* (Vol. 4). John Wiley & Sons.

Stevenson, H. C. (2014). *Promoting racial literacy in schools: Differences that make a difference*. Teachers College Press.

Stokes, E. K., Zambrano, L. D., Anderson, K. N., Marder, E. P., Raz, K. M., Felix, S. E. B., Tie, Y., & Fullerton, K. E. (2020). Coronavirus disease 2019 case surveillance—United States, January 22–May 30, 2020. *Morbidity and Mortality Weekly Report, 69*(24), 759.

Sutcher, L., Darling-Hammond, L., & Carver-Thomas, D. (2016). *A coming crisis in teaching? Teacher supply, demand, and shortages in the US*. Learning Policy Institute.

Su, A. J. (2019). Self-care for leaders: Make restoration a part of the job. *Leader to Lead, 94*, 12–16.

Tillman, L. C. (2004). African American principals and the legacy of Brown. *Review of Research in Education, 28*(1), 101–146.

USDA Economic Research Service (2019). Food security in the U.S. Key statistics and graphics. Washington, DC. www.ers.usda.gov/topics/food- nutrition-assistance/food-security-in-the-us/key-statistics-graphics.aspx

CHAPTER 4

Hard Pivot

Compulsory Crisis Leadership
Emerges From a Space of Doubt

Andrew Phillips, Kelly Grimmett, and Elizabeth Fernandez-Vina

---

EDITORIAL FRAMING

In the first rapid-cycle inquiry of this book, three educational leadership doctoral students take up the call to dig into the collective understanding of what happens in crisis for educational leaders—specifically, what it meant for them and their cohort in the University of Pennsylvania Mid-Career Program for Educational Leadership during the onset of the COVID-19 pandemic.

In this chapter, readers will learn more than just eyewitness accounts of what happened to a group of educational leaders in the pandemic. It will also help readers understand why flux pedagogy as a humanizing tool for support is needed not only for students in our schools, but within our teaching and learning models for adult educators.

While educational leaders often work hard to build camaraderie among collectives of educators through tools like icebreakers, this chapter helps us understand why this is not nearly enough. Instead, we learn that models to build community must work to build collective power through more humanizing tenets and mechanisms that disrupt hierarchies of power. Within flux pedagogy, there is a commitment to enacting critical and humanizing frames simultaneously to support collectives and this rapid-cycle inquiry is a reminder of why this is essential.

As the group writes:

> Yet, a group identity develops that begins to defy dominant cultural constructs. The cohort model helps to disrupt colonialist paradigms of rugged individualism and replace them with collectivism, a shared sense of responsibility for and to one another. Unlike prior

educational experiences, this setting is not competitive. Diverse perspectives enrich thought and experience.

In times of crisis, flux pedagogy is necessary to create collectives that are brave, diverse, and loving. Without a flux pedagogical mindset, these educators would have been ill-equipped to exercise flux leadership within their contexts, to engage in these rapid-cycle inquiries, and ultimately to engage in the leadership practices their communities desperately needed modeled during these times.

Flux pedagogy acknowledges the tensions and complexity in leadership, and that can be seen in how these students analyzed their own experiences: "Yielding/Dismantling, Losing/Finding, Doubt/Validation." Leadership is anything but contradiction, and this inquiry works to help readers better understand what this looks like and how it can be named and moved through in productive ways.

We hope this chapter sheds light on the fact that humanizing teaching and learning models like flux pedagogy are necessary to create the conditions for learning communities to thrive in these moments. For educational leaders, K–12 students, community members, teachers, staff for past, present, and future.

INTRODUCTION

Twenty-five individuals began the Mid-Career Doctoral Program in Educational Leadership in July 2019, an executive doctoral program at the University of Pennsylvania Graduate School of Education. It is a crucible of intensity forging deep bonds. Each cohort member prepares to launch a pilot research study in the context of leadership practice. The coronavirus pandemic lands and waves of COVID-19 closures wash over everything. Overnight, the work, as educator and student, is cast online. People's lives are altered in ways that ossify preexisting equity conditions, compounding the inequities in schooling and life in an acute on chronic assault. As we watch human suffering unfold in full relief, we feel reverberations near and far. The ties sustaining the cohort are stretched taught through screens of glass, adrift in a "state of relational and educational uncertainty, upheaval, and reverberation" (Ravitch, 2020, p. 7). Instinctively craving to contextualize the experience within emergent and humanizing frameworks, as an act of self-care and group care as a cohort of educational leaders responsible to serve whole communities, the chapter authors chose to interview each cohort member (all quotes herein are from cohort members with permission). As the world shuts down, we gathered insights and reflected on the roles of these leaders in a time of radical flux.

ORIENTATION: STRANGERS

July 2019: We sought this space. We sit in a circle. We know generalities: We are a collective situated between leadership and scholarship. We represent every education sector and locale, a range of career trajectories, a cross-section of roles, and a spectrum of social identities. We are 25 education professionals working and living in locations across the United States, plus one from Vietnam, with over 400 years of shared experience. The average age is 43. We are 15 women, 10 men; 10 identify White, and 15 of color. We are the 18th Mid-Career cohort: C18s.

For the next 3 years, we are told, we will deepen our understanding of educational organizations, instruction, and learning while continuing to meet the daily demands of serving as educational leaders who are also doctoral students. The program is designed for diverse cohorts of working professionals in senior levels of educational leadership, aspiring to become more effective while navigating and transforming the status quo. We prepare ourselves, individually and collectively, to deepen our impact, as have hundreds of others in the preceding cohorts. Still, sitting in this circle, we experience doubt. *Do I belong here? Will I be able to fulfill academic demands? How will I fit this work into my already jammed schedule? Will I make it?*

Our program director presents a cautionary tale to conclude the one-day orientation. It sets the tone. Early 20th-century German forestry sought to order trees in columns and rows for efficient harvest. This ordering ignored the intertwining subterranean root systems. The convenience of visual order disregarded the messiness of relationships, and the result was blight. Positivist relational rationality overlooks a potent space in the status quo: the third space, the in-between, the liminal space from which support emerges and sustenance is nurtured. The parable is clear. We will need one another to survive, proliferate, and grow (Brown, 2017) if we are to thrive across these next 3 years and decades to follow. In education, having a deep and lasting impact is not a solitary enterprise, so our work begins together. Who could know how this would be tested in a mere 6 months?

CONVERGENCE: OTHERS

Powell and Menendian (2016) define "othering" as "a set of dynamics, processes, and structures that engender marginality and persistent inequality across any of the full range of human differences based on group identities." By design, our cohort spans physical, psychological, demographic, and cultural dimensions. Convened as a collection of "others" in positions of educational leadership, each member brings a sense of displacement and isolation—an imposter syndrome—and with that: doubt. Belonging is an unspoken question amid the tension of bringing an authentic self to the circle. Yet, a group identity develops that begins to defy dominant cultural constructs. The cohort model helps to disrupt colonialist paradigms of rugged individualism and replace them with collectivism, a shared sense of responsibility for and to one another. Unlike prior educational experiences, this setting is not competitive. Diverse perspectives enrich thought and experience. The cohort dwells in a kind of "third space" (Bhabha, 2004) and plots the dismantlement of the status quo in education. It surfaces and names the "othering" still entrenched within respective professional and personal settings. We didn't know how abruptly we'd soon be forced apart.

EMERGENCE(Y): COHORT

The first year unfolds. As an executive program, classes convene on campus one weekend a month. To attend to the substantial work between sessions, we connect through a variety of media. Classes are not compartmentalized, nor do they follow a conventional semester schedule. It is an ongoing and endless stream of work that overlaps scholarship with practice and interweaves individuals with collective professional experience. Over time, we cultivate a potent, collective power infused with a deep belief in an ability to lead the traversing of educational landscapes while embracing the three intertwined goals: survive, proliferate, grow (Brown, 2017). This belief remains a fragile work in progress.

In March 2020, we prepared to launch the pilot studies, a precursor to our dissertations. Seemingly overnight, the pandemic strikes, and the waves of COVID-19 closures upend our personal and professional lives. Within hours, we close our schools, send the children home, and arrive for class . . . online. It is a surreal and hazy space, full of fear, shock, and pain—suspending us between past, present, and future. The crisis is still unfolding, and we have yet to grasp its enormity as we worry for our students, families, and communities. In this foreign, awkward space, we gather together on a virtual frontline.

Schools are not hospitals. But schools have become a critical vehicle to coordinate and deliver far more than academics. Schools are hubs for social, emotional, intellectual, nutritional, physical, and communicative support for their children and families. The cohort encompasses leaders deep in the trenches of a humanitarian crisis. We have no playbook, precedent, historical reference, or research. The shutdown is an in-between space like no other. Thoughtful agility will be a critical survival skill as we grapple with creating a sense of virtual school order when order appears absent in the physical world. Our flux identities of leader-student are thrust into the radical flux of educational leadership through a pandemic.

After the school closures began on March 13, we huddled—virtually—with our professor, Dr. Sharon Ravitch. In a defining moment of leadership, Dr. Ravitch compassionately supports the cohort and elects to pivot from long-planned individual research. In this watershed moment, we will study educational leadership in action. The burning question: *What will be the inevitable impacts on the American educational landscape and its leaders?*

How do we, as in-service educational leaders, come together as a flux inquiry group to identify and balance our positionalities in the fluidity of the crisis? How do we use flux leadership to make sense of our shifting roles that now require us to respond and console a litany of colleague and community needs? In what ways does engaging in flux leadership reconcile these needs with our personal self-care needs of mind, body, and spirit through a crisis, while determining and setting a course of action for our institutions without the benefit of clear data, precedence, or policy? How does the emergent hybridity of our voices, cultures, and experiences come together as an agentic and creative third space of hybridity, emergence, and transformation (Ravitch, 2020)?

NAVIGATION: LEADERS (IN FLUX)

With a mere toehold in this new mode and space, the cohort begins this inquiry. We are practitioner doctoral students cast into a radically changed landscape, and like everything else, this inquiry approach is uncharted territory; interviews with cohort members are both research and shared compassionate reflection as we learn how to understand our new geography. In this space, crisis leadership is compulsory: Schooling must continue when no one knows how to make that happen. Our intent is to project impact, not simply record history. We do so by offering insight into how this group of educational leader-students moved through the first 6 months of a tectonic transformation in which we too remained mired. Personal and professional responsibilities reveal the lived dimensions of the crisis, and common threads emerge. Leaning into this shared leadership inquiry, our method is both ballast and guide. As the group dynamic contributes to our own sense of empowerment, we frame the cohort's evolution, as students and leaders bridging radical unknowns, to offer something that moves us forward.

Ten weeks into the pandemic and shelter-in-place orders, George Floyd's murder, under the knee of a White Minneapolis police officer, creates another layer of crisis. Floyd's murder sparks global civil actions that erupt into multigenerational civic outrage. Already displaced, social and educational terrains suffer even more profound ruptures. The cohort's felt sense of urgency deepens and intensifies. This chapter offers field validation of these leaders' stories of how we managed as educational leaders during a time of crisis—what we were thinking, feeling, and doing during a pandemic to maintain our sanity, keep our schools functioning, and hold our families intact. It shares how we stay informed, intentional, and thoughtful in the now blurred third space of professional and academic co-mingled with personal life. Our work—the work—is about self-care and caregiving, doubt and validation, rituals and boundaries, urgent calm and forging forward, deciding and inquiring, yielding and dismantling, losing and finding. One at a time, or all at once, in a time of radical flux, there is no choice. Leadership is compulsory. The quotes below emerged from our rapid-cycle interviews.

SELF-CARE/CAREGIVING

I am exhausted most days. I worry about the job I am doing as a parent and doubt my skills as both a mom and an educator.

As the abrupt sheltering-in-place halts established routines, the rupture prompts new resolutions and promises of new beginnings. Commutes, late meetings, and familial commitments are no longer a requirement. Amid complete imbalance, we lunge for stability through reaffirmations: We must take care of ourselves to take care of others. There will be time to build a routine of good habits in the midst of this pandemic. We will balance professional, family, personal, and academic responsibilities. We make these plans; the universe mocks us. We try again. Might the pandemic offer an opportunity for better self-care?

We make new lists, set new goals, try to establish new routines overnight. Longing for a nonexistent routine, we piece together schedules and daily itineraries: work meetings, work time, exercise, study, care for and teach our own children. We expect to be everything to everyone, including ourselves. Crisis adrenaline conjures visions of invincibility: We can do it all, we persuade ourselves. Calendars clear and businesses close. Impending needs rise like tidal waves, crashing through the Wi-Fi.

We try again to pack tasks into a pattern that is not sustainable, asking ourselves *where is the balance?* The lists become endless, renewing each morning: work check-ins, prepare breakfast for our families, throw clothes in the washer, another Zoom meeting, remember to eat breakfast, answer emails, put clothes in the dryer, order groceries, listen to a webinar, practice yoga, another Zoom meeting, draft a letter to staff, make dinner, help kids with homework, and on and on. As for the pandemic offering an opportunity for better self-care—no, not now. We click from meeting to meeting, complete tasks and fulfill obligations as possible, and barely have time to visit the restroom just down the hall.

We deprioritize self-care. It's a bad maintenance plan; we know this. But when we prioritize self-care, it becomes an obsession or a chore, another task on the list. Though we are proximally closer to our families, the overwhelming needs of others spare little time for family. We push toward impossible expectations amid the weight of paradox. We can't keep up, and we chastise our failures. Self-criticism takes its toll. Guilt pervades every action and inaction. Might the pandemic offer an opportunity for better self-care? Uh, well . . .

Lost routines—once dreaded commutes, in-person meetings, family commitments—are now longed for memories. We search for a sense of control, designing concrete tasks with beginnings and ends. We bake and puzzle, drink more, eat more, exercise less, eat less, work more, drink less, and binge-watch television. We hide from families in bathrooms, attend class from a car, and take work calls from bed. As the pendulum swings, we struggle to find stasis. At what point might the pandemic offer an opportunity for better self-care?

The burden of leadership at home and at work is real—everyone wants a piece of us, including ourselves. It takes willpower to give ourselves permission to be human amid the harsh reality that we aren't superheroes. Taking care of the mind, body, and soul requires unanticipated effort. It is easier to care for others. It takes intentionality to maintain self-care and nourishment. We didn't prioritize self-care before the pandemic, and we still don't. Instead, we set lofty goals for ourselves, as we do so often at new thresholds. Aspirations can disconnect vision from sight, and self-care isn't about checking boxes. It is about giving ourselves permission to be who we are instead of what we want to be. Unfulfilled self-care goals ironically induce anxiety. These unchecked boxes cause us to doubt ourselves and our ability to do anything well, such as establishing boundaries or critical decisions. Self-care is about replacing self-criticism with self-compassion—being as gentle, kind, and supportive to ourselves as we are to others. Welcome to this state of knowing. It took us a pandemic to arrive here. How does this space offer an opportunity for better self-care so that our leadership is sustainable?

DOUBT/VALIDATION

I feel, at the same time, afraid and courageous—lost and found. I am both adrift at sea and moored on the shore. I am in a space where I am looking between worlds, both isolated and frighteningly intimate, as we break the fourth wall into people's homes and worlds—in many ways without invitation. I am both an advocate and imposter, a leader with a vision and a wanderer in the dark. I do not know where I stand.

Self-doubt is a curious, surprising leadership malady. We turn a corner and enter a space of professional and personal crisis. It tests us. Doubt is abundant; validation is scarce. Overnight, everything comes into question, underscored by the absence of physical schools. We scramble as the abrupt shelter-in-place forces adjustments to meet an unprecedented leadership challenge. We adapt and respond, with every ounce of intention we can muster, to perform rapid triage and create online learning environments from scratch. The transition exposes and exacerbates so many of the pre-existing inequities within our schools.

Educators are planners, and this is a paradox. Teaching requires nimbleness, yet schools are not nimble places. Schools rely on patterns and routines. As educational leaders, nothing prepared us for this moment; an undercurrent of resentment fuels the doubt. Novice or veteran, we collectively experience isolation while charging forward to navigate a vast terrain of volatile and complex issues. Extant research and historical documents, vital to informed decisions, are no longer relevant. There is no playbook for the overwhelming volume of tasks. As a cohort of leaders, we manifest the transition in unison, experiencing unique circumstances and common fears together. In the safety of early crisis cohort huddles, we share agonies and questions: *Are we equipped to lead in these unprecedented times? Will we manage professional, personal, and academic demands? Will we make it through?* We attempt to project calm as doubt torments. We long for normalcy yet know this is a rare opportunity to promote real change. We work to mitigate immediate challenges, seek validation, and brainstorm strategies to dismantle the falling status quo.

While working and living in a liminal space between past and future, there is no end in sight. There's self-imposed pressure to make the right decisions, while projecting strength and resilience. Yet, we are fighting a downward spiral of personal and professional ineffectiveness. We look in the mirror and tell ourselves to hold it together. We call someone looking for a pat on the back. Then there are times we gratefully receive that call. Validation increases from vulnerability with ourselves and others. It comes from within but is nurtured by staff members, families, friends, and cohort-mates. Self-forgiveness is validating, too. Until we accept that we aren't invincible, that it's impossible to be everything to everyone, we cannot validate our feelings, emotions, and decisions. Acceptance, in this way, requires that we give ourselves permission to be human. From vulnerability grows real strength. This process is a crucial juncture for growing through pandemic leadership. Though the future is uncertain and full of unknowable consequences, it is okay to lean into vulnerability to change course. Our journey is to learn, not to confirm. It is okay to say, "eff it, we're not doing this because it doesn't make sense now," just as our professor did.

RITUALS/BOUNDARIES

I had to step away and create a space where we talked. I asked, "What do we believe is important for our children? How are we showing up as leaders?" We were tired and emotional. I tell my principals, "protect your energy." I build in time for them to share this work.

We create some rituals, like commencements, weddings, and funerals, "imbued with meaning," suggests thought leader Alex Vogel. These rituals mark a time or event as special or important. They connect the present with [the] things in the past and our hope for the future. Equally important, if not more so, are the small rituals. These mundane, secular events organize everyday life, and practicing these small rituals orders our time and space with routine. Temporal human-made apparatuses, like clocks and calendars, help us navigate days, weeks, and months, while creating observed natural patterns. Though time does not exist, against these objects, we track life's passages, note gains and losses, material and otherwise, and plan forward.

Though constructed time is not human's natural state, traumatic evaporation of small rituals is a frequent refrain. The cohort struggles to reconstruct personal and professional rituals that might re-establish measurable patterns. In the early days of quarantine, it often felt hopeless as we were knocked down again and again while fighting to maintain normalcy. Reflective, inquiry-based, proactive endeavors are subsumed by the need for rapid response, reactive decision-making. It is a weak leadership position, but there is no alternative. Pandemic quarantines are not familiar to our small rituals; blind innovation is compensation.

Several weeks into distance learning, the assistant superintendent asks herself, *What can I do differently? What does my community need?* Her predominantly African American community has been hit hard by the school closures. Injustices and inequalities before COVID-19 are magnified. She transforms the meeting space into a place for meaningful dialogue between principals. Among updates and district messages, instruction, and learning reports, the weekly meeting ritual transcends business as usual. This intentionally cultivated space centers both care and compassion. It is an opportunity to strengthen community bonds—a place to tackle social injustice and community inequity and dream together

In the midst of the pandemic, we abruptly experienced our lives absent of rituals. We miss the interstitial glue holding apart—and thus together—defined commitments and life obligations. Physical space is also not inconsequential: We do different things in different places. Some houses have spaces for eating, cooking, bathing, and dreaming. Others do not. Overnight, quarantine creates one-room schoolhouses from homes. The rituals that created boundaries and limited access to us have vanished. Invited or not, we enter into and share together previously private domestic life. Boundaries are a concept, a line struck by a pen to define—thus differentiate—geographic, political, and ideological realms. Unforeseen and unpredicted, quarantine erases physical and identity boundaries while simultaneously reinforcing them: Quarantine rendered them visible.

Pre-quarantine, we routinely traversed vast spaces spread across a region. Physically compressed into immediate domestic and neighborhood spaces, we traveled as voyeurs. The network of spaces through which we moved becomes confused: Different functions overlayer into the same space(s), with few opportunities for transition. Ensconced within familiar domestic spaces, they become unfamiliar by constant occupation. A bedroom is conscripted into a space of work: Teaching and learning occur at a makeshift table. We work in the home space; we live in the workspace. Life rituals, even mundane ones, no longer unfold according to a spatial script. We ad hoc everything to make it work. And our privileges bubble up to us in all of this.

Errands—once a nuisance, but now we discover they served as chances to step away and reflect—are thwarted by business closures. Extended showers and parked cars are now a refuge. These escape sites provide a buffer, replacing lost pockets of time that once separated the person from the professional. For those acclimated to working from home, empty workday spaces are corrupted by the constant presence or hollow absence of family. The home now includes identities once assumed on the other side of the front door. Identities inhabit, are formed by and shaped through interactions within different spaces. Yet, space shapes us as much as we shape it. What remains of life's spatial variety is compressed into one place: the domestic space of the home.

A meal sits before the keyboard; a child sits in the lap; a pet strolls the background. An unmuted mic broadcasts a local siren, applause, and a helicopter surveilling protests. In some houses, a table is nearly a symbol of gathering, offering a setting for celebrations, dialogue, and disagreement. During quarantine, the table surface has tipped up into the vertical screen. We enter one another's homes, devoid of known rituals to honor or welcome such intrusions.

URGENT CALM/FORGING FORWARD

> We had 4 hours to get everyone out of there, get them everything they needed, and the building was shutting down. And we weren't going to be back. Then my role became moving the entire campus to virtual, making sure that everyone in the field was taken care of, helping to manage, to make sure everyone had devices and the setup they needed, checking in with teachers, checking in with students, checking in with families. And just trying to keep everybody calm.

Safety drills are all too familiar in education. The alarms go off, and we stay calm. We walk with purpose to the nearest exit. It is an ingrained survival ritual. Despite this preparation, no drills or practices could have prepared us for March 2020. In this drill, we took shelter in our homes, familiarized ourselves with new technologies, and sought new ways to continue the work.

In March, we went home expecting to return to our schools and districts. Initial teaching measures are stop-gap: 2, maybe 3, weeks of quarantine. Though many are surprised, no one imagines that day is the last in their school or office. Personal belongings, materials, and supplies are left at the end of a school day. Temporary measures become permanent, stretching through the balance of the school year, into the summer and—now—through the fall. Over time, schools morph into ghost towns.

Leading through waves of closures is similar to walking blindfolded, and recovery begins with assessments. What are our resources? Is everybody all right? What is the damage? A flood of questions follow. A massive learning curve accompanies a ballooning workload, and we realize how ill-equipped we are to handle this radically changing landscape. The closest thing we have to a playbook might be a natural disaster, like Hurricane Sandy. But natural disasters are regional, and this is global. Safety does not exist.

A few schools and districts receive advanced notice; they ready their faculty for the long road ahead. Though most pivot to distance learning overnight, chaos and confusion swamp schools and districts as we slowly come to terms with the magnitude of the crisis. Every situation and context is unique, yet the recurring theme is "keep calm and carry on." The simple task of "carrying on" assumes basic needs are met, even if they aren't. Students do not have computers, or printers, or Wi-Fi, or paper, or space, or a quiet setting, or food, or support. Together, we assume the responsibility of distributing work packets and food packages.

Teachers, too, have needs. Geographically dispersed across massive school districts, logistics become a nightmare. The absence of interschool curricular communications is laid bare. Each school has been ensconced in the familiarity of its own building. These norms must give way to new systems found amid a crisis of need. Cross-school-coordination becomes paramount to coherently remap curriculum based not on location but by subject and grade. Teachers across the district begin to meet in virtually collaborative spaces. Solutions won't be perfect, but we have to start. Refinements will soon follow.

Caught mid-process, student teachers, weeks from certification, are systemless. Careers, just about to launch, are stalled in the starting blocks. Test centers close. Assessments, clinical hours, graduation regulatory requirements are no longer possible. State-standardized testing, minimum numbers of school days, and hours of annual schooling are all thrown asunder. Governors issue executive orders. Legislators pass emergency legislation. Education secretaries revise the policy. Superintendents navigate conflicting layers of information. Lawyers parse language for precision accessible to the layperson. They issue modifications and waivers in pieces, undermining the quest for clarity.

School leaders pivot from academic plans to scholastic, social, and emotional unknowns. They examine the unfolding crises and imagine unpredictable paradigm shifts. In the still-unfolding crisis, leaders shift from reactive to long-range planning, now painfully aware that plans are fragile. It is a response, an impulse for the sense of order, to reassure our communities. School, as we knew it, as the locus of learning, is upended. When it is finally back, it won't be back the same. It can't be. And that is both a curse and blessing.

DECIDING/INQUIRING

The immediate focus was on the quick shift that we had to make to get the essentials in place. That's how we phrased it with the cabinet team and my board: How do we keep the idea of "School" going? How do we do this shift to online learning with very, very little guidance from county and state, without a clear model of what that looks like?

Leadership is built around the principle of inquiry stance decision-making (Ravitch, 2020). Experience is not about precedents for repetition; it provides a lens of wisdom to guide choices ahead. COVID-19 leadership looks and feels different because intuition guides thinking and decision-making. Experience operates subconsciously in the background as we react to everything around us. Synthesizing shifting landscapes of reliable information with local contexts requires an inquiry approach to leadership. We observe some common threads. *How do we communicate our thinking to our constituents? How do we keep track of everything? What operational systems remain in place?* The very idea of school—schooling—is called into question.

Part of the job is to anticipate and design solutions ahead of time. Expectations guide this process. Then, comparison: *Are we doing what we said we'd do?* A cohort of over-achievers struggle to perform. We actionize new skill sets and leadership literacies. In this process, nothing is immune to inquiry. The way we conduct meetings, communicate with families and children, and take care of our community all under intense scrutiny. An assistant superintendent, mindful of preexisting inequities, now magnified, assembles her principals to make a list of every vulnerable student, regardless of the reason—social, behavioral, emotional, academic, special needs, counseling, therapy—everyone. Principals assign small groups to faculty and staff. They reach out and touch base with each student and/or parent/guardian *every single day*.

The social purpose of education shifts from learning to a potential positive: connection, perhaps in a way never before possible. The pandemic disrupts not only learning but also power and identity dynamics. Might new relationships be established, built entirely on positivity and support? The phone calls are no longer about issues; they are more fundamental: *How are you doing? Are you okay?* The response to this social shift is immediate. A principal for the poorest school in the city—six projects, three shelters—with students more often out of the classroom than in, witnesses students reaching out to connect. Were school buildings, a fixed norm, somehow blocking our ability to cultivate relationships fundamental to learning? With buildings shuttered, relationship building emerged as an opportunity amid the chaos of quarantine.

YIELDING/DISMANTLING

Watching the ebb and flow of this process reminds me of the ebb and flow of grief. You're doing fine, everything's fine and all under control. You barely even think about it. Then, all of a sudden, you just feel so overwhelmed, like this big wave has crashed on you, and you just can't.

In the material sciences, a yield point is a point on the stress-strain curve at which a material reaches its limit of inherent elasticity and becomes plastic. Before the threshold, a material may deform but revert to its original resting shape once the stress is withdrawn. After the yield point, however, the material will deform and will not return to its original shape. Eventually, increased plasticity under continued or increasing stress leads to structural failure and everything crumbles.

The pandemic has tossed educators into turmoil as they attempt to stand in a space between stress and strain. Parents are screaming, students are missing, family members are ill, children are underfoot at home while their mother is triaging crises beyond. Fundamental systems demand attention, but the usual tool kit is at school.

The virus and community stressors exponentially expand in tandem; they are in a musical call and response toward ever higher pitches. Educators feel helpless while witnessing and experiencing the stressors. The virtual platform is simultaneously a stress trigger and the only means of communication. *What is an educator's yield point? What prevents crossing the threshold?* Bleary-eyed amid fleeting days and nights, leaders share developments, news, information and practices, and memes—desperate moments of levity to lighten the gloom. As the pandemic overwhelms the most seasoned logistical expert, we speak honestly and listen deeply through Zooms, calls, and social media posts. Constant contact is a bridge spanning between marooned local ecologies and the shared global crisis. The cohort supports from a space between stress and strain, buttressing individual efforts, all while affirming: It's real.

Unplanned adaptation emerges from the chaos of urgent need; it clamors for immediate attention, which can't be denied. It is "an audible." The pandemic sets in; "audibles" become the norm rather than the exception. It's untidy and demands that a given system's compartmentalizing walls and partitions—assuming you can discern the difference—be removed or relocated. It can be trial and error or luck, whatever works at the moment. An adaptation's continued use becomes a pattern; the pattern becomes a structure. Until it too is removed or modified as a preexisting condition to some future change. Change begins with the preexisting, set by past trajectories. Planned construction may radically revise the past or setting, but it is not a *tabula rasa*. There are always preexisting infrastructures to accommodate or re-route. Change processes survey and account for preexisting conditions to determine what to maintain and adjust, modify, subtract, and/or add. Ironically, change models rely on continuity to allow for a gradient of change shifting from status quo to new, whether swift or gradual. Pandemics have no regard for change processes.

The word "dismantle" derives from the Old French *desmanteler*: *des-* (expressing reversal) + *manteler* ("fortify," from the Latin *mantellum*, or "cloak"). The pandemic, and ensuing civic outrage over George Floyd, dismantle the present and defortify the familiar. Cracks become chasms, and "There is no white space anymore," a cohort member stoically announces. Enraged citizens fill the streets in an uprising. At this moment, we ask ourselves: *What's the difference between demolition and destruction?* Ruins clear space for the new, and present opportunity to rebuild. The cohort turns its imagination to this horizon. "Let's be really clear, in case you forgot: It wasn't working. I want it all to go away. This would not be possible without the shutdown. This is the catalyst." The work is to establish clarity amid ambiguity, to differentiate between what is technical and what is adaptive. The work requires that we avoid applying technical solutions to adaptive problems while naming this moment and fleshing out our commonalities and differences.

In the throes of building while dismantling, the community maintains its connective tissue. Listening to another's silence is a profound act of giving. Deeply hearing another's speechlessness is a different yielding, which buffers against the looming, threatening strain point. Reassuring silence is both empathetic receiving and cathartic giving—offering a chance to pivot. This moment, filled with painful hope, is situated between loss and life. This is our healing.

LOSING/FINDING

The most inspiring part of my day is this daily morning prayer with this group of folks in my district. It was actually kind of awkward. There was a part of me that just didn't feel comfortable with being me on the call and not the most senior leader. I decided that I had to introduce myself to the group by my first name and be very verbal about that. I told folks, "I'm me, there's no titles in this. We're all part of this community." And then be vulnerable. I mean, to be quite frank, there's people who shared stuff that brought me to tears. And that was a very hard thing for me because there's this internal thing in my head that is like, "you've got to be stoic during those times, you have to be a leader." I've been crying right along. There's this tension between being the leader versus just being another human being on the call.

COVID-19 breached boundaries, cracking meticulously formed identities. Intentional or accidental, these cracks present risks. There are, however, comedic moments: children and pets interrupt the formalities of Zoom meetings. Desperate for laughter, we cling to the absurdity of it all. Humor balances the abundance of solemn moments, where the first response is a deep breath. Communities of color are devastated, telegraphing the systemic racial and ethnic disparities legacied in structural discrimination limiting access to health and resources. A student's family loses four members, he's numb. The sobering reality of a childhood now desensitized to widespread death is haunting. It begs a level of grief counseling that's not part of the training. Adjacent to mass loss, other communities are merely inconvenienced, and this era will be a blip on the radar of memory. "They have lost nothing. Absolutely nothing. There's good reason that if you are of a certain class or educational level, it's entirely possible your kids will come out of this ahead of the game." The cohort mourns the loss of gathering, of being near one another. Our bonds were annealed in the intensity of the first week. Full of strong personalities, "It reminds me of sleepaway camp. Sleepaway camp will bond the most unlikely bedfellows." We know that collective impact requires mutual respect and deep reliance exceeding academic solidarity. This is a space that nurtured the connective tissue, now sustaining the bonds. We worry, *how long will it last?* This is more than logistical separation; it is a source of life.

Yet loss also opens space for gain. Superficialities fall as the hustling grind yields to purposeful efforts. There's a newfound focus that needs time to adjust. There is an ardent hope that transition isn't too swift, that it doesn't overrun what's only just uncovered before there's time to acknowledge, nurture, and grow what has been found. Sudden reversion to previous patterns would be a new loss, eradicating what's just now gleaned. This is the paradox: profound and unvoiced truths are found in the vacuum of tragic loss. Acts of reconciliation, knitting one to the other, remains the work at hand. Once woven, the tapestry's backside should appear no coarser than its front.

ONWARD

This is our crucible; this is our moment, as a group, who have aspirations to go and help shape future generations of young people and probably generations of future educators as well. It's almost impossible for anyone who goes into education to be a pessimist, just by definition. Nobody's like: this is worthless. Even in this really profound moment of uncertainty and difficulty, it's nice to know that other people think there's something that can be done. And that in order for it to get done, we have to do it.

If we go back to business as usual, this experience, this crisis, will have been a missed opportunity. We don't know what the future holds, but we know that the ripple effects will stretch far beyond the horizon. Tough stretches seem like they will never end, but they do, and we emerge. Persisting through the long haul is the challenge. Our collective and communities' traumas have profoundly impacted our minds, bodies, and souls. Feeling compelled to take better care of oneself while being responsible for caring for others is overwhelming. We doubt ourselves even as the pandemic mandates that we address the inequities. We struggle to establish boundaries between personal, professional, and academic lives. We look in the mirror, and for the first time we see every aspect of our lives under a microscope as we grapple with what we knew all along. We can do better. But better does not mean striving for perfection. Better is about having tolerance for ambiguity, allowing ourselves to be human, and truly leaning into that humanity.

Though unknown is scary, it grants permission to reinvent outdated systems so that students, educators, and communities can better educate every child. We look forward with confidence and humility, becoming more familiar with the nuances of what we don't know equally as well as the fears and doubts we do know. Educators and families must accept that perfection is unrealistic and, more importantly, a significant barrier to successful emergence from present circumstances. As leaders, we are restless, eager to respond and move forward quickly. We have learned, however, that the best and only way to proceed is to humble oneself enough to make mistakes—to listen, learn, and be deliberate.

Today's decisions bear distant implications for tomorrow. This moment of uncertainty is an opportunity to benefit from the missteps, frustrations, and realizations of our past. We can correct our course now and in the future by continuing some of the conditions that this moment in history has afforded us: Stop and reflect, slow down, stop checking the boxes, and take—and give—permission to be human. We will never know the best path forward, but what we do know is that we must not move forward seeking perfection. We must move onward.

Rapid-Cycle Research Design

Goals: As educational leaders in a radically changed education landscape, we attempted to make sense of and adapt to new geographies of work and personal self-care and to understand current dimensions while redefining future trajectories, even as the terrain continues to shift.

Guiding Inquiry Questions

What are the cohort members' experiences as they pivot from academic plans to scholastic unknowns? How do the cohort members identify and balance their positionalities as leaders in the fluidity of crisis? How does the cohort define their shifting leadership roles, reconcile colleague needs with personal self-care needs through a crisis while setting a course of action for their institutions without the benefit of clear data, precedence, or policy?

Rapid-cycle data collection

1. Rapid-cycle surveys. At the outset, a survey was sent to take the temperature of the group. We asked the doctoral cohort for words and images to describe their circumstances using participatory methods of visual elicitation.
2. We generated questions, then piloted the questions with each other. We divided the cohort into three groups and each of us interviewed one group, totaling 24 individual semi-structured interviews ranging from 30 to 60 minutes. Unintentionally, our interviews turned into "healing-centered storytelling" (Ravitch, 2021). We conducted the interviews in May when our cohortmates were settling into this new way of life and set of roles.

Rapid-cycle data analysis

1. Rapid-cycle member checks/participant validation happened via text, Zoom check-ins, and conversations.
2. We leveraged each other's strengths: organization, getting ideas on paper, "spitting and polishing." We used Google Docs to comment and write notes back and forth.
3. We used Otter.ai to transcribe the interviews and then coded our interviews using a code list that we decided on together: Work Support, Work Stress, Personal Life Support, Personal Life Stress, Penn Stress, Penn Support, Other Challenges, Mind (well-being), Body (well-being) Spirit (well-being), Mourning, Ritual, pre-weekend, during, after, White Space, Protips, Boundaries.
4. Themes that emerged from coding became headers; eventually we consolidated and renamed these as themes: Family, Self-Care

(control), Self-Doubt/Self-Assurance, Blurred Lines/Boundaries, Rituals (20th FL, coffee, library, commute), Second in Command, Cohort as Caregivers, Being the eye (in the storm), Outlets: Venting, Dismantling.

5. We were in regular communication with each other and debriefed regularly after interviews to discuss emergent themes. We recorded our conversations with each other when we debriefed regarding the process and interviews.

REFERENCES

Appiah, K. A. (2006). *Cosmopolitanism: Ethics in a world of strangers.* W. W. Norton.

Bhabha, H. K. (2004). *The location of culture.* Routledge.

Brown, A. M. (2017). *Emergent strategy: Shaping change, shaping worlds.* AK Press.

Chilisa, B. (2020). *Indigenous research methodologies.* Sage.

Clance, P. R., & Imes, S. A. (1978). The imposter phenomenon in high-achieving women: Dynamics and therapeutic intervention. *Psychotherapy: Theory, Research & Practice, 15*(3), 241.

Imad, M. (2020). Trauma-informed teaching and learning. *YouTube.* www.youtube.com/watch?v=AuRxxPK9Hyc

Morris, S. M. (2020). *A pedagogy of transformation for times of crisis—OEB Insights.* https://oeb.global/oeb-insights/a-pedagogy-of-transformation-for-times-of-crisis.

Powell, J. A., & Menendian, S. (2016). *Othering and Belonging,* 1. www.otheringandbelonging.org/issue-1

Ravitch, S. M. (2021). *Equitable teaching takes time and practice here are strategies to help: How to prepare yourself—and your students—to discuss race, identity, and equity.* Harvard Business Publishing: Education.

Ravitch, S. M. (2020). Flux pedagogy: Transforming teaching and leading during coronavirus. *Perspectives on Urban Education, 17*(4), 18–32.

Vogl, C. (2016). *The art of community: Seven principles for belonging.* Berrett-Koehler Publishers, Inc.

CHAPTER 5

"And How Are the Children?"

Rahshene Davis, Amelia Coleman-Brown, and Michael Farrell

EDITORIAL FRAMING

In this chapter, three district leaders within the School District of Philadelphia take on a rapid-cycle inquiry that works to examine the underpinnings of the COVID-19 pandemic and the racial reckoning and how that has impacted the equity dimension as it pertains to students. In urban districts, we argue that the flux leadership tenet of a critical inquiry stance is required to not only examine structural impacts of our leadership decisions but also to surface the narratives that underlie these crucial choices: the ones of children.

These authors bravely embody the critical inquiry stance required to dive headfirst into storying the gap by asking School District of Philadelphia principals how child safety and well-being were during this crucial moment. Their recurring question at strategic points: "And how are the children?" becomes a crucial inquiry and moves to surface data points that sometimes become missed in school climate surveys in our schools. They continually ask their principals these questions throughout March, April, and May. In turn, readers will witness the intertwining of impacts related to racial trauma and the pandemic within these responses. This inquiry will remind readers that leadership decisions are always nested and enacted within the dynamics of structural, social, and organizational power. While this is often difficult to navigate, these authors demonstrate that embodying a critical inquiry stance can help bring clarity in how to move forward during these times by sharpening our focus on questions that most matter within our context.

Additionally, the authors discuss the importance of brave spaces, an essential aspect of flux pedagogy and flux leadership, and how that positioned all stakeholders to feel safe enough to share their stories. While they argue that without a responsive and humanizing leadership response or a commitment to acts of distributive wisdom, it cannot be enough for long-lasting change, they remind us that flux pedagogy is positioned with love, which can pave the path forward. This inquiry is grounded in love and commitment to all children, and as the authors note, this type of leadership stance will help leaders grow in the ways that are required to become the leaders and learners our children deserve.

INTRODUCTION

The title of this chapter is inspired by an African fable that describes the traditional greeting of the Masai warriors. The greeting *"Kasserianingera"* translates to *"And how are the children?"* This greeting exemplifies the high value the Masai always place on their children's well-being. Even warriors with no children of their own would always give the traditional answer: "All the children are well." This response meant that priorities of protecting children are still there—that peace and safety prevail and that the Masai society has not forgotten its "why" or its responsibilities as a people. Having a greeting that asks, *"And how are the children?"* keeps the well-being of our children a priority, even when we face our most difficult challenges in a state of flux. As leaders, we must protect children first, always considering *And how are the children?* in all that we do.

During the COVID-19 pandemic, school principals became even more essential within the communities we serve. As we reacted and responded to the uncertain times, the needs of our students emerged—needs that were not new but exacerbated under even more dire conditions. In addition to COVID-19, the civil unrest sparked by the public lynching of George Floyd shed light on the systemic racism that exists in policing and U.S. civic life more broadly. The national civil unrest around policing opened the door to the country coming together. As educators took to the streets, joining the uprising, we saw the responsibility to look within our education system and challenge ourselves to name the antiracist leadership practices that we would embody to dismantle our own system. In this state of flux, on behalf of the children, we examine how specific school contexts and individual school leaders' lived experience impacts their response. And we continue to ask, *"And how are the children?"*

To explore the lived realities of our colleagues, we set out to examine urban leaders and their ability to keep children first during these times of flux like COVID-19 and the national civil unrest that erupted after the public murder of George Floyd. Racism and injustice plague our country and every system within it. The education system is not exempt from this racism. It is our leaders' responsibility to enact antiracist leadership practices that dismantle the systemic racism that creates barriers for our children (Khalifa, 2018). We looked to leaders across the School District of Philadelphia, our leadership home, who serve high-needs populations to hear and learn from how they lead through this crisis.

We spoke with many School District of Philadelphia principals and asked how they had kept children's safety and well-being at the forefront of their consciousness when so much was happening around them. We began interviews by asking, *"And how are the children?"* and then asked follow-up questions to find out what it would take for each leader to be able to answer, "All of the children are well." Our goal in these shared inquiries was to explore what conditions need to be present to ensure that, indeed, *all* the children are well. How are leaders ensuring that their actions, amid a time of global flux, center the well-being of the children and keep them the top priority? As we interviewed school leaders throughout Philadelphia, asking each one the question *"And how are the children?"* responses varied, yet several powerful, generative themes emerged.

"AND HOW ARE THE CHILDREN?"

Leaders provided commentary on their frustrations as they described equity issues that were not new but were intensified. "In some communities, not everyone has access," one said, "Everyone did not have access to healthy foods, technology, and internet connections and for many parents working daily was essential to their livelihood" were emblematic responses. While COVID-19 presented a new set of challenges, the inequities that already existed were illuminated due to the sudden shutdown of schools. Students left school on Friday, March 13, beginning a weekend, not knowing they would not return to their school building for 6 months or longer. Perhaps ever. Students were not sent home with books and other essential learning materials. In the days following, it became clear that students needed access—to books, to learning materials, to meals.

The District and City were commended for their rapid response of setting up food distribution centers throughout Philadelphia, ensuring that tens of thousands of students could pick up two meals daily. This effort highlights the point that schools are not only places of learning but also serve other basic humanitarian needs. Schools and the adults in them are part of many students' support systems, which requires seeing each other face to face. While the District quickly provided academic learning packets to students throughout the City, leaders began to ask about technology access for students, as it became clear that the rapid shift was going to become more long term than anyone initially thought. The District took on the challenge of ensuring every student had a laptop as it made plans to shift all learning online. As this undertaking occurred, leaders found it painfully ironic—because it is—that the CEO of our city's largest internet provider made a $5 million personal donation to the District to help purchase laptops. Yet, many families with these new donated devices in hand still could not access online learning due to no or limited internet access in their own homes—a struggle for equity that continues. The lack of justice in education continues to perpetuate a cycle of societal inequities that stem from systematic racism and oppression. Through March, April, and May, we asked, "*And how are the children?*" only to hear back, "*We don't know—the children are not signing on.*"

Once laptops were distributed, the District tried to track and measure the number of students signing on each day to the learning platforms. When schools and individual teachers began to track participation formally, the powerful concept of student–teacher relationships was foregrounded. Many barriers prevented families from connecting to the internet, and, for many students, a lack of motivation and connection also kept them from signing on or putting cameras on for lack of privacy.

We continued to ask, "*And how are the children?*" Leaders shared stories about seeing children the same day we interviewed them, meaning that it was a regular occurrence. Leaders shared their connections to individual students and communities and how sustaining they were in powerful ways that showed their commitment and the power of their emotional and relational bonds with students and families. Countless leaders found a way to continue the strong connection they had with families throughout the pandemic—it is brave, really, the ways that these educators extended themselves during a time of profound fear and trauma for everyone, including themselves and their own families, to their students. They shared ways they supported their students and communities in ways that are nothing short of heroic. Through phone calls, texts, emails, and messages on newly created social media accounts, leaders found and created the touchpoints that so often easily and seamlessly occurred in person. They made these a reality online and in person—this required incredible commitment and stamina.

At the beginning of the pandemic, several leaders chose to mask and glove up to visit families at home when they were concerned about students making the transition and then throughout the stay-at-home orders. While the District did not endorse these visits, leaders felt called to do so given a range of issues and struggles their students faced. "Oh, the children. I *think* they are OK . . ." Leaders reported that on the outside many students "looked okay, but do we *really* know?" One principal stated, "It's often overlooked and normalized and expected that children are resilient. While many of the District children looked and appeared to move about their respected communities the way they normally would, we had no true measure to know how they were *really* doing. Amid the tyranny of the urgent—distributing food and laptops—have we forgotten about the children . . . ?"

After listening to our school principals, the most influential leaders in the city, we have a renewed hope. Through purposeful collaboration and centering all students' needs, including our most marginalized ones, we, the system, and village, can ensure a crucial answer. Our hope is that when this storm passes there will be a new horizon. And when we ask the question, "*How are the children?*," we will all first *see* the children, and we can ask *them* how they are doing. And we keep asking them, long after the pandemic has passed. We know their names. We know their stories. We know their hopes and dreams. And, right now, we can confidently say we know *the children are much better.*

> Things are not getting worse, they are getting uncovered. We must hold each other tight and continue to pull back the veil.
>
> —Adrienne Maree Brown

The COVID-19 pandemic brought with it a new deadly virus and exposed an old historical disease our country has been suffering from for centuries: racism. During both uncertainty and unrest, Black school leaders and their White allies leaned into these present challenges with intentionality and grace. The flux framework and rapid-cycle inquiry process helped the leaders in Philadelphia transition into the 2020–2021 school year in a full virtual setting in a more planned and prepared manner. In March, when schools closed abruptly, teachers and leaders had to "build the plane while flying it," and there was no time for preparation. The knowledge gained from the introduction of flux pedagogy in April allowed leaders time to process it over the summer and use this new knowledge to plan for a virtual school opening. My leaders first leaned into Radical Compassion and Radical Self-Care (Ravitch, 2020) to ensure they were checking on their well-being, the well-being of the staff under their charge, and the well-being of the students and parents at home.

Our district created schedules that included a 30-minute morning meeting for each classroom, where teachers could build relationships with students. Meetings also created time for lessons for socioemotional learning, and space for students to process their feelings about these stressful and uncertain times we were all living through. Leaders devoted time during teacher meetings to talk about their feelings and check in on how they were doing during these difficult times. The onset of the pandemic created this new meeting space in our schools, and practicing self-care was front and center for the first time. "Practicing self-care has never felt more urgent than in these socially, politically, economically, medically, environmentally, and spiritually troubling times; it has become part of many people's lexicon, yet few consider its deeper vicissitudes, its relationship to social identities and issues of structural discrimination, and the promise it holds for transformative education that can support optimal human development" (Ravitch, 2020).

We needed the practice of radical self-care when many students in our school communities witnessed on the news media the killing of Walter

Wallace Jr. in front of his mother. Both unarmed, Wallace's mom pleaded for the police not to kill her son, who was suffering from a mental health crisis. Many students experienced this trauma by watching it play out on the news or by living in the same community. The next day, they came to school ready to discuss the trauma they experienced and ask questions as to why police killed another unarmed Black man. Many children in our communities were not well after experiencing this trauma more locally and relating it to the slayings of George Floyd and Breonna Taylor they had seen from afar. This death was close to home, but the children had the same questions.

School leaders have found that we cannot support our children in the ways they need support if we are not supporting our teachers as well. This work of self-care and making space for reflection and processing of feelings is needed for all. We find ourselves constantly asking, "And How Are the Children?" The insurrection on the U.S. Capitol building aired on television, unfolding before our very eyes. The world was able to see White privilege on display, as a riot incited by our president among his White supporters, was able to happen with little to no opposition from the police or our national security. We all witnessed how these protestors were treated the opposite of Black Lives Matter activists. The response from authorities or lack thereof was astonishing, painting a vivid picture of how America continues to uphold and protect White supremacy. This turning point in our nation's history was traumatic, and leaders found themselves asking, "How will we help our children process this trauma, and how will we support teachers who have endured trauma during this time?"

Issues of systemic racism, caught on camera for all to see, have confronted educators and students before. This racial trauma for people of color is real during these times, and we must allow ourselves the grace to say, "I'm not okay," while taking the needed steps of radical self-care. Holding spaces and resisting the business-as-usual mindset during this time is an act of bravery for every educator engaging in this essential work. While we have pockets of excellence in schools and classrooms around our city, we are still operating in a very reactive mode. Our system has not yet done the work to make sure we are proactively laying a foundation for our students to help them understand and recognize when race, power, and privilege are at play in all situations. This proactive approach in education will ensure our students have the critical thinking skills necessary to challenge ideas and process trauma. This is the necessary work that must happen at a systems level in education. This pandemic and civil unrest have taught us that our educators can do virtually anything to make sure our children are well. They need to be equipped with the necessary knowledge and skills to impart to our children because you cannot teach what you do not know. As we get stronger and smarter about the necessary work of dismantling systemic oppression, our students resultantly become stronger and smarter. The time is now. All educators must meet this challenge, as we have so many times before. Our children are counting on us.

*   *   *

Much like most of the world, educational leaders deal with the emotional and mental anguish of the pandemic and the harsh public realities of racism simultaneously. As leaders of color, and White allies, the national re-unveiling of White supremacy pierced my heart, soul, and mind in nondescript ways. Nonetheless, it remains our moral and professional responsibility to leverage our lived experiences and make sure that we make a difference in the lives of the children we serve. Kouzes and Posner (2010) write, "The first truth about leadership is that You Make a Difference. It's the most fundamental truth of all." After listening and learning from principals about what actions mattered most, my leadership stance "fluxxed" and, perhaps more than before, "Making a Difference" on behalf of the children of my network became my standard. *Are our actions making a difference?* What are the children, teachers, and principals experiencing, and is it making a difference? Our efforts must have a positive, longstanding impact once the pandemic ends. We leaned into two values that have made me the leader I am today: love and learning. We leaned, intentionally, into love.

Leaders were encouraged to extend love to themselves and others with purpose. We slowed things down and encouraged leaders to take the time to get to know themselves a bit more intimately so that they could be of better service to others, and we did the same. Goleman, Boyatzis, and McKee stated in their book *Primal Leadership* (2002), "In complex times, emotional intelligence is a must. Emotionally intelligent leaders can build relationships because they are aware of their emotional makeup and are sensitive and inspiring to others" (p. 31). We also worked to model ways a leader embodied self-love and extended love across their school communities. Across the network, we adopted Wellness Welcomes at the start of meetings and adopted ways for school communities to check in on each other.

We nurtured and embraced spaces that allowed members of the school community to share how they felt, and these spaces were created for all stakeholders, students, teachers, and leaders alike. We can't make a difference if we don't show each other and ourselves that we matter. We recognize that these technical add-ons to a school or network agenda will only live if the reasoning is understood across the hearts and minds of people. You can't fully commit to something you don't believe in. Flux pedagogy reminds us that "this crisis moment requires that educators learn new skills and mindsets for designing and enacting relational and transformative pedagogies with our students and colleagues even as we lead and teach them specific topics and content areas" (Ravitch, 2020).

Simultaneously as we leaned into love, we also positioned ourselves to learn more from those around us and those we serve. During the summer of 2020, we embraced the inquiry stance on purpose, and positioned ourselves to listen and learn to best respond to the needs of the children we serve. How are our children? How can we make a difference? Adrienne Maree Brown (2017) reminds us that "we are socialized to see what is wrong, missing, off, to tear down the ideas of others and uplift our own. To a certain degree, our entire future may depend on learning to listen, listen without assumptions or defenses." As we continue to enact flux to make a difference, we are more curious to learn of the experiences taking place across the schools we serve, regardless of whether they are physical or virtual school spaces. We are eager to learn more intentionally of the experiences of the teachers and students that I serve and to utilize that knowledge to make a difference at scale. "Leaders need opportunities to learn from the 'inside' of other leaders' experiences, doubts and all." Inquiry stance offers the "potential for site-based leaders to identify issues and problems that are locally significant, previously unrecognized, and rarely given the systematic, intentional study that an inquiry-based approach to leadership affords" (Lytle, Johanek, & Rho, 2018, p. 157).

*   *   *

When we entered our doctoral work together, we anticipated that our new learning would bring challenges. None of us could imagine a global pandemic taking shape and disrupting our lives, during our doctoral program. Yet, we found our most profound learning has been at the intersection of our doctoral community of practitioners, research interests, and current realities. As we consciously and subconsciously mourn the loss of some of the elements of what was a connected, grounded inquiry, practitioner identity emerged. The flux of our lives and the interconnectedness of our personal, professional, and academic moments supports a new clarity, a new purpose, a new ground in the state of flux.

As the pandemic evolved, we found ourselves reminding one another and those around us how many of the challenges emerging, especially around access for our students, were not new but truly getting uncovered. Our voice as antiracist leaders, shedding light on the inequities, became interconnected to our beliefs and identity as researchers. Our identities as leaders and learners became fluid, naturally showing up in spaces with an inquiry stance (Cochran-Smith & Lytle, 2009). The more we embodied the approach, our collective capacity as practitioners—and the knowledge that we generate with others—was the way through the pandemic and beyond to work toward justice.

As we stepped into our inquiry stance, we noticed a freeness, a boldness in the actions that we began to take as leaders. An inquiry stance, grounded in the belief that relational learning is essential, dismisses the hierarchies that often govern the systems and practices that often hinder student support and success (Ravitch, 2020). By shifting our leadership to be grounded in a flux leadership mindset, we became adaptive, generative, and compassionate—and gave permission for others to do the same. The reality is that no one has the playbook for what comes next. Yet we're empowered to adapt and create something new. We do so by centering the expertise, voices, and passion from the school leaders we work with.

As we reflected on and listened to the stories, sensemaking, and action of leaders throughout our district, we again found ourselves reminded of the power and purpose of storytelling. As we purposefully interviewed principals or sat in spaces with our colleagues, the fruits of the inquiry stance became clear. The most beautiful moments were not those of concrete action or the genius ideas that emerged from schools but watching the approach of racial compassion and self-care emerge as a way forward. As we shared space for ourselves, and our leaders authentically—to share, to cry,

---

RAPID-CYCLE INQUIRY

Goal: To explore the lived realities of our colleagues, we examined urban leaders and their ability to prioritize children first during times of flux like COVID-19 and the national civil unrest that erupted after the public murder of George Floyd. We interviewed leaders across the School District of Philadelphia, our leadership home, who serve high-needs populations to learn from how they are leading through this crisis.

Rapid-cycle data collection and analysis

We engaged in informal interviews with School District of Philadelphia principals and asked how they have been keeping children's safety and well-being at the forefront of their consciousness when so much was happening around them.

We began interviews by asking, "And how are the children?" and then asked follow-up questions to find out what it would take for each leader to be able to answer, "All of the children are well." Our goal in these shared inquiries was to explore what conditions need to be present to ensure that, indeed, all of the children are well. How are these leaders ensuring that the actions they take through this time of such flux in the world ensure the well-being of the children and keep them as the top priority? As we interviewed school leaders throughout Philadelphia, asking each one the question, "And how are the children?," responses varied, yet a number of powerful, generative themes emerged that were recorded and vetted by the leaders, each other, and members of our doctoral cohort.

to process, to heal—we noticed leaders extending this space of authenticity to those around them.

As we continue to ask, "*And how are the children?*" we grow as leaders and learners. In these moments of listening, we are reminded of the power of storytelling that strengthens our practice of centering students and those who support them most closely. In continually asking about the children, by extension we ask, *How are the adults?* And in extending our care for others, we must also ask, *How are we ourselves?* This practice invites us to lead and learn with grace, permeated by an ethic of care for all. In this space, we will heal and transform ourselves, and, collectively, heal the children around us.

REFERENCES

Brown, A. M. (2017). *Emergent strategy: Shaping change, shaping worlds.* AK Press.

Cochran-Smith, M., & Lytle, S. L. (2009). *Inquiry as stance: Practitioner research for the next generation.* Teachers College Press.

Goleman, D., Boyatzis, R. E., & McKee, A. (2002). *Primal leadership: Realizing the power of emotional intelligence.* Harvard Business School Press.

Khalifa, M. (2018). *Culturally responsive school leadership.* Harvard Education Press.

Kouzes, J. M., & Posner, B. Z. (2010). *The truth about leadership: The no-fads, heart-of-the-matter facts you need to know.* John Wiley & Sons.

Lytle, J. H., Lytle, S. L., Johanek, M. C., & Rho, K. J. (Eds.). (2018). *Repositioning educational leadership: Practitioners leading from an inquiry stance.* Teachers College Press.

Ravitch, S.M. (2020) Flux pedagogy: Transforming teaching and leading during Coronavirus. *Perspectives on Urban Education, 17*(4), 18–32.

CHAPTER 6

Real Talk

Teaching and Leading While BIPOC

Deirdre Johnson Burel, Felicia Owo-Grant, and Michael Tapscott

---

EDITORIAL FRAMING

In this chapter, a group of doctoral candidates take on a rapid-cycle inquiry that examines what it means to teach and lead while being Black, Indigenous, or a Person of Color (BIPOC) across a variety of educational contexts, including traditional public schools, charter schools, and independent schools. Their work includes interview excerpts that will help readers better understand the importance of the flux tenet of racial literacy in whatever context in which they serve as teachers and leaders. As mentioned in Chapters 2 and 3, racial literacy is the ability to read, recast, and resolve racially stressful encounters and navigate identity-related stress (Stevenson, 2014). This chapter reminds us that the flux tenet of a critical inquiry stance is fundamentally premised on one's ability to understand their own racial identity and its connection to the surrounding context in which they serve.

   As they discuss, they work to provide readers with a "narrative rendering" of a wide swath of BIPOC individuals to shed light on what the educational landscape looks like at a particular moment in time—in this case, during the COVID-19 pandemic. Navigating identity-based stress becomes a central focus for these educators within these moments of flux and paints the backdrop of how they navigate to support their students and stakeholders within their educational context successfully. While racial diversity has tremendous benefits for educational systems at large, these stories pinpoint tensions that one who identifies as BIPOC navigates daily. These stories help readers understand how the dual impact of the pandemic and the George Floyd protests forced an evolution in their leadership. It forced leaders to lean into aspects of other aspects of flux leadership including crisis agility and humanizing and responsive leadership to support a diversity of stakeholders. As you will read, many BIPOC leaders interviewed had navigated these types of stressful situations before. As the authors write:

> The lived experiences and ability for minoritized people living within White supremacy culture to thrive, against all odds, provides an advantage for navigating in crisis. One could contend that the various leadership styles necessary to traverse the tides of adversity have been developed within BIPOC in America in order to survive.

This chapter provides a unique lens and perspective that can help readers better understand that leading while BIPOC in a crisis brings forth equity, deficit, and identity issues in both familiar and unfamiliar ways that will feel resonant. It also provides readers with recommendations for approaching both this moment and the future in ways that are more culturally responsive and increasingly relevant for stakeholders, such as thinking about how these data might influence the ways in which we think about pedagogy and school climate. At the end of this chapter, the authors conclude by saying that we should be reimagining K–12 education in ways that can allow our full identities to exist in ways that are equitable for all, which embodies an essential commitment of flux pedagogy. We believe that this inquiry brings to light the stories that deeply illustrate why flux pedagogy is necessary for the future of schooling—because a school grounded in tenets of antiracism and love gives all stakeholders the humanity they deserve.

INTRODUCTION

In March 2020, the growing global pandemic forced the country to respond quickly. Businesses, schools, and other institutions shut down; U.S. cities went into quarantine; and schooling moved into the home. While the transition to online, remote learning contributed to some students making significant educational progress, for others it exacerbated structural inequities, magnified familial dynamics and shifting pedagogies, and contributed to significant losses in learning. COVID-19, however, was not the only transformational crisis that children, parents, and educators would face.

On May 25, 2020, George Floyd's murder by Minneapolis police officers was the latest publicized instance of police brutality against a Black person. Floyd's murder sparked a movement across the country in the fight against anti-Black racism. For our children, the incessant killings of Black men and women have become normalized in their lifetime. My 8th-grade students recall the murder of Trayvon Martin in 2012 when many of them were only 6 years old, Eric Garner in 2014, and more recently Breonna

Taylor in 2020. For Black and Brown children, the message is clear: Their lives are expendable. For parents and educators, the fight against anti-Black racism is most critical.

The roles of teachers and educational leaders are difficult enough as it is. When you include a worldwide pandemic and a seemingly endless reel of bolstered and violent anti-Black racism, teachers and educational leaders of color are shouldering the fears, tears, and anxieties of those around us. Meanwhile, we must "push through" with resilience in turbulent and threatening times. It is vital to explore and share the stories of the emotional and psychological toll on us because we matter. This is not sustainable.

We spoke with and heard the stories of teachers and school leaders working in traditional public, public charter, and independent schools. They have an average of 15 years of experience, hailing from the midwestern, northeastern, and southern regions of the United States. We sought to understand what they experienced during this season of unrest. How did they teach and lead through it, and what was the distinct lens their social identities helped bring to their work? We were sobered, heartened, encouraged, and enlightened by their experiences. Many BIPOC leaders bring with them a culture of struggle and resilience. They are not new to addressing or facing adversity. Arguably, grit is in the DNA of living as a minoritized person within White-supremacy culture.

What is teaching and leading like in this season? BIPOC leaders and teachers have something to say! *The field would do well to hear from them.* They offer insights on leading with people at the center, removing the artificial walls of the schoolhouse, and moving more fluidly into relationships with students and their families. BIPOC leaders discussed the role of race and ethnicity in how they teach and lead; they identified discrete challenges of leadership, delineated how they leveraged formal and informal supports to undergird their mental health, shared insights on navigating shifting pedagogies for diverse learners, and offered recommendations on what their lessons portend for classrooms and schools in the coming months and years.

WHO THEY ARE: VOICES FROM THE FIELD (A SNAPSHOT)

In our first term as doctoral students at the University of Pennsylvania, we had the privilege of reading Michele Foster's (1997) book, *Black Teachers on Teaching*. As chapter authors, the impact of what we read transformed us, and it influenced the topic we chose to write about and the voices we wanted to include. Like Foster's work, we hope to share a "narrative rendering" of the experiences of BIPOC teachers and school leaders in different areas of the United States. You will hear from Angela, Tony, Carlos, Tiwa, Kourtney, and Michelle. We hope that these accounts will increase our capacity to understand the dynamic experiences of BIPOC teachers, and school leaders, and encourage other BIPOC teachers and leaders to share their journeys.

Angela: Public Charter School Teacher, Southern Region

"I think as a Black woman who grew up during the desegregation movement and I was a part of . . . being my school I was removed from my neighborhood school and at the time I guess my parents and people in our neighborhood thought it was a good thing that we were going getting on the bus and going across town to the predominantly White school. But I do feel that that had . . . I think I was in 3rd grade. And so being so young, that was a lot to handle, and I did it for 3 years. I remember having one really good teacher who I felt was really kind and sincere. And I can remember the days when I had my hand up and I didn't get called on any other things that I can remember about that experience that were truly hard. I go to the water fountain and the little White girls wouldn't drink behind me because they thought they were going to turn Black. So there were some things. And so for me, working at a school that is diverse I really try to make sure that I'm treating my students as fairly as possible."

Tony: Independent School Leader, Midwestern Region

"I started my teaching career at 22. I've been in independent schools exclusively. I went to a private school from 7th to 12th grade, then went off to college, and had been basically teaching in one way or the other or in education for the last, now, 23 years. Which is kind of a trip to say out loud. And then often what's fun for me is, if I'm in a room with White folks, which happens a lot, and then we're talking about kind of independent school experience, invariably I'm always the one that probably has the most. You know I have an undergrad from a private institution, and then I have a couple master's degrees. And so I've been ensconced, kind of, in private education some way or another since I was 12 years old. So now, I'm entering my, you know, my 33rd year, essentially, being a part of independent schools."

Carlos: Independent School Leader, Southern Region

"I think I consistently have that lens on of what it means to be a person of color. So, when I'm doing admissions, you know, I'm thinking about, not just the number of people of color on campus, but how are those kids being retained and what is the attrition of that group? What does our faculty look like? What's the experience of students around discipline? How do we use data? I keep my own records to look at who's being disciplined? Who isn't being disciplined? And how do we evaluate that as a team? So, I think the lens is always there for every single piece of work that I do, not only from my perspective as a Latino male, but also when I think about people who are different in our community, right. What is their experience? And how does each part of our program impact them, or maybe not impact them? How do we address those issues? So, I think about it a lot in terms of hiring also. Like, who's on my team? How different are they from me? And that could be across gender, it could be across race, it could be across age, but really thinking about the people that I'm working with. How different are their perspectives? Making sure that I have a really different set of folks in front of me making decisions."

Tiwa: Public School Leader, Northeastern Region

"My role as a school leader is one that is multifaceted. I set the example and the direction of everything, every nuance that we do. To push myself to always take in the many perspectives of all stakeholders before making any decisions big and small. My role as a school leader, I feel that I take on the emotions and the underbelly and everything that happens in that school. I feel that my job is to manage the temperature, stress level, and anxiety at all times and try to push and navigate my students through. Being a person of color influences how I lead. I have a school that is a majority Black or African American. Being a Black person, you naturally learn how to code switch. Being a leader, I find that I can easily navigate and code switch when I have to because most of my students are students of color. With the state of how my community is changing. I mean the gentrification is starting to happen at my school, but not so much. And so being a person of color, I am worried about what happens when the gentrification is taking over a school that has been so highly coveted within the Black community in my ward. And so already I am being mindful of advocating and celebrating the loveliness of my Black students but I am also pushing myself to be cognizant of not having barriers up that other students may feel because they are not a person of color. So I do empathize with the few students that don't identify as Black at my school and that causes me a little stress. I am trying to appease everyone."

Kourtney: Public Charter School Leader, Northeastern Region

"I am intentional about the community that I support. My vision as a school leader is to support Black and Brown children and I am a leader of color. [My student population is predominantly Black.] I would also say from the perspective that my school is a bit diverse. We do have some scholars who are Caucasian and a few students that are Pacific Islanders, so there is diversity so not to say we served all, but as far as being a leader of color making sure that those kind of cultural competencies are not only myself embodied but my staff embody cultural competences to be able to support our scholars. Really just making sure that we are in tune with the backgrounds of our students and really knowing them deeply. I am a firm believer that we have to support the whole child. So beyond what is happening in our school we do support families outside with whatever resources they may need. Whether that be mental health support, whether that be food on their table, whether it be technology support, whatever we can do to eliminate any barriers that may inhibit education. It is my role as a school leader to make sure that happens and to make sure that my staff have the capacity to also make that happen for all of our students; and leading with that in mind."

Michelle: Public School Teacher, Southern Region

"Why I decided to teach is because I believe that I had a very great education in a very broken system. And I had like teachers who showed up to work. They were professional, they were articulate. They taught us about perseverance. They had this really magical way of building our mindsets and shaping our mindsets without all of the tools that we have today. I can remember attending ABC high school and never going on a college tour, but anybody who attended ABC school will tell you that some way, subconsciously, we knew that we were supposed to be successful, we knew that we were supposed to attend college or wherever it was that we landed. We believe the non-model second to none. We believe that we were the best person for any job they put us in front of. But also I had amazing white teachers, you know, really urban really impact our city. And so for me I just felt like what I learned from both sets is something that I wanted to give to students."

IDENTITY

Even before the threats of a worldwide pandemic and escalating racial tensions, teachers and educational leaders of color had many obstacles to overcome. While studies show that racial diversity among teachers and educational leaders has significant benefits for all students (Khalifa, 2018), showing up unapologetically as oneself when you identify as Black, Indigenous, or a Person of Color (BIPOC) is a daily challenge. The feelings of identity management and to code-switching to be better received are struggles that W. E. B. Du Bois (1968) conceptualized in his double consciousness framework. It is a deep tension and source of racial stress and trauma that BIPOC folks continue to battle (Pak & Ravitch, 2021). Tony described his challenges with this tension:

> One of my challenges that I've been told as a leader when I do these
> leader profiles, I've been told a couple times that I could be a leader

despite my profile, which is kind of funny. Right, because I have certain qualities that are not considered "leaderly." And, talk about race, we can go there. What is the view of a leader? What's a leader even supposed to be like, you know? And, what are they supposed to sound like and feel like?

You know my first big meeting as a senior administrator, I remember saying, we worked on a project that was really challenging and I said, this is a challenge. This is a project that's going to be really challenging for us. We're gonna feel some of that. And the rest of it was, but I know that we got this, like right. We're just gonna rise to the occasion and do this. The feedback I got was, some people in the room felt like I wasn't very confident. And my response to that feedback is, I come from a tradition of struggle. So, our talking about struggle, right, and our talking about journeys and talking about, things that are sometimes uncomfortable. That's a part of a way, I think, that you can really inspire and lead to have people persevere. But I think it can also be viewed as not confident, not steady, too emotional, you know.

Racial diversity among teachers and educational leaders has significant benefits for all students (Khalifa, 2018). Educators of color are seen as positive role models for students of color, are more likely to have higher expectations of students of color, to develop trusting relationships with students of color, to develop and enact culturally relevant curricula, and to play a critical role in ensuring equity (Egalite & Kisida, 2016; U.S. Department of Education, 2016). This relational and developmental work is critical for helping all students succeed, especially students of color who do not often see themselves reflected in the teacher workforce or administrative offices (Stevenson, 2014). We observed from our discussions with teachers and school leaders that their identities and experiences shape how they choose to lead.

LEADERSHIP: TRANSCENDING ADVERSITY

The role of educational practitioners—leaders and teachers—requires the continued ability to negotiate between one's own needs and the needs of the community served. For all leaders, knowing how to shift their language, tone, and approach to meet the intended audience's needs is paramount to the success of the school community. For BIPOC leaders, these issues become intensified, given the structural racism of schools (Ravitch, 2020) and the racial trauma and stress experienced by many Black people in America. A connective thread across all the practitioners with whom we spoke was the leadership attributes they embodied that manifested as pillars of strength during this global health and nationally heightened racial crises. In these extended moments of crisis, these leadership characteristics are a true differentiator: They can help a community ride the turbulent waves of tension, uncertainty, and discomfort.

Several of the leaders interviewed discussed the idea that the ability to evolve is a critical component of effective leadership and that evolution in times of crisis becomes even more important.

> Yeah, I mean I think part of it has to evolve right because I couldn't be leading the exact same way. It just wouldn't be effective in many ways to just, you know. First, I think timelines are different. There's an urgency now, of what needs to be done and by when. Right. It's also once again there are times when I have to say, I hear everyone's feedback. This is the road we're going to, right. This is the path we're going down. So, sometimes it may, at times, mean that I have to step in and be really thoughtful and get everything on the table that people are feeling and navigating that. And you always have to do as a leader, but right now, there is a different urgency that there may be real disagreements in terms of how people feel about something. And right now, we have to make decisions, right, and that there is not a lot of time to say, well let's still think about Model A or Model B.
>
> There's a timeline that's different in terms of families need to make, we're thinking about our own pressures but also we have families that have to decide what am I going to do with work? If you're, if you're canceled, right, not canceled but if you're online, come in the Fall, how am I gonna handle that, if, if my kid needs to be in school and I have work, right? So, right now, I think it's a little different because the impact on our families is greater than a lot of our other decisions that aren't necessarily, right. Like, sometimes it may impact you if we go to live grades. Sure, that'll have an impact on how you feel. But our impact on whether or not we're going to go virtual or not has an incredibly deep impact that needs to be decided for families in a way that it's a direct impact. So, I think it's different to lead right now, right. It's being able to once again process and hear people out and also pushing people through that to navigate them to a place where we'll still be successful as a community and as a school, even though it may feel incredibly tiring. —Carlos

A teacher described the evolution of her role amidst the COVID-19 pandemic and how she had to sacrifice instructional time to curate celebratory moments and events for students within the virtual classroom. Further, another leader shared that the uncertainty and unpredictability of these unprecedented times have limited the ability to anticipate changes, sort of like changing the rules of a chess game midplay.

Before I used to having time to anticipate the changes and, you know, we started to have meetings over the summer and we can hit these thoughtful planning sessions. We can invite you know the instructional team and core people to kind of put structures in place. I feel like with COVID, I never would have guessed that on March 16, which was our last day in our brick and mortar school that that would be the last day for the rest of the school year I never anticipated I thought we were going to be out for a couple of weeks. Work package. We're going to be. And so I had to quickly, quickly. Try to adjust in learn so many new platforms with Microsoft Teams in office, Zoom and virtual everything. Beyond an experience, honestly, it has been beyond experience, and experience. And if I can even share I'm pretty sure more questions will lead into this, go for it. I was surprised that I had more anxiety than what I would have anticipated bleeding through COVID. In a brick and mortar school, even though they're there different kinds of crazy things happen, but you still use the same type of unpredictable things happening right so I know what to anticipate. However, once we transition to COVID, and this virtual learning platform. I remember waking up and just having a sense of anxiety building to go downstairs to begin my day because I could not predict what I was going to walk into every day during this virtual plan. What new responsibility or new task I needed to learn in order to get through that day, or what I had the answers to the numerous questions my staff members weren't asking. And so it was causing some anxiety in me. —Tiwa

The demands on schools to change their entire model have occurred instantaneously, and foreseeable failure is on the horizon for leaders and teachers who cannot adapt to this cataclysmic shift. Michelle shared a story of her school leader's inability to shift his leadership style during the last months of the academic year when schools were forced to flip to virtual learning rapidly. During the interview, she described her leader as one whose primary leadership approach is delegation, describing an environment where the principal has hired capable instructional leads and experts—but he does not listen and learn from these experts. The current state of the world, however, amplified this issue within their school community, and the space became intolerable for her and other staff.

I think there is a lot of room to develop [my principal and assistant principals] levels and layers of support. So that the team itself can be more effective holistically. When you are a leader you have to be willing to, like I said before, roll up your sleeves and get your hands dirty. Leadership is not just about delegating, leadership is about following. So you know I think that when we are communicating

via text and they are saying great job, you all are moving so quickly, that's support but to me if I ever wanted to become a leader; I don't want to ever leave the classroom, this is where my heart is, but if I ever wanted to be a leader I know that my leadership style would be more supportive. . . . It is the idea that support having to be more than celebratory. I don't just want a text from you saying hey you are so amazing. Thank you for that but what else can be done. What else needs to be done. How can I assist you all in this; is the best form of support . . . In my time in ABC school district I have seen a lot more leaders . . . who lead through delegating and not lead through following. And I think that is extremely important for an effective leader to understand that when you are really great at what you do it is when you are following the experts you put into the position to enhance your knowledge . . . I have seen [my principal] do a great job of hiring experts but not listening and learning from these experts.
—Michelle

The idea of evolution is biological at its core. As humans, the need to evolve is inevitable; however, the ability to do so within oneself is difficult and even more complex when leading others through evolutionary times. In leadership, evolution seems to be couched in two primary leadership pedagogy: crisis and adaptive leadership. An adaptive leader can adjust to changing environments and respond to recurring problems while leading others through turbulence. The BIPOC leaders interviewed all shared experiences of how they have manifested and wielded their adaptive leadership skills to support their communities—both during the pandemic and amid other challenges their communities have faced.

Grit, reflection, care, communication, empathy, and resolve were character traits revealed as the leaders shared their experiences of leadership amid a pandemic and heightened state of racial tensions in America. The lived experiences and ability for minoritized people living within White supremacy culture to thrive, against all odds, provides an advantage for navigating in crisis. One could contend that the various leadership styles necessary to traverse the tides of adversity have been developed within BIPOC in America to survive. However, little research on leadership specifically or leadership in education has focused on the distinct intersections of leading while BIPOC.

However, the broader literature on leadership does offer some interconnectivity. Bennis and Thomas (2002) explore the notion of what makes a leader. They propose that the skills required to conquer adversity and emerge stronger and more committed than ever are the same ones that make for extraordinary leaders. "Crisis leaders are effective because they possess the awareness of themselves and others in the context of dynamic, tenuous, and shifting situations" (Powley & Taylor, 2014, p. 562). Embedded in Bennis and Thomas's (2002) framework is the idea that crisis leadership is about who a leader is and how a leader responds to crisis. Leadership of this kind has been represented in constructs such as adaptive leadership (Heifetz, Grashow, & Linsky, 2009), servant leadership (Spears & Lawrence, 2004), relational leadership (Uhl-Bien, 2006), spiritual leadership (Fry, 2003), authentic leadership (Gardner, Avolio, Luthans, May, & Walumbwa, 2005), fundamental states of leadership (Quinn, 2004), resonant leadership (Boyatzis & McKee, 2005), and eighth-habit leadership (Covey, 2004).

These constructs propose a kind of leadership that is internally directed, other-focused, externally open, and purpose-centered, where the leaders act selflessly and transcend self-serving needs in favor of serving others (Quinn, 2004). As research begins to examine the racialized experience of BIPOC leaders more closely, we should look toward the inherent tools BIPOC leaders possess as a result of adapting to living as a minoritized person within White supremacy culture. Some of these adaptations allowing BIPOC leaders to ascend to leadership may undergird their ability to lead. More research in this area is needed to deeply explore what and how these tools can be more explicitly named and intentionally cultivated as there is likely variance among BIPOC leaders predicated on other types of (or lack thereof) experiences and supports.

IDENTITY

While studies show that racial diversity among teachers and educational leaders has significant benefits for all students (Khalifa, 2018), showing up unapologetically as oneself when you identify as Black, Indigenous, or a Person of Color (BIPOC) is a daily challenge. The feeling of having to manage our identities and to code-switch to be better received are struggles that W. E. B. Du Bois (1968) conceptualized in his double-consciousness framework. It is a deep tension and source of racial stress and trauma that BIPOC folks continue to battle (Pak & Ravitch, 2021). A Latinx, male head of school described his challenges with this tension:

> One of my challenges that I've been told as a leader when I do these leader profiles, I've been told a couple times that I could be a leader despite my profile, which is kind of funny. Right, because I have certain qualities that are not considered "leaderly." And, talk about race, we can go there. What is the view of a leader? What's a leader even supposed to be like, you know? And, what are they supposed to sound like and feel like?
>
> You know my first big meeting as a senior administrator, I remember saying, we worked on a project that was really challenging and I said, this is a challenge. This is a project that's going to be really challenging for us. We're gonna feel some of that. And the rest of

it was, but I know that we got this, like right. We're just gonna rise
to the occasion and do this. The feedback I got was, some people in
the room felt like I wasn't very confident. And my response to that
feedback is, I come from a tradition of struggle. So, our talking about
struggle, right, and our talking about journeys and talking about,
things that are sometimes uncomfortable. That's a part of a way, I
think, that you can really inspire and lead to have people persevere.
But I think it can also be viewed as not confident, not steady, too
emotional, you know.

There is a duality embedded in mental health—on the one hand, BIPOC
leaders are used to dealing with adversity, and as a result, we adjust quickly.
On the other hand, there are also challenges within the personal response.
We often push through our emotions and our challenges with little attention
to our feelings because we feel we have to. It was also clear throughout our
interviews that both the formal and informal support available to teachers
and school leaders of color were largely curated by themselves. Carlos described the importance of building networks of colleagues to contact with
questions or concerns:

> There are a number of other either division heads or heads or other
> people that I reach out to and we just talk about things. Part of it just
> commiserating. It's like, let's just get together and recognize that this
> is difficult, right, and that this is tough. I think I use my network for .
> when questions come up, right. So, if I have a question that I need to
> put out there and say hey I need an answer, that's an easy text to a
> group of people and say, what have you thought about this scenario?
> Can anyone give me some feedback? The network thing is huge.

Tony shared his experience with an executive coach who holds him
accountable:

> I have an executive coach. Having a woman of color help me through
> this period has been game changing because I think her instincts to
> get a feeling and an understanding for what it is that might be really
> gnawing at me, and then my ability to not have to, at all, code switch
> and just be me has been a real gift. I trust her. The first thing she
> always asks me is, "Are you taking care of yourself?"

NAVIGATING ANXIETIES, TEARS, AND FEARS

The transition to remote learning adds additional stressors to our lives.
Teachers and educational leaders shared difficulties with time, self-efficacy,

and managing the fears, tears, and anxieties of those entrusted to our care while we work through our own. Time creep was a common thread among all the teachers and educational leaders with whom we spoke. A leader shared, "One of the biggest stressors for me is feeling like if I have any downtime in my schedule that I'm not working hard enough. If my schedule is not stacked with meetings, I'm not working." Another said, "Being home and working virtually during this pandemic, [there] wasn't a hard stop time for me for the first few months. I felt like my day bled on until 8 or 9 o'clock at night. It wasn't a hard stop. Like, I'm done with work, and now it's time for me to be home with family." In managing our obligations to others, BIPOC often sacrifice self-care, and the boundaries between work and home life blur or disappear altogether. The consequences affect everyone around us.

> Once we transitioned to this virtual learning platform, I remember waking up and just having a sense of anxiety building to go downstairs to begin my day because I could not predict what I was going to walk into every day. What new responsibility or new task I needed to learn in order to get through that day? Would I have the answers to the numerous questions my staff members were asking me? It was causing anxiety in me. Then just trying to manage the family. I remember this one day . . . and this was the day I just lost it. I just shut down my computer. I went upstairs and I'm like 'I'm getting ready to have a breakdown.' I have kids and, like many educators, we are trying to do this work while we have children in the home. I'm assuming my kids are doing what they need to do. It's weird because I'm at the computer—this is the main cinema, but there are all of these short cinemas that are happening around me and I am trying to navigate all of this and lead through so many distractions and wonderings and anxieties. It's been a lot for me to manage.

As teachers and educational leaders, we are often tending to the needs of our different constituencies, be they students, families, the board of trustees, or other stakeholders. Managing the anxieties and fears of others is exponentially more difficult when everyone and everything is in flux. Many of us are concerned with making the right decisions for literally life-or-death situations. As teachers or school leaders, we know there are unknown variables that we can somewhat anticipate from day to day, from year to year. Right now, there are so many additional unknown variables that we cannot predict and are beyond our control. A school principal shared, "It's just a very solemn time. It's difficult to lead through adversity while still having to push through." She continued:

> It's like not being set up with the tools for success. There are a lot of people who are also dying from [COVID-19]. It is scary. It's scary

to even know the staff members that have COVID-19, will they pull through? And I think, you know, "My gym teacher's healthy. He works out." He may have asthma. He may get pneumonia. You don't really know. It's really tricky.

We are often required to make decisions without knowing all the contributing factors. Specifically, in the COVID-19 context, some folks are not comfortable with sharing their medical history. For others, culture and customs prevent them from openly sharing their needs. For people of color, it is difficult to ask for or receive help from others. Carlos shared his understanding with families who find it difficult to accept help, and highlights the gravity of the situation in which we all find ourselves:

I know a couple of families of color that were impacted by COVID, but that their refusal to accept, unless I really pushed on it, any kind of help was really there when in reality they needed it. Right, like, but it was it was they're proud families who you know are not used to asking for any assistance, right. So, that comes into play when I'm thinking about a family that's dealing with COVID and is out of work. It's like, now it is not an option. You need to accept this right, because I clearly see that you, and I know that this feels weird and awkward, because you're not used to it, but I can see that you absolutely need assistance during this time.

Many families struggle with covering essentials like food, rent, child care, and basic needs, but school and district officials may not know the extent to which these families are struggling. Some may ask, what is in the scope of the school's responsibility to families? The more appropriate question, especially during prolonged moments of crisis is, *How do we ensure that we are taking care of one another?*

TEACHING AND LEADING WITH PEOPLE AT THE CENTER

Black, Indigenous, or People of Color (BIPOC) bring a unique lens to their roles. While there is an abundance of research on leadership, very little of this research captures the unique and distinct perspective and approaches of leaders of color. As COVID-19 and the nation's racial unrest took hold, we were keenly aware that the unique lenses of BIPOC leaders were further magnified and that learning from their experiences is generative in real time.

As the nation transitioned into distance learning, discussions emerged about the potential impact distance learning would have in exacerbating existing inequities. There is a delicate line between acknowledging and addressing inequity and weaponizing inequity so that it further deficit-izes children and their families and resultantly exacerbates such inequity (McDermott, Raley, & Seyer-Ochi, 2009). Research aiming to bring greater visibility to inequity and frame the challenges faced by BIPOC communi-ties, in the absence of doing so with a critical or culturally responsive lens, often ignores the assets and funds of knowledge that BIPOC communities bring to bear on their educational experience. In so doing, those assets go under-utilized in supporting children's learning. This project created a prox-imal opportunity to engage with BIPOC educators (teachers and leaders) to understand if and how culturally responsive ways of working deepened understanding of community's assets and challenges, while also informing how these educators did their work.

BIPOC leaders and teachers recognize and emphasize the delicate balance of partnership between home and school. They respect the agency of fami-lies while inserting pedagogical expertise and developmentally appropriate practice to optimize children's learning experiences and academic growth. It was not surprising to find that BIPOC leaders centered people, framed and sometimes explicitly named a theory of action that anchored the holistic well-being of their school communities. The BIPOC leaders we spoke with weren't afraid to take decisive action early, to center themselves as leaders by making themselves more proximate and accessible to their communities. In this way, their leadership could be seen, touched, and felt. Further, their students, teachers, and families understood their ways of working. BIPOC educators were keenly aware of providing a sense of "I'm in the trenches with you." All of them were agile in their leadership; they were clear to bal-ance providing stability to their communities while also acknowledging that this was not business as usual. Writ large, their approaches were grounded in centering people—teachers, students, and parents. Likewise, their central focus was anchored in ensuring that as the work advanced, the children would be well—academically and socioemotionally—in both the short and long term. One leader framed what we would call his theory of action as the three Cs: care, curriculum, and community.

> I said we're going to focus on three Cs and if we execute these three Cs well we're going to be okay through this period. The first C was care. I said care is number one. You know, I said care is number one. I don't think my predecessor would have said that, you know. We will figure out the academic piece of it of course, you know, but care, how we're going to care for our kids? Find out what their challenges are? —Tony

Tony led with care and acknowledged this framing of the school's ap-proach helped faculty prioritize working more closely and intensely with parents. Other educators amplified the value of relationships and expressed deep concern for the distinct challenges of supporting vulnerable students (e.g., homeless). The inability to hug a student or catch a student in the hall takes away the ability to leverage relationships in a manner that helps students stay connected academically. To that end, BIPOC teachers discussed the importance of the school building as an insulating variable that helped to support students and faculty alike.

> I just think that the world now sees how important teachers are. And how important a school environment is because when they get to school. If they see Miss Williams that changes their day they get out of the car and they had a bad day, it changes. This is the same for me. I could get into with my husband . . . when I walk into this cool. I'm excited. I'm happy it, everything changes. And I don't think that people outside of education understand the power of those buildings.

How people (students and teachers) experience a school is arguably at the heart of a school's value proposition. BIPOC teachers and leaders have a keen awareness of the multiple ways this value proposition comes to life in a school building, keeping learners connected and school relevant. We were struck by the fact that none of the leaders we spoke with worked from a "business as usual" premise. They recognized the need to pivot and asserted ways to help their teams or students adjust.

CULTURALLY RESPONSIVE TEACHING AND LEADING MATTERS!

BIPOC educators highlighted how broader perceptions of who students and their families are impacted how the school handled technology dissemination. One educator specifically discussed how the school had one-to-one technology but didn't send it home with schools initially. While there wasn't an explicit articulation about race/ethnicity or socioeconomics, there was an undergirding sense that the children's background (i.e., low income) delayed the school's willingness to send home the computers. Likewise, one teacher expressed a pointed disconnect and lack of awareness between the White school leader's approach to education during the pandemic, including not having children of his own, and gaps in what he thought was a reasonable expectation for children.

> They have a lot of stress, the parents are saying, hey, those dishes you use only doing even now, you're doing them all day because everybody's eating all day. And I don't care that you have to get on Zoom with your teacher, I need this done, the stressors that the parents

are going through, of course, reflect on to the students. And we tried to communicate that . . . But there hasn't been anything that he's received. So, of course we do our jobs and we get on and we help the kids. We work with the kids.

It was particularly noticeable that BIPOC educators expressed a keen awareness of how all types of students were faring, particularly those facing more difficult situations. They reflected compassionately on the stressors facing families, without vilifying or deficitizing parents and asserting the need for a more balanced, developmentally appropriate approach. For example, educators recognized parents' desires to help students get the work done and the resulting frustration in the process. One leader spoke of the need for balancing "getting the work done" with creating an environment that encouraged students to take academic risks. She recognized this skill as one that educators, rather than parents, are more equipped to deliver because of their training and pedagogical expertise. However, this leader also grappled with how there might be a broader articulation of this academic risk-taking value that could be communicated to the whole school community (inclusive of parents).

BUILDING A PATH FORWARD: RECOMMENDATIONS FOR NEXT SCHOOL YEAR AND BEYOND

The global pandemic of COVID-19 converged at a radical intersection—what some are calling the 1619 pandemic—the United States' ongoing battle with White supremacy and its related casualties. At the junction of this global pandemic and racial reckoning, BIPOC leaders faced a daunting escalation as they navigated the personal impact of these events and helped support their students, families, and schools in moving through the storm. While many were pressed and stressed in new ways, they leveraged informal networks and their past experiences in leading through adversity to chart a path forward with culturally responsive leadership approaches. In their synthesis of the literature, Khalifa, Khalil, Marsh, & Halloran (2019) discuss culturally responsive leadership (CRL) as promoting an inclusive environment, particularly for minoritized students. Moreover, this type of leadership addresses the needs of students, teachers, and parents. From the classroom to the head of school, the BIPOC educators we talked to anchored CRL even without calling it by name.

In alignment with their anchoring in culturally responsive leadership, the BIPOC educators interviewed called for or were planning to build inclusive teams to help develop plans for the upcoming school year. They recognized the need for broad and diverse stakeholder engagement in crafting a re-entry plan. Many of them had valuable lessons learned from the fourth quarter of the 2020 school year to inform the path forward. We share a few of those recommendations here:

Recommendations on Parent/Stakeholder Engagement

- Plan to include/engage parent(s) deeply throughout the year; plan new virtual parent meetings to build on newly forged connections with families.
- Engage all stakeholders in building re-entry plans, especially teachers, who can serve as ambassadors and champions with students and families.
- Employ distributive leadership models as a standard way of working, throughout the school year; these models may also serve as informal/mental health supports for faculty.

Recommendations on Relationships, School Climate, and Instructional Models

- Prioritize new students in re-entry planning. If all students can't return to the building, consider bringing an entry grade to a school (e.g., kindergarten in K–6 schools, or 6th-graders in middle schools).
- Balance technology with tactile learning tools (esp. for K–3). Ensure students have books and other tools so that technology is a complementary tool, not the only or most essential tool. Using print materials may also be helpful in places where broadband access is challenging.
- Facilitate more relational continuity with approaches such as looping; continuity in teachers from year to year will ensure teachers and students are well acquainted and can foster a more seamless transition to new academic material. Likewise, teachers have a greater command of students' academic strengths and weaknesses.

While BIPOC teachers and leaders offer powerful insights on managing adversity and planning for the upcoming year, we collectively acknowledge there is much about the way we deliver K–12 education that could benefit from reimagining. This moment affords such an opportunity to create new ways of being and working that ensure schools become places where all students can thrive. How do we invite students and their authentic identities into school—permanently erasing the hard lines between school and home? This question carries particular importance for BIPOC students. Moreover, can this moment help us chart a course for more effectively incorporating students' and families' funds of knowledge in ways that make more relevant connections between the classroom and students' lived experience? In what

RAPID-CYCLE INQUIRY

Rapid-cycle research design

Goal: Black, Indigenous, and People of Color (BIPOC) bring a distinct lens to their roles as educators and leaders. We wanted to understand how their social identities shaped their motivation to teach, their educational philosophies, and how they are supported in their roles. This chapter explores their experiences, challenges, successes, and lessons learned during the tectonic shift of COVID-19 and its broader implications for the future of education. During COVID-19, we surveyed six teachers and six educational leaders spanning the South, Northeast, and Midwest. This article frames the common themes identified in those interviews.

Guiding inquiry question: How do people of color experience teaching and leading in traditional public, public charter, and independent schools during COVID-19?

Existing knowledge, role of literature

Stevenson's RECAST Theory, Critical Leadership, Culturally Responsive School Leadership

Rapid-cycle interviews

1. We discussed the number of participants and context of participants. We wanted participants who worked in different educational settings and who were situated in different places geographically.
2. We developed pre-interview talking points.
3. We conducted 12 semi-structured interviews via Zoom that lasted approximately 30 to 60 minutes. Each interview was recorded, and the researchers watched all interviews.

Rapid-cycle surveys

1. We created a survey to capture demographic information and developed driving interview questions. We captured descriptive information from respondents, including race/ethnicity, years of experience, gender, site of practice, grade configuration of school, and grade(s) taught.
2. The goal of the survey was to provide background on participants, qualify them for participation, and inform the interview discussion.

Rapid-cycle analysis

1. We used transcription software. Each participant transcript was read by two members of the team, each of whom identified major themes.

> 2. Researchers read and/or watched all interviews that led to the grouping of themes that we refined through researcher dialogic engagement.
>
> **Rapid-cycle knowledge sharing and dissemination**
>
> 1. We disseminated articles via LinkedIn, Facebook, and Twitter, and shared them with senior leadership staff.
> 2. The knowledge gained through the research, interviews, and dialogic engagement has been used formally and informally in our work (e.g., leadership team meetings at our educational institutions).

ways can this shift also invite students to build toward a more transformative vision of our nation?

Our real-talk conversation with BIPOC teachers and leaders illuminates much about stressors, adaptive tools, resilience, and inclusive ways to respond to these current crises. Unfortunately, what is also clear is that there is a need for greater visibility of the unique needs and challenges these leaders face and how to support them. Likewise, there is a significant need for research on the distinct experience of teaching and leading while BIPOC. Research in this area can inform the work of BIPOC educators and the broader leadership and education fields. In striking contrast to the challenges that some assume might hold back BIPOC teachers and leaders living within White supremacy culture, they instead harness a distinct set of advantages and assets that make them uniquely qualified to lead through adversity.

REFERENCES

Bennis, W. G. & Thomas, R. J. (2002). Crucibles of leadership. *Harvard Business Review, 80*(9), 39–45.

Boyatzis, R. E., & McKee, A. (2005). *Resonant leadership: Renewing yourself and connecting with others through mindfulness, hope, and compassion.* Harvard Business School Press.

Covey, S. R. (2004). *The 7 habits of highly effective people: Restoring the character ethic.* Free Press.

Du Bois, W. E. B. (1968). *The souls of black folk; essays and sketches.* Johnson Reprint Corp.

Foster, M. (1997). *Black teachers on teaching.* New Press.

Fry, L. W. (2003). Toward a theory of spiritual leadership. *The Leadership Quarterly, 14*(6), 693–727. https://doi.org/10.1016/j.leaqua.2003.09.001

Gardner, W. L., Avolio, B. J., Luthans, F., May, D. R., & Walumbwa, F. (2005). "Can you see the real me?" A self-based model of authentic leader and follower development. *Leadership Quarterly, 16*(3), 343–372. https://doi.org/10.1016/j.leaqua.2005.03.003

Heifetz, R. A., Grashow, A., & Linsky, M. (2009). *The practice of adaptive leadership: Tools and tactics for changing your organization and the world.* Harvard Business Press.

Khalifa, M. (2018). *Culturally responsive school leadership.* Race and Education Series. Harvard Education Press.

Khalifa, M. A., Khalil, D., Marsh, T. E. J., & Halloran, C. (2019). Toward an Indigenous, decolonizing school leadership: A literature review. *Educational Administration Quarterly, 55*(4), 571–614.

McDermott, R., Raley J. D., & Seyer-Ochi, I. (2009). Race and class in a culture of risk. *Review of Research in Education, 33*(1), 101–116. https://doi.org/10.3102/0091732X08327163

Pak, K. & Ravitch, S. M. (Eds.). (2021). *Critical leadership praxis for educational and social change.* Teachers College Press.

Powley, E. H., & Taylor, S. N. (2014). Pedagogical approaches to develop critical thinking and crisis leadership. *Journal of Management Education, 38*(4), 560–585. https://doi:10.1177/1052562913519081

Quinn, R. E. (2004). *Building the bridge as you walk on it: A guide for leading change.* Jossey-Bass.

Ravitch, S. M. (2020). Why teaching through crisis requires a radical new mindset: Introducing flux pedagogy. *Harvard Business Publishing Education.* https://hbsp.harvard.edu/inspiring-minds/why-teaching-through-crisis-requires-a-radical-new-mindset

Spears, L. C., & Lawrence, M. (2004). *Practicing servant-leadership: Succeeding through trust, bravery, and forgiveness.* Jossey-Bass.

Stevenson, H. (2014). *Promoting racial literacy in schools: Differences that make a difference.* Teachers College Press.

Uhl-Bien, M. (2006). Relational Leadership Theory: Exploring the social processes of leadership and organizing. *Leadership Quarterly, 17*(6), 654–676. https://doi.org/10.1016/j.leaqua.2006.10.007

CHAPTER 7

Systems of Emotional Support for Educators in Crisis

Carla Haith and Jeannine Minort-Kale

EDITORIAL FRAMING

In this chapter, two doctoral candidates take on a rapid-cycle inquiry that examines what was happening behind the scenes with educators navigating the COVID-19 pandemic. As the authors state in their thinking behind conducting this inquiry, they observed the survey data collected from over 5,000 educators in March through a research effort between Yale Center for Emotional Intelligence and the Collaborative for Social-Emotional and Academic Learning. The data from this survey showed that the five most frequent words that teachers used to describe their feelings were "anxious," "fearful," "worried," "overwhelmed," and "sad." For these two authors, this data heightened the sense of urgency to conduct this rapid-cycle inquiry in order to better understand what was happening with educators behind their computer screens.

In turn, these authors went on a journey to "story the gap" and gather stories around the emotional needs of educators during the pandemic. As mentioned in Chapter 3, there is an urgency to gather contextualized data within our contexts on the ground in order to inform our decision-making in more responsive and humanizing ways. A primary goal of flux leadership is to collect and gather essential data that otherwise might be silenced or missed within moments of change or crisis.

These authors model this type of data gathering within this chapter. They take on timely questions: How did the shift to distance learning impact educator emotions and time? How were school systems working to support these educators' emotional well-being? Finally, how did educators feel about the impacts of these supports, or lack of, on their well-being and ability to do their jobs? These interviews capture educators' feelings of resilience, loss, and stress that the pandemic exacerbated. Haith and Minort-Kale detail powerful vignettes that help echo the importance of the flux tenet of responsive and humanizing leadership to create systems needed for educators to feel supported and sustained in these moments. In many of these vignettes, leadership supports with the flux tenet of radical compassion were often missing, and educators had to find ways to survive without them. As the authors remind us: "It is critical to keep human well-being at the center of our work in education." We could not agree more. This chapter illustrates both the importance of enacting responsive and humanizing leadership within moments of flux but also what can transpire when this tenet of our leadership practice is not practiced during crisis situations in schools.

INTRODUCTION

One of the things I am grateful for—and it is still a work in progress—is that it became apparent very quickly that the mental and emotional toll of distance learning has impacted each of our constituencies differently. And as an admin team, this crisis is asking us to really lean into work we may never have even thought of doing.

—New England School Leader

The shift to distance learning in response to COVID-19 was accompanied by various degrees of planning at the local, district, and school levels. The limited available preparation time was generally, and appropriately, dedicated to logistical aspects—like identifying virtual online platforms, daily schedules. The limited available preparation time was generally, and appropriately, dedicated to logistical aspects—like identifying virtual online platforms and daily schedules. Preparation time also now required planning for student support aspects such as the continued availability of school lunch to families in need and addressing the emotional loss experienced by many students. Suddenly, the onset of loss from the removal of their social networks and missing significant events, such as graduation, presented its own set of unique and time-consuming challenges.

Thus, less intentionally discussed and planned for, in most settings, was the emotional needs of educators within the school system. Like many adults, educators expressed significant feelings of anxiety and stress during this time. Survey data was collected from more than 5,000 educators in March as part of a collaborative effort between the Yale Center for Emotional Intelligence and the Collaborative for Social Emotional and Academic Learning. The data showed that the five most frequent words teachers used to describe their feelings at that time were "anxious," "fearful," "worried," "overwhelmed," and "sad." Those feelings can impact their ability to appropriately respond to both the academic and socioemotional needs of their students. As leaders ourselves, we set out to learn about the experiences of education practitioners in both the private and public sectors, with a focus on three main questions about their experiences during this time:

1. How has the pandemic crisis and shift to distance learning decreased, increased, or adjusted the emotional and time demands on you as an educator?
2. How have school systems been supporting your emotional well-being while you adapt to the rapidly changing demands of distance learning while balancing other aspects of your lives also in flux?
3. How do you feel these supports, or lack thereof, have impacted your well-being and ability to meet the expectations of your roles?

Education as a field is in a permanent state of emergency, and on the edge of total catastrophe. Educators internalize this sense of panic and stress at all levels and work tirelessly to try to be all things to all people. Similar to other systems of human service, already stressed in the pre–COVID-19 world, the pandemic intensified the overwhelming and multidimensional demands placed on both the education system and educators. While the educators we spoke with generally reported that distance learning increased the time and emotional energy needed to perform their jobs, their response to questions about support varied based on the educators' expectations and supports offered by their organizations. This variation held especially true when those supports were offered by someone with direct influence over the educators' day-to-day responsibilities.

We want to emphasize the overarching finding from our inquiry that it is critical to keep human well-being at the center of our work in education. True, the demands of education across the United States and the world changed dramatically overnight. We need to distribute computers! We must buy computers to distribute! We must find money to buy computers! What about the students who rely on school lunches? The needs were significant, and surges of sustained energy were required to meet them. Still, some organizations allowed the state of urgency that accompanied this pandemic to keep them from responding to the needs of people, including educators and parents. We should never underestimate the potential impact of asking someone how they are doing. Not simply in casual, polite conversation but in a way that allows a person to feel seen, take a deep breath, and choose whether to respond. The critical importance of that supportive atmosphere and personal touch appeared repeatedly in our conversations; it affected the ability of educators to manage the demands on time and emotions thrust upon them during this crisis.

We asked educators to share their thoughts about the shift in demands placed on them as a result of everything happening in the world. We present excerpts from those conversations nested within emergent themes from our educator interviews.

SOCIALLY DISTANCED LEADERSHIP—MISS A

One of the challenges for many was feeling removed from the work and students they love so much. Miss A is a highly respected educator of color who has been in the field for over 20 years. She's worked in public and private settings as a teacher and administrator on both coasts of the United States.

> Distance Learning has absolutely been one of the most challenging things. I'm an educator. I'm for the kids, and so not seeing the kids every day has been hard. You start to, you know, forget why you're there, or why you're working so hard. I am working so hard. However, you see the fruits of your labor when you have the opportunity to see and be with the kids. You see the kids; they stop by your office. They want to have lunch with you, they see you at recess duty, they see you at carpool, and they bring that rejuvenation of spirit and rejuvenation of energy and you're not getting it on Zoom. When we were in person, I hosted a Friday "luncheon with Miss A" every week, and one week we would play a game and the other week we tell jokes, so that was a lot of fun. And then I was also popping into classes, because I have to still observe and evaluate my faculty. So I was seeing the kids in these very short spurts. But, you know, when you look at your calendar, it is daunting. I look at my calendar it's like Zoom call after phone call after phone call, and there's no kid interaction there. It's just, business, business, business, and that's really hard, right, super hard and super challenging! I think another piece that's really challenging about this is that there's no end in sight. We've had other crises in the community, in California, there are fires. And so, that's a crisis where it's like a snow day on the East Coast, we have to shut down the school, however, there's an end in sight. So, this is definitely challenging because we don't know how it's going to end or when it's going to end.

Educators love to work with young people. They celebrate the success of their students and feel pain when they see their students in distress. The feelings of disconnect from the children, who many educators view as the more important part of their work, creates wear on educators that impacts their ability to keep doing necessary work in meaningful ways.

MAINTAINING FLEXIBILITY—MR. T

Mr. T teaches secondary math. He is also an athletic coach, adviser, and the parent of two young children, one of whom was born during the COVID-19 crisis. He has worked at his current organization for his entire teaching career. He is well regarded for his ability to connect with any child and his willingness to meet them wherever they are academically or socially.

> My wife is also a teacher and we both decided to shorten our parental leaves and teach during the spring. So we basically traded off the kids. If I was not in class, I had them and if she wasn't in class, she had them. It was hectic. I would often start at 7 a.m., trade off during the day, and then work after the kids went to bed from 10 at night until 2 or 3 the next morning.
>
> It was definitely tough in the classroom because everyone is trying to navigate a new system, new demands on their time, and new expectations on how to use their time. We were tasked with making sure that students were doing ok but it wasn't always easy. As someone who wanders around a lot in the classroom to check in and see how people are doing. It was difficult because some of the younger kids would turn their cameras off because they were super self-conscious and didn't want to stare at themselves. Some students just had issues with working technology. Some kids just struggled to transition because they were social kids and started just doing the minimum.
>
> We have one administrator whose job it was to provide us with educational technology support. He was great about the issues I ran into. I didn't really hear from anyone else, even when my child was born. I didn't even know who was covering my classes during the short period I took off. No one was responding to my emails. No one reached to see if I needed anything simple like a textbook or the document camera that was in my room. So I ended up buying one. I also didn't expect much, so I am not upset about it. I will figure it out.

What struck us most about the conversation with Mr. T was how even-keeled, even optimistic, he was about his ability to continue to do what was needed to support his students and navigate his own childcare challenges. The resilience he demonstrated, however, was consistent among all the educators we contacted. While each teacher felt their challenges, not one had given up on their commitment to their students. They never stopped finding ways to serve them.

THE CHALLENGE OF BOUNDARIES—MS. F

Ms. F has taught in independent schools for the last 16 years. She worked in DC private schools, and then moved to the New England Area, where she has worked in three independent schools. She has taught kindergarten and 2nd grade, and she is now the assistant head of lower school. She shared how her school offered support to teachers during these challenging times.

> Well, one of the things as a community that we talked about with the faculty and staff when we reviewed some data that was taken during remote learning this past spring was that we need to really be conscious about when people were available and when people were not. Realizing that there is some fluidity because people can contact you anytime. Really respecting individual needs of people. For instance, if someone from your team was not available to make it to a meeting, suspending the judgment around why and just assuming goodwill, that there was a reason they couldn't be a part of that meeting. Also being conscientious about when you are sending emails and when you are what you are asking of folks, because it's very easy to push send on an email and say, "Hey, meet me in this Zoom meeting" because we can't assume what people have going on outside of their work schedules and work life so we have really trying to be conscientious of that and keeping that at the forefront as we do planning and as we set up professional development. As well as if we have to continue with distance learning. In August we will continue to talk about this, really making sure that the social-emotional well-being of the constituents in our community are taken care of during the first 6 weeks of school in a way that will be different than, if we were just coming back to the school building, so I think that there's been a lot of ongoing conversations around that for our students but also for our faculty and staff. We are trying to find out right now who is comfortable with being back on campus, or are there people who are not going to be able to return and really just looking at the human side of things and the emotional side of things, so that when we do come back together, whether that is virtually or brick and mortar, we have a better sense of how people are feeling mentally and emotionally going into it, and so really thinking about those first 6 weeks to establish. What does it mean to be part of a community in a physical sense? We've all been away from each other for so long.

Armed with information from distance learning in the spring, school administrators had the opportunity to use what they learned to prepare teachers to move into distance learning at any given time. Ultimately, they understood that boundaries needed to be at the forefront of every decision. Self-care in this way ensured teacher and student social-emotional health and well-being. Plans to have ongoing conversations are extremely important.

TEACHERS AS PARENTS, PARENTS AS TEACHERS—MS. B

It was evident that educators were carrying the weight of worrying about the impact of this loss of classroom time on student learning while also balancing the needs of their own children. Ms. B is a classroom teacher in an urban public school setting, where she has worked for more than a dozen years. Her students revered her for a demonstrated commitment to them and the sense of community she creates in the classroom.

> I am doing pretty well today. We are going on 4 days in a row of sleeping through the night, so I should go play the Lotto. Getting a full night's sleep makes me weird, like what does it mean to be this well rested? I guess that says something about my life. When I am at school, that is my only job. There can be a lot, but that is it. At home with two kids, it becomes split between being a teacher, a mother, and the mother of a student with special needs, and making sure that everyone is getting all their work done. I have learned to relax a bit and take the position of what gets done, gets done. I keep thinking that every student, not just my students at school but my own kids and their classmates, is going to be so far behind. That allowed me to relax a bit because it meant that they were not at a disadvantage the same way. Even so, I have cried. One of my students emailed me to ask if I still liked her because she struggled in class and hasn't been turning in the online assignments. Our school social worker has put out a Google Meet for anyone and everyone, so even staff could come in and talk with her. That helped.

In addition to learning how to innovatively teach and lead, many educators were the primary caregivers for their own school-age children. Some expressed that they felt this part of themselves was not seen or understood, which weighed on their mental health and well-being. This weight was of vital concern to the durability of their work and well-being.

THE EDUCATOR TECHNOLOGY GAP—MS. C

A school athletic director in Virginia talked about the difficulties she encountered based on the technology her school provided her and the virtual platform she was asked to use. She has worked in three independent schools, two in Massachusetts and her current school in Norfolk, Virginia. She started as an elementary 4th-grade teacher. As a former collegiate athlete, she has always been passionate about sports. As an athletic director, she oversees the athletic department, teaches K–8th-grade physical education, and 6th-grade health. She also coaches basketball, volleyball, cross country, and soccer.

> I will say that initially the school was on the Google Meet platform. And we had a consensus from a lot of the teachers, and I know for the PE department Zoom worked a little bit better, because we were able to see several students on the screen as opposed to the Google Meet. If you didn't have the extension, you were only seeing one person on the screen. So they did jump on that fairly quickly and got all of the teachers the Zoom license. Sure, so we were able to use that platform, and it actually worked great for me, so I was glad that they were able to support us and hear us out and meet our needs that way.

Did the school meet all your technology needs?

> I would say, no, not really. Because again, I did go to the school, and I got a Chromebook, I got a laptop initially, and the audio was not working on the laptop, so yes we did get the Zoom licensure, but at the end of the day I still had to use my personal iPad. And so, yes, I would say, they tried in that sense, but the technology just for me was like I said a little frustrating. I think that it was also a little challenging at times because I do have two young kids at home that I had to help navigate with their distance learning and while we only had specials on Friday. My role was only to teach PE on Fridays. You know when you think about, you know, three people in the home, being on Zoom. At the same time, and our Wi-Fi and that kind of thing. I mean, you know, it was challenging sometimes. So, I think that I would say that piece was one of the things that if we had to do this again, I think my family and I would have to think about, you know, probably more broadband with our Wi-Fi system. And I think again being a parent of two younger kids was challenging at times. And they do attend the school that I, I teach at so I'm having to navigate their schedules and having to, just be a support for them not that I'm not a support for them during, if they were in school, but this was just more I had to be a little bit more hands on with them and making sure that they were able to get on their Zooms at the time, they needed to get on complete their assignments and making sure that they had everything that they needed to have as well. So, at times that was challenging.

Technology has been a pedagogical imperative during this global pandemic. The technology teams in schools must test all the devices that students and teachers will need in the event that distance learning needs to be in place in moving forward. The hardware and the online platforms students and teachers use need to be established, which requires schools to offer professional development in these areas. Mrs. C's interview makes clear the work that we must do, now and in the future, to close these loops.

WEARING MULTIPLE HATS—MS. J

It is generally acknowledged in the educational world that few people "just teach." There are the informal hats that many teachers wear—counselor, tutor, intermediary, coach. There are also educators who perform multiple formal roles in a school. Ms. J is one such teacher. In addition to teaching science in an independent school, Ms. J runs a large enrichment program that serves over 600 students.

> There is not enough time in the day for what I have been asked to do. I teach a reduced load because of my additional responsibilities. My additional responsibilities doubled in terms of demand because that had to go virtual too. The program is smaller during the school year, so we used the spring as a tester to see how well we are reaching out to our students before the larger summer program. And what that required was a lot of technology resources and budget criteria that had to be met and shifted. Like if we saved $30,000 on buses, how much of that money could I then use to send Chromebooks home? It's like this panic. To avoid missing somebody falling through the cracks, whether it is my science students, my enrichment program students, or my own kids.
>
> I am easily putting in 12 hours of work, but I have been strategic with my breaks. I try to make sure to sneak in an online yoga class in the morning before things get crazy. Sneak in a walk. Then I am back online until 9 or 10. I am also on a few task forces at school to address certain aspects of all these different scenarios we have to plan for. It dawned on me that I need to carve out time for myself and my kids have been seriously neglected by me over the last couple of months, especially my 6th-grader, and I want to find ways to make this summer enjoyable for them.
>
> My school has tried to support me. My leader called me just to check in. Still, a lot of the supporters have missed their mark with me. I think I have seen my colleagues more virtually than I ever saw them live. For some people, it was a great opportunity to connect, but it also felt directionless at times. It was hard for me because I knew that I had other things to do, and this was taking time away from me having that time with my family later on.

Ms. J was somewhat excited about the challenges that distance learning presented because she felt it allowed her to grow in ways she has been interested in pursuing. Some teachers thrive on the forced opportunity to grow and change, and leaders should think about how support for these pressure-driven educators may look different.

LESSONS AND MOVING FORWARD

Education is for improving the lives of others and for leaving your community and your world better than you found it!

—Marian Wright Edelman

As schools fell more into the uneven rhythm of distance learning, some leaders and stakeholders scrambled to fill what they saw as evolving gaps in support for educators. School leaders and board members worked to develop ideas that would create "bright spots" for faculty and students. Discussions began to occur about how the demands of schedules coupled with screen time fatigue presented true challenges for educators. Some of the educators we spoke with talked about things that the schools did to show appreciation. We heard about teachers receiving individual check-in calls, Amazon gift cards, treat boxes full of snacks, and wine delivered to their homes, as well as notes of gratitude.

Still, many expressed that these tokens helped only to a degree, and several said that offers of support felt absent or insufficient. Educators continued to carry the weight of concern about how the students would potentially suffer. It was disheartening for them to think that students were not progressing the way they would be during in-person instruction. Was the summer slide starting months earlier? What would this mean for the future? Am I fulfilling my obligation to improve student performance? These questions keep educators and administrators awake at night. We have no answers.

Although the educators we spoke with were in different roles and different settings, each vignette told a story of educators working in a system that was more focused on survival than thriving. While several of the educators described feeling a strong sense of disconnect and helplessness, many also shared what helped them feel tethered and focused during this time of uncertainty. These stories provide lessons for educators to carry with them even once we can all return to a physical school.

1. Educators who worked in schools with well-established school–family partnerships reported feeling more successful. This connection helped educators feel more grounded in their work and students, while also reducing the fear of academic loss. Thus,

schools should take deliberate steps to re-establish meaningful relationships with their parent communities. Too often, these are neglected. Ways to do so range from sending out weekly emails, via Google classrooms, to a system of checking in with families by phone one or more times weekly. The goal is to keep the human connection alive during a challenging time.

2. Educators who were already comfortable with technology reported feeling less stressed in the shift to distance learning and were less reliant on support from their organizations. Schools should develop comprehensive technology professional development plans geared toward helping teachers integrate technology into their daily practice in purposeful ways that are efficient.

3. Educators shared that they believe this crisis may be the ultimate motivation to finally abandon old-fashioned teaching and learning methods that have not worked for students in quite some time. Educators now know that they need to have a plan because part of the "new normal" means that they may be asked to shift to distance learning at any time. This uncertainty can induce anxiety if leaders and schools are unwilling to abandon existing systems—such as rigid grade calculations categories for participation and homework or failing to lead the way in showing teachers how to utilize new and evolving tools that re-create systems of collaboration and assessment.

4. Professional development is a good thing, but meeting schedules must value teachers' time and respect the burnout that many can feel from being on camera all day. Schools should think carefully about having conversations or learning asynchronously, what must be discussed live, and what can be optional. Planning in this way requires a differentiated approach to communicating information but is worth the effort.

When we began this project, we sought to provide a space for teachers and leaders to authentically share how teaching and leading during COVID-19 impacted their work and personal lives. While we found that educators did not have a monolithic experience, their feelings of detachment were fairly consistent, as was the significant need for emotional support. As identified at the start of this chapter, we must center human well-being, even when other interests compete.

When we initially had our conversations with educators, no nationwide plan or consensus existed for fall schooling. As we write this in August, plans for the upcoming school year continue to ebb and flow dramatically as COVID numbers rise and fall in various parts of the country. Rather than approach the situation as temporary, schools have considered how the educational landscape generally, and teaching specifically, will change more permanently. Conversations and news media speculation about families planning to homeschool their children, or set up learning pods with similar families, has caused public schools to worry that they will face a decrease in enrollment-based funding, consequently threatening to add additional depth to the achievement gap. Independent schools worry they will lose families that they depend on for their budgets if they do not create an educational plan that fits their brand. Currently, three different learning models have emerged: all students returning to school in person, a hybrid model where children go to school in person a few times a week and participate in virtual learning when they are not on campus, or fully remote schooling.

Educators are at the mercy of both waves of political pressure and shifts of national thinking. Their mental health and well-being are not the only things at stake. *Time* magazine reported in July stories of early retirement

---

RAPID-CYCLE INQUIRY

Rapid-cycle research design

Goals: To better understand the shift to distance learning in response to the COVID-19 crisis as it relates to planning at the local, district, and school levels. The limited available preparation time was generally, and appropriately, dedicated to logistical aspects—like identifying virtual online platforms and daily schedules. Preparation time also now required planning for student support aspects such as the continued availability of school lunch to families in need and addressing the emotional loss experienced by many students. What was less intentionally discussed and planned for were the emotional needs of educators within the school system. Like many adults, educators expressed an increased feeling of anxiety and stress during this time. Those can impact their ability to properly respond to both the academic and socioemotional needs of their students. We wanted to understand this phenomenon in real time.

Rapid-cycle data collection

1. We discussed the need for leaders from both public and private schools to participate.
2. We developed interview questions.
3. 12 individual interviews, each about 30 minutes long.

Rapid-cycle analysis

1. Use of transcription software.
2. Researchers participated in intensive dialogic engagement sessions for data analysis.

when teachers decide the COVID-19 risk to return to in-person instruction is not worth taking (Reilly, 2020). In August, CNN reported that teachers in Gwinnett County, Georgia, chose to resign rather than enter classrooms under current conditions. New Jersey worries about the impact of substitute teachers. Teacher shortages have already made it difficult to hire in a way that would allow for recommended class sizes.

We do not assume the position that these issues are hopeless, even if there are no perfect solutions. The problems discussed in our interviews are clearly far from resolved, but there is information and data, both anecdotal and research-based, that schools can use to create a blueprint that supports every adult and child in the community proactively. We hope that leaders keep these stories in mind to ensure that educators at all levels feel cared for and connected so they continue to do the work needed to support our kids.

REFERENCES

Reilly, K. (2020). With no end in sight to the coronavirus, some teachers are retiring rather than going back to school. https://time.com/5864158/coronavirus-teachers-school

CHAPTER 8

Listening Leadership

The Student Voices Project

Manuela Adsuar-Pizzi

EDITORIAL FRAMING

In this chapter, Manuela Adsuar-Pizzi, an educational leader at an independent high school in New York and doctoral candidate, discusses what it means to lead in crisis and where students fall into this dire picture:

> We were building the boat in deep water, throwing life jackets as we saw people drowning. Students were ripped from their schools, teachers, friends and support structure—without any warning . . . The veil was torn separating home and school, society and self, revealing deeply embedded social structures rooted in inequity and, at the heart of this, lie the students.

At the heart of this rapid-cycle inquiry, the author brings to light the power of story within educational leadership practice through an approach that invites students into an initiative called the Student Voices Project. This invitation centers on a single inquiry question: "Who was listening?"

On the surface, one can see the powerful engagement of students during a time of crisis. This collaborative, informal storytelling initiative allowed students to share their experiences. It also provided something even more invaluable: the unapologetic truth-telling of students, which reflects the deeper commitments of the flux leadership tenet of distributive wisdom. As introduced in Chapter 3, the distributive wisdom approach serves as an alternative for schools to build stronger knowledge capacities in their building—by seeing student voices as critical data within school improvement, leaders can enact humanizing change in more authentic ways. Within this chapter, readers will see how this could be possible.

The author writes about how students conveyed their stories through videos, drawings, photos, and other media on social media platforms, such as TikTok, Instagram, and Facebook. This became a powerful way

---

to recenter student stories and combat deficit perspectives that often plagues students in these moments. These stories and narratives are interwoven in a manner that prompts deeper questions for the author within the chapter: How do students ask questions when confused? Could a series of videos ever replace in-person instruction?

The answers to these questions are far less important than the questions that arise from centering these student perspectives. By seeing these stories as invaluable and humanizing data points, this chapter prompts larger takeaways around how student sense-making of crisis moments and time of change are essential within flux leadership. Distributive wisdom is an active process working to influence the social dimensions of leadership around equity and justice. Shifting our leadership stance to do more to incorporate student voices in how we run our schools will provide educational ecosystems with the proactive change they have been searching for.

The last day of school came, and I plainly said bye to my friends as if I were coming back the following week. Little did I realize, those days would turn into weeks, then suddenly into months. Interacting with others has been impossible, and I'm not going to lie, I'm not too fond of quarantine. Looking at the news seeing empty boardwalks, subways, and cities has impacted the way I view the overall situation.

—8th-grade student, Sussex, NJ

Only the human heart, telling its stories, brings language back to life and taps into the power of the Word "as an instrument of creation." That changes everything—sends the blood of life pumping through our words. Personal story changes language/writing from a mere subject in school into a tool for survival and peace. But the "telling is not all"—there must be another there to listen.

—Lynn Nelson, 2000

"YOUR TEACHER HAS PLACED YOU IN THE WAITING ROOM"

I am the head of school at an alternative, independent high school in Brooklyn, serving a population of students with diverse neurological and cognitive complexities, when the COVID-19 pandemic sweeps brutally and swiftly across the boroughs, causing the city of New York to abruptly enter a shelter-in-place mandate. It is the first week of pandemic virtual instruction, and we have set up a virtual "roam" document as a leadership team. Each day we drop into classes to see how they are going, answer any "in the moment" questions, and touch base in any way we can with our students "in the field." Today, however, I am not in drop-in mode. I have been asked to meet with a teacher and student because the teacher is worried about what is happening in the household and how it affects the student. Since the start of quarantine, this student has logged into each class in her closet. It is the only space she has peace and quiet and where she feels she can be herself. Teachers have reported hearing screaming and fighting in the background during classes and occasionally the sound of crashing objects. We are worried about her, but we cannot reach her. I am online, and the host has placed me in the waiting room. I am by myself in my home office, waiting to connect. All I can think is that our kids are in crisis and we cannot reach them.

As I wait in virtual limbo, I think back to the last day we were all together in the school, to the student announcement board, on which is still written in bold blue letters, "Welcome! Today is March 13, 2020." That day began like most others, except that calls and meetings to address the "threat of pandemic" filled my calendar and loomed in our newsfeeds. At 12:05 p.m., we began our weekly faculty meeting via Zoom to run a rehearsal on the platform if we needed to shift to virtual instruction in response to the rapidly changing conditions related to the COVID-19 pandemic. At 1:12 p.m., I received a text from my district leader: "Gather your entire school for an emergency meeting. We're closing schools. Everyone must pack up and be ready to go virtual by the end of the business day." A return to school would be pending. At 1:13 p.m., I called my leadership team into the office. "We're closing. We're going virtual. Assemble everyone in the building for an all-school meeting. I will give the announcement at 1:15, since everyone will be back in the building for their classes at that time."

It is an odd state of affairs to be a principal during a crisis. As a leader, you need to stand firm, yet be cheery enough to fit the circumstances and break the ice—particularly for the students and teachers prone to panic, anxiety, and stress. So I stood there that day, looked each person in that room in the eye, and told them what was happening. I told them our plan and explained how we needed to take all our belongings home so the building could be cleaned. I explained that we needed to set up a space for them to process together; share contact information; check out needed books, supplies, and devices; and work with teachers on practice runs with Zoom. The student lounge where we were meeting instantly took on an air of business, with a tinge of excitement. One student exclaimed, "This is great! I don't have to go to school anymore!" I jokingly retorted, "D, I know where you live, so if you don't log in for class, you know you'll see me knocking on your door!" After a few laughs and jabs back and forth, we settled again into the rest of the afternoon, teaching classes and tying up loose ends. Little did we know. Little did we know.

ACKNOWLEDGMENT OF CONTEXT— CRISIS LEARNING PLANS IN THE TIME OF COVID-19

In the fall of 2019, the National Center for Educational Statistics estimated that 56.6 million children across the United States were expected to attend an elementary, middle, or high school, across sectors. In the middle of March 2020, every single one of these 56.6 million children was sent home from school and told not to return "until further notice," pending the spread of the COVID pandemic sweeping swiftly across the globe. On March 16, 2020, the U.S. Department of Education issued a Fact Sheet titled "Addressing the Risk of COVID-19 in Schools While Protecting the Civil Rights of Students" (USDOE Office for Civil Rights, 2020). In this document, the USDOE outlines guidance for schools and administrators regarding compliance across CDC, Section 504, Title II, and Title VI standards such that "compliance with CDC's recommendations should not create civil rights concerns. Section 504 of the Rehabilitation Act of 1973 (Section 504) prohibits disability discrimination by schools receiving federal financial assistance. Title II of the Americans with Disabilities Act of 1990 (Title II) prohibits disability discrimination by public entities, including schools. Title VI of the Civil Rights Act of 1964 (Title VI) prohibits race, color, and national origin discrimination by schools receiving federal funds" (www.nces.ed.gov, 2020).

Almost overnight, schools and administrators across the nation got to work developing and implementing emergency school continuity plans that could protect students' rights to health care and rights to educational access. We developed plans in the midst of a national crisis—an unprecedented pandemic. We were building the boat in deep water, throwing life jackets as we saw people drowning. Students were ripped from their schools, teachers, friends, and support structures—with no warning. Through this planning, it became evident that schools provide much more than just a learning space for 8 hours a day. Schools are the backbone of the social system, providing and accountable for more people than any other public institution in the country. And, at this moment, as Americans placed a microscope over this system, it reflected something alarming: deeply embedded social structures rooted in inequity, with students at its center. Wading through social distancing, quarantines, and online classes, students who began to find their footing (and not all did) started speaking out, sharing their opinions and experiences, but who was listening?

THE PROJECT AND INVITATION

The Student Voices Project began to answer this very question. "Who *was* listening?" This imperative contends to reposition student reflections and experiences as central narratives in the discourse on crisis education during the COVID-19 pandemic. The project, designed as an informal, collaborative, storytelling initiative, started in April 2020 to encourage students of all ages to share their school experiences during the COVID-19 outbreak. Invitations to participate were sent out digitally via email and social media platforms, encouraging students, parents, and educators to collect student stories through videos, drawings, writing, photographs, and other media. In this chapter and my reflections, I draw on information gathered across my professional networks by asking students to submit written, audio, video, and/or artistic reflections and responses via Google forms and Flip Grid. Additionally, I look to social media platforms such as TikTok, Instagram, and Facebook to survey the myriad of ways student stories have been told during this time.

All these platforms assume a level of privilege and access to participate in the sharing of these stories. I recognize the need to interrogate the norms of crisis-schooling frameworks dependent on device and internet access that have left a large portion of our student population without access to educational continuity in a virtual setting. Based on this, I seek to acknowledge the missing voices in our stories, highlighting that this erasure of experience is in itself a narrative that must be heard and attended to in education. Reflecting on these trends, I seek to recenter student experiences and narratives, those shared as well as those absent, as a lens through which we as educators can examine and create more meaningful ways to engage student knowledge and needs in our schools and classrooms and to reflect on our perceptions and practices.

By centering students in this way, I hope that these reflections can serve as a call to dismantle deficitizing discourse related to student identities and experiences. Further, I hope these stories inform a greater understanding of students positioned as central agents in the national narrative on education. I do this from my positionality as an educational leader, literacy teacher, and mother. My positionality as a White, cis-gendered, economically advantaged woman in education must also be centered on the imperative to actively dismantle White supremacy culture in my work and life, and to lead with an antiracist stance that reflects on my own experiences of privilege, complicity, and implicit bias. Continually, I seek to notice, name, and push against these aspects of privilege.

As a colleague and ally on this journey, I invite you to participate in a "radical listening" and "critical listening" stance as you read through the testimonial quotes and excerpts in this chapter (Cruz, 2012). This space is freed from a pattern of pathologizing student experiences and open to healing justice frameworks visible within the testimonies as you read between the lines. It is no doubt that this period of "radical flux" has tapped into varying levels of vulnerability in our personal lives and practices as adults.

I engage in this reflection to safely and bravely invite student vulnerability into this space.

Radical and significant life changes continue to burden our students during this pandemic year. Alongside the pandemic, economic upheaval, civil unrest, and the ongoing daily impact of institutionalized racism permeate the fabric of our nation. I seek to offer the tradition of merging student testimonios and critical witness frameworks (Campano & Ghiso, 2010; Dutro, 2019) into the discourse on education. In so doing, this work can hold a powerful potential to empower and recenter student voice in participative decision-making reimagining education in a post-pandemic nation.

The deeply rooted tradition of testimonio can also, as Cruz (2012) contends, develop "the potential to undermine the larger narratives that often erase and make invisible the expendable and often disposable labor and experiences" of individuals within a system (p. 460). Thus, it can be utilized as a powerful pedagogy of practice meant to decolonize, disrupt and (re)form educational experiences. Student voices can often be characterized as marginalized and deficitized in education and the classroom (Lefstein, Pollak, & Segal, 2020) and are rarely centered despite the potential to create a space of empowerment and collective action (Woodward, 2018). While I do not claim nor appropriate the genre of testimonio as the core of this piece, I do want to recognize and honor the wisdom in the tradition and call forward its potential and power to engage student voices as "Stories, ideally of coincidence and heartache and the sweetest tiny moments; . . . And just a glimpse of tomorrow, either in the face of an innocent or the realization of a dream" (Brown, 2017, p. 109). Thus, this wisdom of practice (Shulman, 2007) comes to bear as the connective tissue of this piece.

Student Submitted Original Poem:

"Don't Give Up"

One day everything is normal, and then it's just not.
Spring is over and warm weather is supposed to be coming, but it's
    just not.
I'm with my friends, sharing laughs at the mall, and then we're
    just not.

Everyone is scared, people are sick, they're supposed to be staying
    home, but they're just not.
We should be happy, we should be at school with our teachers
    learning new things, but we're just not.
We need to stay positive, we need to be strong. When everything is
    against us we should just give up . . . but we're JUST NOT!
                                            (8th-grade Student, Vernon, NJ)

A PERSONAL HISTORY OF COLLECTIVE TRAUMA

A little over 20 years ago, in May 2000, Lynn Nelson wrote in "the shadow of the tragedy of Columbine High School" of images "locked now in our collective memories, congealing our previous vague anxiety and concern" (p. 42). I cannot help now but conjure this sentiment amidst these words. As a college student, I will never forget my initial reactions of repulsion, fear, and uncertainty as I watched the news scenes unfold that day to cover the story of the shootings. A little over a decade later, I remember sitting with my newborn daughter in my lap, watching the news as the Twin Towers came crashing down in lower Manhattan, remembering that same combination of repulsion, fear, and uncertainty. Both moments claimed a stake in the national timeline—a time "Before Columbine" or "Pre-9/11." Both moments changed our national narrative and language. As a student, mother, teacher, and eventual administrator in New York City, both incidents, while in the past, occupied a perpetual space in my present, peppering every choice and action with the potential of crisis. Anyone who lived in New York following 9/11 can attest to the "on edge" feelings at every turn—a stalled subway train due to a bomb threat or a helicopter or plane flying too low, too loud, causing you to question.

When the COVID pandemic hit the East Coast in March 2020, I was accustomed to crises. We pushed through challenges of 9/11, both as a city and nation. I created a slew of protocols and practices to guard against school shootings. The terms "lockdown" and "shelter in place" became ubiquitous in our work and lives. As one kindergarten student I spoke with so eloquently stated, "Lockdown means someone bad is in school and wants to shoot everybody, so you have to lock the doors and put all the desks up and hide, but I wanna fight like 'Schoom, Schoom' [articulates warrior moves with arms]" (kindergarten student, Indianapolis, IN). So, in March 2020, when Governor Cuomo placed all NYC residents into a mandated "shelter in place" order, associations with school shootings and 9/11 awakened within me once again.

Each day in March, my children and I awoke to news channels roll-calling the dead—another 1,000 today, and another, and another, accompanying the mandate to shelter in place. Was this the Zombie apocalypse all my middle school students rooted for? Were we entering the prelude to a dystopian state? I grew up in the Midwest, where some towns did not exceed 1,000. Each day during COVID-19, I woke up to see a town, a neighborhood, a network of families obliterated by this silent enemy. I began to lose hope and feel despair. I knew this pandemic hit very close to home for so many of my students who had already lost family members in 9/11, and who now had family members on the front line. This moment, this time, was a space of collective trauma. We were all suddenly thrust into it;

yet, our collective experiences and shared stories of grief and perseverance, brought forth by 9/11, Columbine, Sandy Hook, and other events, brought to light the power in sharing the narrative: "Our stories sit in us, waiting to be told, to be acknowledged" (Nelson, 2000, p. 44).

WHO IS LISTENING?

"I will tell you something about stories, [he said.] They aren't just entertainment. Don't be fooled. They are all we have, you see, all we have to fight off Illness and death" —Leslie Marmon Silko (1977)

"But when we are allowed to write our stories and when someone actually listens to us, powerful language begins to emerge. Voice emerges. Sense of self grows. Maybe that is all we need (could it be so simple?)—all we need to become powerfully literate and to heal ourselves." —Lynn Nelson (2000, p. 45)

"I really do wish the teachers knew how much this is affecting some people. Kids are getting really depressed over this and harming themselves. Not me personally, but I hear it down the grape vine. It's a really stressful period and having a butt load of schoolwork piled on top really gets to some of us. I don't mind staying at home, but it's really the fact that the virus is straying closer and closer to my family is what I'm worried about." —8th-grade student, Lancaster, PA

The Student Voices Project grew from wonderings about how students were coping with the abrupt changes in schooling and the choices that were undoubtedly impacting them. These choices were made by educational leaders overnight with no input from the students themselves. As I collected stories and reflections, it became clear that each student, unique in their own identities and contexts, experienced pandemic virtual schooling on a deeply personal level. One student, anxious and confused, reflected on the uncertainty of the time, mixed with the constant flux of her school's continuity plan:

"In the beginning I felt very, very stressed and annoyed by the fact my school kept changing what we were supposed to do but now I have gotten used to it and it has been a lot easier to manage. I wish my school teachers would acknowledge how hard it's been not only for them but for the students and that most of the work had been catering neuro-typical students."—8th-grade student, New York, NY

What is so poignant in this reflection is the student's ability to recognize the limitations of pandemic virtual schooling that her middle school chose to follow. As leaders made choices on how to continue schooling, they also made assumptions about how students are expected to function virtually. Despite what we know about the social and emotional aspects of learning, alongside the impact of dynamic social interaction and collaboration in classrooms, all seemed to go out the window when transitioning to virtual instruction. The transition left some students scrambling on their own to develop their social literacy in a virtual space. Particularly, this uniquely challenged students with cognitive or neurological complexities.

Another student noted how adjusting to "reading the virtual room" was difficult at first. He describes how these adjustments leave him worried about the impacts he'll face as a learner moving forward:

> "I like staying home and sleeping, but I don't like that we can't just raise our hands and ask questions like in an actual class. I think it will be weird going right from being home for what feels like forever right into high school. Honestly, I do like being home so I really wouldn't mind if we don't go back to school in fall. I am wondering though how this is going to affect our classes and things that we are and aren't allowed to do when we do go back to school." —8th-grade student, Vernon, NJ

This reflection, like many others we received, points to the value students place on knowing how to navigate the norms of educational spaces. As educators, we create these norms at the beginning of the year to enable students to participate in the classroom community effectively. Thrust suddenly into unfamiliar learning spaces, many students became unsure how to participate as agents in their learning. What were the expectations placed on them? How could they interact with each other and their teachers or ask a question when confused? Could a series of videos really replace in-person instruction? What happens to "in the moment" adjustment, adaptation, and responsiveness to learner needs? Finally, how can students engage in best practices as learners when there is no common or consistent framework for schooling?

Indeed, students' experiences varied tremendously throughout school closures. Some students who had technology provided by their schools had no internet to access content. Some parents stayed home, some lost their jobs, and others fought the front lines daily as essential workers. Some students received packets from their schools while others were thrust swiftly and without training into online classes. Through it all, the children were ferried through the cattle shoot of whatever plan for learning their school or district created.

One student shared in an informal conversation about how her school sent students home with only a photocopied packet. They were told that they would not receive any direct instruction in classes for the remainder of the school year. She shared that after the last day of school, she had no idea what happened to most of her teachers or classmates due to the shelter-in-place mandate. Like most high schools in New York City, her school is primarily a commuter school, so few if any students from her school live near her neighborhood. That, combined with the public transportation closures, left her feeling isolated and on her own. She noted that while the school had voluntary check-in times, no one was taking advantage of them. She worried that when she returned to school, she wouldn't be ready to begin preparing for college. She felt so far behind.

Another student echoed this sentiment and dove further into the social complexities of schooling, worried that the transition back to "normal" may leave many students exposed to a variety of social and academic vulnerabilities that for some may have otherwise been mitigated at home:

> "I don't know how to feel about going back to school. I want to learn how we used to without the drama that follows. The question I have is the education worth the drama and mean kids it comes with. Going back to school is uncharted territory. Will it be the same as we left it? Will we be the same? After the pandemic has completely gone away, if it does, the lessons they teach us must be somewhat different from the lessons they used to teach to fill in some blanks that we must have missed during online school. I wonder how they will approach this in a way to teach us to keep pushing us forward but also teach us the things we missed without getting stuck in a grade below we should be." —8th-grade student, Brooklyn, NY

As an educator, this project has shown me the ways students take agency over their individualized learning. The extent to which our students reflect upon, know, and understand what does and does not work for them as learners has powerfully emerged in this inquiry. As the primary decision-makers on educational frameworks, policies, and pedagogical methods, we should take the time to invite students to the table to share what is meaningful and what is needed for them to thrive in our shared educational spaces—virtual or otherwise. Additionally, through these reflections, I have come to understand our role as educators in providing structures for ritual, routine, and rites of passage. Childhood and adolescence are times marked by a substantial amount of transition and change. In light of the global and collective uncertainty we face as individuals in this world right now, it is even more essential for students that we continue to provide the assurance and support these rituals, routines, and rites of passage that mark our students' lives. I thus leave us with a call and a question: Our students are speaking—it's time to *listen!* Are you ready to do that?

Goal: The purpose of this project was to invite students to share their accounts and reflections of their experiences with the first few months of COVID-19 crisis schooling to bring their voices to the table when reimagining education in the "new normal."

Focus: This project draws upon literature grounded in Critical Race Theory, culturally sustaining leadership theories and critical and transformative storytelling frameworks. The project also centers students as agents in their learning, honors student knowledges and expertise in their own lives and learning, and is founded on the belief that through critical listening and witnessing, leaders may learn from student stories and experiences.

Rapid-cycle data collection

1. We set up a "landing page" with links to a series of Google forms that invited students to "share their stories" through multiple media formats. During this cycle we reached out to our networks and utilized social media platforms to promote participation. We recognized that the limitations of outreach—namely, using a social network and the barrier of privileged access to technology platforms—limited the representation of voice in this project.
2. This project is a clarion call for the need for more work on healing-centered storytelling frameworks for research, both as a method and as a praxis.
3. Field notes for this inquiry were limited to personal autobiographical reflections based on personal experiences as a leader during this time, which were analyzed in relation to students' counter-narratives.
4. Participants were directed via email, texts, and social media channels to come to a "landing page" here: https://mailchi.mp/upenn/studentvoicesproject, where they could follow links to provide their contributions through an audio recording, Google form upload via text, video, art, or contribute to the FlipGrid. Some participants chose to send responses via text or email directly or call to share their stories.

Rapid-cycle analysis

1. Student personal data were not collected or associated with the contributions, so follow-up was not possible.
2. Thematic coding of emergent themes.

REFERENCES

Brown, A. M. (2017). *Emergent strategy: Shaping change, shaping worlds*. AK Press.

Campano, G., & Ghiso, M. (2010). Immigrant students as cosmopolitan intellectuals. In Wolf, S., Coats, K., Enciso, P., & Jenkins, C. (Eds.), *Handbook of research on children's and young adult literature*. Routledge.

Cruz, C. (2012). Making curriculum from scratch: Testimonio in an urban classroom. *Equity & Excellence in Education, 45*(3), 460–471.

Dutro, E. (2019). *The vulnerable heart of literacy*. Teachers College Press.

Lefstein, A., Pollak, I., & Segal, A. (2020). Compelling student voice: Dialogic practices of public confession. *Discourse: Studies in the Cultural Politics of Education, 41*(1), 110–123.

The NCES fast facts tool provides quick answers to many education questions. (n.d.). National Center for Education Statistics. http://nces.ed.gov/fastfacts

Nelson, G. L. (2000). Warriors with words: Toward a post-Columbine writing curriculum. *English Journal, 89*(5), 42–46.

Shulman, L. S. (2007). Practical wisdom in the service of professional practice. *Educational Researcher, 36*(9), 560–563.

Silko, L. M. (1977) *Ceremony 2*. Viking.

United States Department of Education, Office for Civil Rights. (2020). Fact Sheet: Addressing the risk of COVID-19 in schools while protecting the civil rights of students. www2.ed.gov/about/offices/list/ocr/docs/ocr-coronavirus-fact-sheet.pdf

Woodward, B. (2018). Centering the voice of Black male urban high school students on effective student–teacher classroom relationships. *Journal of Urban Learning, Teaching, & Research, 14*, 63–72.

Global Engagement, Perspective Sharing, and Future Seeing in and Beyond Global Crisis

Drew Cortese, Kiet Hoang, and Clare Sisisky

Editorial Framing

In this chapter, three educational leaders explore the fundamental importance of global experiences and transnational identities in shaping the flux leadership tenet of crisis agility. It cannot be overstated how COVID-19 reminded the educational leadership community that educational impacts are not merely limited nor shaped by our local context. While educational leaders might be alarmed or despaired by this reality, these authors shed light on how a global perspective can be an affordance in times of radical flux. In this chapter, interviews from educational leaders across numerous countries—Australia, Brazil, Canada, China, Denmark, France, India, United Kingdom, United States, and Vietnam—provide compelling data to support those intercultural competencies necessary in shaping leadership abilities that can adapt to the current moment and the future.

These authors ask tough questions on what it might mean to decolonize education and how global perspectives influence who we are and our leadership choices. In this rapid-cycle inquiry, a counter-narrative emerges: one that pushes back against the idea of global competition within education and one of knowledge-sharing and respect for one another. In these interviews, leaders recount sharing and learning across borders. They passed on information on what worked in navigating school closures and adapting to the pandemic movement to support other educational leaders. Within these interviews, readers can see how distributive wisdom can exist between school contexts in ways that are authentic and humanizing. As we saw in Chapter 3, distributive wisdom is a relational approach that helps elevate important self-work with the understanding that it is essential to seek out thought-partners in continuous self-improvement. As the chapter illustrates, within the pandemic, this approach could not have been more important across global contexts.

The authors also discuss that living in an interconnected and complex world means reflecting on America's role and how that fits within overarching narratives of equity, justice, and change. Ultimately, the patterns in the data surface that educational leaders must draw upon their global thinking through genuine partnership and collaboration to navigate change and think toward the future. As these authors mention, many of the leaders interviewed demonstrated an inquiry stance, and we believe, a critical inquiry stance, in thinking about how systems of power and interconnectedness in the global world we live in shape the lives of our students and K–12 education more broadly. By reaching out to networks across borders and leaning on international partnerships, a more humanizing alternative provides the adaptability and resiliency that times of radical flux demand within educational leadership. Through these global perspectives being surfaced, educators can think more deeply about their educational values and continue to be pushed by insights that are different from their own.

OVERVIEW

In this chapter, we wrestle with how our own experiences as educational leaders with global experiences and identities have shaped our view of educational leadership at this incredibly complex time in the world. We draw inspiration from scholars framing ways of being, thinking, learning, teaching, and leading that center transnational experiences and identities. We identify and share patterns from our interviews with other educational leaders with global partnerships and identities about how their leadership and view of education have been impacted by perspective and knowledge sharing across national borders during the COVID-19 global pandemic and the consequent educational disruption.

PROLOGUE

The challenge, then, is to take minds and hearts formed over the long millennia of living in local troops and equip them with ideas and institutions that will allow us to live together as the global tribe we have become.

—Kwame Anthony Appiah

It's the summer of 2020 when we find ourselves in the grips of a pandemic catalyzing a worldwide public health emergency. Each day, this pandemic claims more lives—nearly a million and counting thus far. A decimated global economy continues to lose trillions of dollars. The education of over a billion students in pre-primary, primary, and secondary schools (UNESCO, 2020) enters a state of emergency. Our current reality resembles something out of Polonius's tragical-comical-historical-pastoral genre, as it certainly feels as if we are being tested on a spiritual level by all of this, too. It's a source of much frustration for the cooler, calmer minds of our colleagues in the education space that know in their bones that it didn't have to be this way. Humanity has been here before, existing as it were "at the brink of the end of the world," as medical anthropologist Christos Lynteris calls it (2018). Today, it appears as if we've arrived there again, teetering on that precipice, especially in the United States. Had we paid attention to the histories, stories, voices, experiences, and insights across physical and cultural borders, Americans—and American education—might be in a very different place right now.

INTERCULTURAL COMPETENCIES AND THE MANCHURIAN PLAGUE

In the fall of 1910, reports out of Manzhouli, a Manchurian border town straddling the divide between Russia and China, were unnerving: "A mysterious illness had afflicted the people of Fuchiatien" (Goh et al., 1987) as the Chinese portion of the town was known, carrying with it an alarming case fatality rate of 100% (Lynteris, 2018). As the fall turned into winter and the incidence of the Manchurian plague continued to rise, the Chinese imperial court sent 30- year-old Dr. Wu Lien-Teh to lead anti-plague efforts (Goh, Ho, & Phua, 1987; Lynteris, 2018). How a Malaysian-born, ethnically Chinese, Cambridge-educated doctor, who had completed fellowships in France and Germany, found himself at the epicenter of an outbreak, sprung from the amateurish hunting practices of a marmot-fur boom meant to satisfy fashion trends in the United States and Western Europe for those who could not afford sable (Goh et al., 1987), that threatened a hotly contested region rife with competing international interests from Japan, Russia, and China, and managed to prevent this epidemic that claimed over 60,000 lives from reaching pandemic proportions, might be one of the best recommendations for why one should cultivate a robust intercultural skill set. That it also carries with it a warning of how the deployment of such competencies must always be done ethically suggests that our shared humanity, the very thing that should bind us together, can so easily be manipulated to split us apart.

It's an understatement to say that Dr. Wu faced truly bleak circumstances. A strange disease tore through the local population alongside harsh winter conditions, with temperatures between 25 and 30 degrees below zero Fahrenheit. Further, he dealt with a lack of proper medical facilities to treat and care for patients—a "public bath-house" had been converted into a make-shift hospital—and a skeleton crew of medical professionals, seven in total, to treat a population of 24,000. His task to overcome a set of cultural norms and societal practices also hindered the young doctor from introducing some of the methods he had learned and helped develop in London, Paris, and Berlin (Goh et al., 1987). We argue that Dr. Wu's robust intercultural competencies—honed in the operating theaters and research laboratories of some of the world's leading hospitals, where his ability to connect with colleagues truly was a matter of life or death—helped to shape him as a transnational actor with adaptive resilience to multiple locales, shifting cultural mores, and his own, ever-changing positionality, character-istics that equipped him for the challenging task at hand.

Dr. Geérald Mesny, a French physician and the head of the Peiyang Medical College, had extensive experience fighting previous outbreaks of bubonic plague and balked at the suggestion from his younger Chinese col-league, Dr. Wu, that the Manchurian outbreak was pneumonic in nature and that masks should be required to stop its spread (Goh et al., 1987). The two doctors clashed, with Mesny exploding into a racist tirade that prompted Wu to tender his resignation. Mesny was, like Wu, educated, well traveled, fluent in multiple languages, and, indeed, a gifted medical professional who had ended plague outbreaks in Hong Kong and India. His mindset, how-ever, wasn't comparable. Dr. Wu accumulated and incorporated knowledge wherever he went, and Mesny held fast to the belief that local knowledges would never trump his own understanding. His utter dismissal of Wu's re-search led him to charge into the hospital the next day to examine patients, without a face mask. Six days later, Mesny was dead, and Wu was back in charge. The Chinese government shut down access to Northern Manchuria and required masks for those in the region (Goh et al., 1987; Wu, 1959).

HISTORY REPEATS ITSELF

COVID-19 is nothing if not globally competent. The pandemic is at ease beyond any borders; it's understood in all languages and able to make deep, personal connections with everyone it meets. The pandemic has had the un-intended consequence of bringing humanity both figuratively closer together (in terms of a shared threat to our existence) and farther apart (by at least 6 feet). What it's also made abundantly clear to us as educational leaders is that the world-spanning skill set that's allowed COVID-19 to profoundly disrupt, dismantle, and, in some cases, destroy so much of our daily lives is the very same tool kit we need to be sharpening to rebuild our learn-ing communities, damaged as they are from a pandemic that not only shut down their operations but glaringly exposed the structural flaws in their foundations. We've long advocated for a more global perspective within the education space, one that acknowledges the interdependence of our modern societies and strives to collaborate across the differences it celebrates. What this pandemic reminds all of us—especially educators—is how inextricably connected our planet is politically, socially, and economically. This connection endures regardless of considerable rhetoric attempting to break bonds of cooperation and claim otherwise.

The confluence of these human operating systems demands a level of international collaboration that we, as educational leaders, have grown accustomed to in our personal and professional practices. This collaboration is shaped over the years through the perspectives and relationships that our transnational experiences have accessed. Considering the future of our field in light of recent events—the disruption of an entire generation's system of formal education by a global pandemic and the murder of George Floyd—the meaning we create from this moment appears through our transnational worldview. Because of the immigration and migration stories of our families, because of the educational and work opportunities we pursued, and because of the professional and personal communities we have cultivated, we have sharpened our ability to understand multiple perspectives and adapt in changing and ambiguous situations. We embrace and hone what are sometimes referred to as global competencies or global literacy (Boix Mansilla & Jackson, 2013).

We emphasize that the development of these much-needed global and intercultural competencies isn't achieved by increasing the number of stamps in one's passport. It's cultivated through the acknowledgment, appreciation, and sharing of the various funds of knowledge and cultural dexterity brought to bear by the individuals and communities one encounters (Moll, Amanti, Neff, & Gonzalez, 1992; Paris & Alim, 2017). Many within our educational communities—students, parents, faculty, staff, leaders—come fully equipped with transnational identities that access the very intercultural competencies and global relationships that are true assets in times of global crises. That these individuals and communities are not tapped for the wealth of resources, including the learned skill sets that often accompany transnational lives, they provide in their respective educational communities (Skerrett, 2015). We must examine why educational institutions do not seek out more input from colleagues with global perspectives, networks, and identities, in connection with the anti-racism work imperative to all educational institutions. Through this critical examination, we decolonize our frameworks for school leadership (Khalifa, Khalil, Marsh, & Halloran, 2019).

Considering this confluence of era-defining change—a pandemic that's tested the bonds of international cooperation as certain nations question if isolationism isn't the better strategy after all and the long-overdue challenges to systemic racism and oppression that this most recent state-sanctioned wave of violence against Black Americans has prompted—we're compelled to work tenaciously toward a future for education that acknowledges the interdependence of our societies and strives to collaborate across differences it celebrates, both for the students and families we seek to impact and for our fellow educators who seek to build these learning communities. As we discuss, debate, and decide what our students need from us now in order to be prepared for their futures in this interconnected and complex world, we draw from the work on global competencies for students (OECD, 2018) as well as Kwame Anthony Appiah's (2006) cosmopolitanism, which emphasizes the universality of our interconnection while embracing our cultural differences. We want our students to both understand and value human interdependence, and also to be prepared for a changing and challenging world. We are intensely aware that one potential for this moment is a turn toward the familiar, to seek the comfort of the known.

Yet some of the familiar narratives in America, some of the "knowns," are also in flux in the current moment, provoked by how this global pandemic has transitioned in the mind of many Americans from a natural disaster to a man-made disaster. The myth of American exceptionalism has long been called into question by many Black, Indigenous, and People of Color in America. How the United States is handling this global pandemic has pushed most Americans to question our understanding of America's superiority and our nation's standing in the world. A recent *New York Times* article described how "interviews with more than three dozen historians, writers, and Americans from all walks of life expressed a struggle to reconcile the crisis with the nation's self-image" (Schuessler, 2020). Scholars and observers outside of the United States perhaps see this even more clearly; in the words of Canadian anthropologist Wade Davis: "COVID has reduced to tatters the illusion of American exceptionalism" (2020).

The paradox of this moment has become deeply personal for us as we witness the intentional scapegoating of Asians and Asian-Americans living in the United States. This paradox, exemplified by the federal policy shifts intended to ostracize international students (Specia & Abi-Habib, 2020), continues to generate spikes in anti-Asian hate crimes (Ormseth, 2020).

We also personally witness how educational institutions have failed to respond in supportive and sustaining ways to international students. The rapid onset of COVID-19 has increased their need for support, which exposed institutions' prioritization of financial calculations over humanitarian values in their relationships with international students who arrive in the United States for academic and economic opportunities. The struggle to reconcile America's promise with her reality is not new. Continued failures of the American response to this pandemic, across so many sectors, embarrassingly reveals our nation's identity crisis. This crisis exists within how we think and feel about our response to it and how we understand what it indicates about inequity and systemic racism—particularly in health care and education.

Even cursory awareness of our daily news cycle yields multiple stories about national desires trending toward disentangling global alliances. However, disentangling limits opportunities for relationships across borders and marginalizes those whose identities or experiences embody these relationships. An educator we interviewed from India describes "countries turning inward because of health and safety," but warns that "they are also putting boundaries around themselves in terms of ideas, concepts, and skills—and this will lead to the burning down of the global exchange of ideas" (personal communication, June 12, 2020).

What happens if, as with the recent SpaceX launch, the innovations meant to benefit humanity's understanding of the world and beyond are available only to the select segment of the 1% who can pay to access them? Issues of access are also central to the Black Lives Matter movement, which continues to illuminate the horrific system of oppression intentionally designed to deny Black Americans and people of color their rights and liberated existence. To say this all concerns us deeply is an understatement. While dialogue is a critical first step, ultimately, we must take action to fulfill the potential of what this moment might mean for the future of education. We must embrace the unfamiliar while recognizing the privileges and limitations of true interdependence. This recognition will help us to communicate and collaborate across borders, tackling the impact of this global pandemic on our students' lives. When we actively lean into this work, our field can address the compounding effects of hundreds of years of systemic racism by truly internalizing that Black Lives Matter across the globe. In this moment, we begin the world anew, placing at the core of all we do, the knowledge, skills, dispositions, and supports all our children need to thrive (OECD, 2018).

GLOBALLY EMERGING PATTERNS

To recognize the value of learning from and with others worldwide requires that educators take seriously the tremendous benefit that global partnerships, connections, and experiences bring to educators themselves. This recognition requires that we place a higher value on the identities and personal relationships that immigrant and transnational educational leaders bring to their leadership. Through our interviews and conversations with various educators, we identified how some patterns concerning the impact of global relationships, global partnerships with peers, intercultural experiences, and/or transnational identities had on their thinking and leadership during this crisis. We spoke to a wide variety of educational leaders (principals, head of school, assistant heads of school, department or division leaders) from numerous countries (primarily working in Australia, Brazil, Canada, China, Denmark, France, India, United Kingdom, United States, and Vietnam) with one or more of the following:

- Global partnerships
- A global network of peers

- Personal or professional experiences living outside of their country of birth
- Immigrant or transnational identity

Through these interviews and conversations, we identified a number of skills, mindsets, and competencies that educators self-reported to be beneficial and generative to their thinking, understanding, and leadership during the COVID-19 crisis: Global Systems Thinking; Future-Seeing; Perspective-Seeking; Adaptability.

Global Systems Thinking

Educators reported seeing how what was happening in one part of the world would inevitably impact other areas of the world, often well before their peers. This demonstrates a strong understanding of how the movement of people and consequently viruses connect different parts of the globe. As an educational leader from Australia articulated, "the pandemic has warned us of the fact that we live in a world without borders, where our happiness depends on global cooperation" (personal communication, June 8, 2020). Some leaders and educators within every large educational umbrella will likely have a strong understanding of the global movement of people either through their own experience or through that of their family, for any number of reasons varying from family members' business travel to personal history as a refugee.

Educators also had a deeply ingrained sense of how different world areas connect (economically or otherwise). Resultantly, they could hear, read, and discuss with a network of peers or family members what was happening in the early months of the pandemic and reported translating this skillset and mindset to their work. For example, an educational leader from a school in Canada described an ongoing practice beginning in the early months of the pandemic. Due to strong ties in Asia, he spent one to two hours every morning reading newspapers from around the world, noting that what he read in the *New York Times* differed from what he read in the *South China Morning Post* (personal communication, July 16, 2020). His foundational knowledge, gained from reporting insights in East Asia connected to his school in Canada. Diverse knowledge provided him with a more robust understanding of the complexity of the crisis. We also heard from other educators that their personal connections provided firsthand insight into the pandemic and how communities and educational institutions responded. These educators brought the global systems thinking their experiences provided to them into the classroom. They also embraced an inquiry stance and sought to find information, knowledge, and insight both from traditional outlets and personal relationships. One educator called this "thought partners," which describes the ways we position everyone as a knower while widening their understanding of both the crisis and the global interconnections that bind us to one another in this moment (Cochran-Smith & Lytle, 2009).

Future-Seeing

Educators who have strong global partnerships reported feeling more prepared for what might be coming because they could hear about and learn from the challenges of their partners and friends before they were faced with similar challenges in their context. For example, American and European educators with strong partners or relationships in East Asia reported feeling better prepared for the early months of the COVID-19 impact locally because the effect of the virus on schools and communities had been on their mind through dialogue with their coworkers since January. When the virus began being documented in Europe and the Americas, educators reported reaching out to their network in East Asia and learning from their experiences of leading during weeks of unprecedented school closures. Through these conversations, they gained insights and ideas about how to transition to remote learning, while sharing resources to support teachers through this disorienting change.

For one of the authors of this article, their organization (a world school with multiple campuses in New York, São Paulo, and Shenzhen) had a campus in China directly impacted by a COVID-19 closure month ahead of its U.S. and Brazilian sister campuses. To have firsthand institutional knowledge available on navigating what was for many schools completely uncharted territory gave us a distinct advantage in preparing both our campuses and our communities for the challenges that would inevitably span the globe. Among this network was a constant flow of communication from a reliable internal network of connected educators that could report accurately about conditions on the ground in Shenzhen. Similarly, interactions occurred in São Paulo, where their campus recorded one of the first known cases of COVID-19 in all of South America. The ways that U.S. educators, teaching in the New York campus of this school, learned from those in São Paulo created conditions for CNBC to call its back-to-campus playbook "the best reopening strategy" in the United States (Dickler, 2020).

The border closing and changes to immigration policies and procedures have caused additional stress, uncertainty, and fear for students studying outside of their country of citizenship. As an example of future-seeing as an invaluable asset at this time, an educator based in the United States reported hearing from Australian colleagues about changes to Chinese international students' re-entry status to China before similar challenges were faced by institutions in Canada and the United States. Additional time to prepare and more profound insight into the challenges these border and immigration policy shifts would create were due to the relationship generated between a Vietnamese educator, now living in the United States, and an Australian colleague specializing in partnerships with China.

As we write, school leaders across the United States struggle to determine if, when, and how they should reopen schools. Educators we interviewed and those in our personal networks and ourselves actively engaged in reaching out to schools outside of the United States that have already reopened to see into the future and learn from their experiences as we work to make decisions, craft options, and communicate with stakeholders. During a July 2020 panel organized by Global Education Benchmark Group, school leaders worldwide engaged in discussion on lessons learned from school reopening. A school head in France shared that when he was preparing to reopen his school, he reached out to school leaders in Denmark and Germany. These schools had already reopened, and their insights helped others to better understand their challenges and opportunities. He also shared that he found the connection and dialogue with peers in Germany to be most helpful because they lived in a similar political climate within their local community context, which demonstrated the need for understanding of cultural context in order to maximize beneficial insight (personal communication, July 16, 2020). This ability to connect with schools adapting and adopting new leadership practices in response to a challenge or crises has proved a tremendously valuable asset in these complex and fluctuating times for educational leaders.

Perspective-Seeking

Educators with experience working and living in a multiperspectival, multicultural, and/or multilingual ecosystem shared that when faced with a complex challenge, these previous experiences and their current global partners pushed them to seek out and understand perspectives in addition to the ones right in front of them. An educational leader who currently resides in the United States but grew up in India shares that Indians have "300 years of living in two frameworks." Her willingness to wrestle with the complex adaptive environment generated by this pandemic draws on her ability to look at anything and everything from multiple angles (personal communication, June 12, 2020). She shared that that many Americans find difficulty "to see the value in a perspective or a culture that is not their own." A common American mentality, she has observed, is to "value other perspectives only after I value my own," adding that "we are seeing America burn now because of this." From her insights we can understand how we can all benefit from seeking out and learning from perspectives "that have worked for other people in their own context—physical, economic, and cultural" (personal communication, June 12, 2020).

A call to reframe leadership competencies and decolonize how we envision and value educational leadership is modeled by Paris and Alim (2017). They propose that "linguistic and cultural dexterity" are promoted because "it is no longer only about equally valuing all of our communities—it is also about the skills, knowledges, and ways of being needed for success in the present and the future" (Paris & Alim, 2017, p. 5). If and when we can elevate those educators who can seek perspectives from within their multiple frameworks and networks, both internal and external, our educational leadership in moments of global crises (and always) will be more adaptive and resilient.

Perspective-seeking also happens in moments of practice when an educator leads with an agile inquiry stance, seeking out knowledge, deeper understanding, and wisdom from colleagues and friends across borders (Ravitch & Carl, 2020). For example, an educator in Denmark reported that she quickly learned from speaking with her family and professional network outside of Denmark that "different countries understood things differently about this virus at different times." She spent some of her valuable time during this crisis seeking out insight and dialogue from various "thought partners" in numerous locations around the world, which helped her bring more depth, nuance, and diversity of thought to leadership and decision-making at her institution. She shared that "as Danes, we are generally risk tolerant, so it was helpful to be able to benchmark and get a feel for decisions and communications" in other places (personal communication, June 16, 2020). These comments also demonstrate a key aspect of perspective-seeking: the ability to understand your cultural context and how that shapes your perspective. Most of the educators we spoke with spent time living outside of the cultural context they would identify as their primary culture. Living outside of their norm helped them demonstrate the ability to see themselves and their culturally influenced perspective as one of many perspectives beneficial to understanding. Further, it enabled them to comfortably seek out other or additional perspectives—even amid ambiguity that may create tensions or conflicts between them.

Adaptability

Educators shared that their ability to be flexible and adaptable was of great value to them during this time of uncertainty. They learned these skills, out of necessity, from living and working in multiple countries or distinct cultural contexts. An American educator discussed her approach to leadership amid a pandemic. She encouraged her team to be ready and willing to adapt, skills she internalized from years of living in South America. Her mindset, she described, pushed back against those in other departments within the organization who actively worked to protect and maintain programs, schedules, and policies created pre-pandemic. Another American, previously serving as a head of school in Japan and Indonesia and now working as a senior adviser to a world school with campuses on three continents, recognized that "a lot of the adaptations are uncomfortable" when schools and their communities are under duress. He believes, however, this moment is when leaders must rethink the assumptions and equations for how school happens. "Design for these spaces, be thoughtful about the parameters, recognize the loss that is felt in the community, and determine what's essential and what's not . . . what makes a school a school?" (Carr, personal communication, May 29, 2020).

Some of the educators we interviewed also spoke of the previous crises and complex environments they have navigated in the past, both personally and professionally, by drawing on their community's (and their own) adaptive resilience in these uncertain times. For example, one educator described being comfortable not knowing everything or having all the information but still feeling confident to make decisions in the best interest of students. She explained this as something she learned from years of working within the complex contexts of schools in Tehran and Jakarta and now brings it to the leadership team of her school in Miami. Another educational leader described his experiences as an immigrant to the United States as informing his ability to understand fear, especially fear that comes from the unknown, and his ability to persevere through that fear or uncertainty. These educators identify how their global experiences and identities helped shape their leadership agility, an essential skill in times of crisis. Ravitch and Carl (2020) describe leader agility as inner resources that educators learn or cultivate based on their own life experiences or choices, providing them with a calmness and confidence in the face of ambiguous and rapidly changing parameters within which to make decisions and guide others. Even as we think about our own lives and leadership in this context, comfort with ambiguity and not being paralyzed by not knowing or controlling much of what transpired around us day to day are familiar mindsets and competencies. Though we would not choose these current challenges—of closed borders and closing minds, of government leaders prioritizing politics over science (and human life) in their decision-making, of educators and frontline workers bearing the brunt of leadership and sacrifice, of systemic racism and inequities perpetuated by our lack of social safety net—we are grateful for the experiences that have taught and forced us to adapt, persevere, and lead with agility.

As we think about these valuable skillsets and mindsets that global educators bring to their institutions, our interviews also reveal two factors necessary for beneficial global partnerships at this crucial moment. First, there is the importance of a relational approach and the intercultural competence of the partners. We believe these patterns are key to highlight because they reflect both a pattern from our interviews and what we have seen in our work with global partnerships. Aligned with humanizing leadership, educators shared that the nature and dynamic of each global partnership was the most important factor in determining whether it made a meaningful impact on their thinking and leadership during this crisis. Global partnerships with the greatest impact were *relational and not transactional,* and some educators specifically described mutual trust and respect as essential. Resultantly, educators connected with both the formal global partners of their institutions and with their personal or familial networks. Second, we identified that conversations with global partners only led to greater perspective and insights when educator's model intercultural competency, including critical and deep understanding of the partner's local cultural context (Deardorff & Ararasatnam-Smith, 2017).

When educators model both these factors, inspiring examples of how global partnerships improved learning outcomes for their students begin to emerge. For example, during the pandemic, a school in the United States and one in Denmark were both able to develop a multinational virtual exchange embedded into one of their courses; a school in the United Kingdom was able to offer summer school courses that enrolled students from five continents. Educators in Vietnam were able to improve online learning and access for their students after learning from international partners. These are examples of how successful global partnerships, which involve relationships between interculturally competent educational leaders, impact the educational leaders themselves and students at their schools.

There is an unusual convergence of awe-inspiring events happening today that make it impossible to believe that the world is not on the cusp of a significant paradigm shift. A change is coming in education. Part of our tremendous responsibility as leaders is to assist our constituencies in recognizing that returning to the way things used to be is a fruitless endeavor. As we consider the leadership demands of this moment and the necessity of making the "next" normal a better one, we find ourselves awestruck by the generosity of spirit exhibited in the conversations we've had, both with each other and our fellow educators from around the world. There's a superpower unleashed when you harness the collective imagination of global educators. The ideas, solutions, pitfalls, and inquiries that were revealed through our series of interviews contained multitudes that no single individual could have had the capacity to come up with on their own or to skillfully monitor and manage alone. Collaboration is the key forward. It drives a humility within us that that recognizes how great ideas begin anywhere. To access a brilliant idea, a leader needs a network of sharp minds that are not solely their own. The time is now to reposition ourselves while embracing the multinational and intercultural relationships, connections, and identities that will bring us out of twin pandemics. Though we have crumbled, this does not mean that we cannot reemerge with the strength to re-envision education to ensure our students' futures.

This work *at this time* undoubtedly shapes how we approach our responsibilities as educators now and in the future. This moment requires that we listen and learn from perspectives and experiences beyond our immediate video calls. Voices and stories that bring us insight and strength from within our communities and from as far beyond, such as the story of Dr. Wu. The

RAPID-CYCLE INQUIRY

Rapid-cycle research design

Goals:

1. To better understand how educational leaders with global identities/experiences/networks leveraged these generated competencies to inform their approaches to leadership within their respective sites of practice during COVID-19.
2. To better recognize educational leaders with immigrant or transnational backgrounds, who are often undervalued, overlooked, or simply not recognized for possessing a robust skill set composed of the very intercultural competencies most needed to steady an organization through a global crisis.
3. To promote interconnectivity between the people who populate school communities and the broader communities that lay adjacent to these formal learning environments, and to recognize the benefits of cross-cultural and cross-border collaboration and the importance of the skill set required to maximize those benefits.

Rapid-cycle data collection

1. Rapid-cycle semi-structured interviews on Zoom, 45–60 minutes in duration, conversational.
2. Rapid-cycle healing-centered storytelling. As collaborators, each of us took turns sharing our own reflections and recollections from our personal experiences as educators and human beings, with a focus on how these experiences influenced our approach to leadership during this pandemic. These intimate conversations shaped our approach toward the interviews we conducted.
3. Rapid-cycle observational field notes in a webinar with global educators designed for a U.S. audience to address the challenges of reopening schools as seen through their points of view (i.e., educators based outside of the United States who had successfully reopened their campuses during the pandemic providing their perspectives on what worked, what didn't, and what they might do differently).

Rapid-cycle analysis

1. Rapid-cycle member checks/participant validation. Ongoing dialogue with several participants throughout this crisis has affirmed and deepened the initial learnings from this inquiry.

2. Open coding as a team, recognized the patterns that emerged from the interviews, and then analyzed the data using these codes. Read the interviews and grouped concepts into thematic buckets refined through dialogic engagement in collaborative sessions.

Rapid-cycle knowledge sharing and dissemination

Opening Speaker at a conference on global education for 350 education leaders from around the world—featured inquiry findings in talk. In discussion with colleagues at our sites of practice. LinkedIn/Twitter—sharing of article with wider community, especially of interest to global educators to help them feel seen at a challenging time

crisis of the COVID-19 global pandemic humbly began a universal course correction while the responsibility of the movement, borne out of George Floyd's murder and the murders of so many other Black people—ignited a powerful and tragic reminder that any global mindset we seek to attain will undoubtedly be borne out of our personal and national experiences. These global and national crises drove us into uncharted territory, a space of uncertain suspension. Still, we reemerge as a community of leaders, forever changed, and fully prepared to blaze a trail forward, together.

REFERENCES

Appiah, K. A. (2006). *Cosmopolitanism: Ethics in a world of strangers*. W. W. Norton & Company.

Boix Mansilla, V., & Jackson, A. (2013). Educating for global competence: Learning redefined for an interconnected world. I H. Jacobs (Ed.), *Mastering global literacy, contemporary perspectives*. Solution Tree.

Cochran-Smith, M., & Lytle, S. L. (2009). *Inquiry as stance: Practitioner research for the next generation*. Teachers College Press.

Dickler, J. (2020). The most expensive high school in America may have the best reopening strategy. CNBC. www.cnbc.com/2020/08/04/americas-most-expensive -high-school-may-have-the-best-reopening-plan.html

Davis, W. (2020). The unravelling of America. *Rolling Stone*. www.rollingstone.com /politics/political-commentary/covid-19-end-of-american-era-wade-davis-1038206

Deardorff, D. K., & Ararasatnam-Smith, L. (2017). *Intercultural competence in higher education: International approaches, assessment, application*. Routledge.

Goh, L. G., Ho, T. M., & Phua, K. H. (1987). Wisdom and Western science: The work of Dr. Wu Lien-Teh. *Asia-Pacific Journal of Public Health, 1*(1), 99–109.

Khalifa, M. A., Khalil, D., Marsh, T. E. J., & Halloran, C. (2019). Toward an Indigenous, decolonizing school leadership: A literature review. *Educational Administration Quarterly, 55*(4), 571–614.

Lynteris, C. (2018). Plague masks: The visual emergence of anti-epidemic personal protection equipment. *Medical Anthropology, 37*(6), 442–457.

Moll, L., Amanti, C., Neff, D., & Gonzalez, N. (1992). Funds of knowledge for teaching: Using a qualitative approach to connect homes and classrooms. *Theory into Practice, 31*(2), 132–141.

OECD. (2018). *Global competency for an inclusive world.* OECD.

Ormseth, M. (2020). Rise in hate incidents toward Asian Americans during Coronavirus crisis, officials say. *Los Angeles Times.* www.latimes.com/california/story/2020-05-13/hate-crimes-and-incidents-directed-at-asian-americans-rise-during-pandemic-county-commission-says

Paris, D., & Alim, H. S. (2017). *Culturally sustaining pedagogies: Teaching and learning for justice in a changing world.* Teachers College Press.

Schuessler, J. (2020). Will a pandemic shatter the perception of American exceptionalism? *New York Times.* www.nytimes.com/2020/04/25/arts/virus-american-exceptionalism.html

Skerrett, A. (2015). *Teaching transnational youth: Literacy and education in a changing world.* Teachers College Press.

Specia, M., & Abi-Habib, M. (2020, July 9). Maybe I shouldn't have come: US visa changes leave international students in limbo. *New York Times.* www.nytimes.com/2020/07/09/world/international-students-visa-reaction.html

Ravitch, S. M., & Carl, N. M. (2020). *Qualitative research: Bridging the conceptual, theoretical, and methodological.* (2nd ed.). Sage.

UNESCO. (2020). *COIVD-19 impact on education.* UNESCO Institute for Statistics Data. https://en.unesco.org/covid19/educationresponse

Wu, L. (1959). *Plague fighter: The autobiography of a modern Chinese physician.* W. Heffer. https://hdl.handle.net/2027/mdp.39015007150702

Teaching and Leading During COVID-19

Lessons from Lived Experiences

Karen D'Avino, Muronji C. Inman-McCraw, and Curtis A. Palmore

---

EDITORIAL FRAMING

In this chapter, three doctoral candidates tackle a rapid-cycle inquiry that examines what adaptive leadership looks like in the COVID-19 pandemic within their respective sites of practice. As noted in the tenet of critical inquiry stance within flux leadership, these authors illustrate that adaptive leadership requires a critical perspective, given the intertwining impacts of the COVID-19 pandemic and racial injustice. A critical inquiry stance must be intentionally antiracist and intersectional to account for how structural power manifests within the range of variables that influence our school communities daily. These authors recognize this within their own reflections. And as the authors dig into what adaptive leadership looks like within their own context given these realities, it begins to emerge that the importance of responsive and humanizing leadership cannot be overstated in these moments. As mentioned in flux leadership, responsiveness is fueled by a deeper humanity for ourselves and stakeholders rather than a leadership stance grounded in fear.

Additionally, this team of doctoral candidates wrote about their work from an ethnographic perspective, shedding light on the importance of narrative and vulnerability in best capturing what leadership looks like in crisis situations. While there is an urgency in crisis, especially in schools, rapid-cycle inquiry provides an opportunity to slow down events in order to take a better snapshot of the stories transpiring around you. This team started their rapid-cycle inquiry with a vignette of Curtis Palmore's context. This vignette provides an in-depth examination of what adaptive leadership moves looked like at that moment in time, but it also provided another element to the inquiry: humanization.

Rapid-cycle inquiry pushes back against the idea that school improvement is all about static data sets. By centering story and narrative, this vignette starts by drawing readers into the historical and present context of Paterson, New Jersey. By providing a grassroots perspective, we can remember the stories behind us and in front of us. Ultimately, leadership practices are not siloed. This vignette discusses how after Curtis's district leadership team got everything in place for distance learning to begin, COVID-19 related losses started to spread through the community, impacting how adaptive leadership was exercised. Their vignette works to remind us that leadership moves should not ever respond to numbers. Leadership should respond to the hearts of the community it serves.

INTRODUCTION

Interviews were conducted in the three different contexts, in the Vernon Township School District located in rural, northwestern New Jersey: Two Rivers Public Charter Schools, a charter school in Washington, DC, and Community Charter School of Paterson, as well as related charter schools in Paterson, New Jersey. Public school teachers and administrators responded to questions about the COVID-19 pandemic, its impact on teaching and learning, how pedagogy has been shaped and will continue to be influenced by the pandemic, and the flux leadership that school administrators have enacted throughout the COVID-19 pandemic. They discussed systemic racism and the responses of school leaders and teachers during this time. These reflections serve as a compass for school leaders and teachers who wish to serve students with compassion and empathy. It reflects a desire to somehow deliver curricula (in a standards-based, accountability-ridden public education model) during life-changing pandemic events that will forever impact how we teach and lead.

Throughout these interviews, we sought perspective on adaptive leadership moves throughout the pandemic. We hope these experiences offer leaders affirmation, guidance, inspiration, and hope to lead in their contexts in the coming years. The chapter is broken down into a vignette of discussing context followed by the adaptive leadership themes that emerge across all three respective contexts examined. The purpose of starting with the vignette is to anchor the inquiry in an educational setting where readers can envision themselves in a related context. The themes that emerged impacted core values and beliefs, collective effort and urgency, shared leadership, loss, connection, family partnership, uncertainty, and hope.

LEADERSHIP VIGNETTES

In 1791, Alexander Hamilton founded Paterson, New Jersey, as America's first planned industrial city. The city of Paterson became a hub for immigrants who sought opportunity and a stake in the American dream. Today Paterson is the third largest city in the state of New Jersey, home to diverse groups of Latin American immigrants and large African American and Bangladeshi populations. Over the last couple of years, the city has grown considerably by focusing on major infrastructure, community, and educational improvements under the leadership of the new mayor, Andre Sayegh. While these improvements are helping to move the city forward, like many urban cities, Paterson experiences high levels of crime and drug use, and one of the lowest college graduation rates of any city in New Jersey.

Paterson serves over 30,000 students in traditional public school and charter school districts. This section will outline the leadership moves made by three public charter school district leaders and their respective teams. Amidst the COVID-19 pandemic, charter schools in Paterson scrambled to find pathways to provide instruction and resources for families that they serve. We tapped into the adaptive leadership found with leaders, teachers, and support staff of three public charter school district leaders in Paterson— The Community Charter School of Paterson, iLearn Schools, and College Achieve of Paterson.

> COVID-19 and the impact that this will have on our district is unknown. We don't have a playbook or policy to follow moving forward. However, we have an opportunity to re-envision what it means to provide high quality teaching and learning to our 900 plus students. It's important that we all lean on each other in the days and weeks to come.

This passage details part of the superintendent's introduction at the all-staff conference call for the Community Charter School of Paterson. The Community Charter School of Paterson is a three-campus public charter school district that serves over 900 students in Paterson, New Jersey. On this call, Mr. Curtis Palmore, the district CEO, provided encouragement for the future, while uncertain about what was to come. Dr. Lisa Lin Schneider, the director of Curriculum and Instruction, mapped a plan for online remote instruction, with clear guidelines for the new "distance learning" program. The abrupt shift from brick and mortar to online instruction accompanied a high level of ingenuity and drive to keep academics moving forward for students and families. Days before the formal closing of schools Dr. Schneider shared the following:

> I believe we are facing a crisis. It has become imminent we will be closing down schools for an extended period of time. It's critical that

we act with urgency and develop a plan which allows our students to continue learning throughout an inevitable campus shutdown. As we develop our plan, we need to be sensitive to potential crisis situations for many of our families and provide synchronous and asynchronous learning experiences. This flexible model will result in the highest levels of participation, thereby increasing equity in implementation for our students.

Within days, CCSP assessed the community's needs by surveying families to identify who needed laptops, internet hotspots, and necessities such as food and water. Leaders and support staff worked to have all family needs identified and to have support plans in place. Together, those at CCSP organized a massive mobilization effort. Over 650 laptops were distributed to families, including in some cases having devices brought directly to the doorsteps of families' homes. When connectivity issues arose, school personnel partnered with parents and worked directly with Wi-Fi providers like T-Mobile and AT&T to ensure that families would have Wi-Fi access. Unlike any yearly campaign or cause, the synergy and collective effort to support one another across the district ran true for all stakeholders.

After getting the foundational pieces in place for distance learning to begin, the district was hit hard with three fatalities within the community. Sadly, three CCSP family members passed from COVID-related illnesses—a grandfather, an uncle, and an aunt. Many of the CCSP families live in communal homes that house extended families, meaning the loss and level of trauma was especially difficult for the community. During this time, a host of staff members also contracted COVID-19. Daily, stakeholders across the school community shared stories of COVID-related losses. Dr. Ford, a campus leader at CCSP, shared anecdotally that all the teachers on his team had multiple family and friends infected and/or impacted by COVID-19.

Messaging for all stakeholders throughout the district was a crucial part of the distance learning strategy during COVID-19. Given the shortcomings of traditional communication models, the district leadership sought alternative ways to communicate directly with all stakeholders. Campus leaders at CCSP lead efforts by creating special YouTube channels for parents and students that provide daily video updates, including the traditional school-wide morning announcements, teacher and student profiles, and highlights of student work.

Additionally, senior district leadership also stayed connected with parents and students by hosting Home School Council virtual meetings and sharing updates for families via video broadcasts on their social media sites. The Home School Council meetings are a staple part of the district. However, shifting the meeting to an online recording format allowed many families the ability to join and actively participate. Curriculum, teaching, and food distribution were topics discussed at these meetings. Finally, local media played a role in district communication as well. The CEO published articles in the local online newspaper about the district's efforts and promoted these communications among the school community. These alternative forms of communication were welcomed and important for keeping the district together as a community.

Driven by the old proverb, "Seek God's will in all that you do, and He will show the path to take," a voluntary interfaith daily prayer group was established for staff at the CCSP community. This group sought to pray for the school community members that COVID-19 adversely impacted. Meeting daily on a conference call, the group prays for ailing community members and direction for the school district. These conference calls that are still in existence are considered by the CEO "a lifeline for the direction of the district and healing within the school community."

Academically, CCSP spearheaded efforts to provide high-quality synchronous teaching for all students in the district. CCSP defined synchronous teaching as an approach where teachers provide remote instruction via a Zoom call, and students are active participants and view the lesson in real time. Together with district leadership, teaching teams, and the teacher union, CCSP collaboratively refocused teachers planning to address the new realities of teaching remotely. Leaders addressed new challenges of teaching new forms of technology to adults and students in a rapid format with targeted support and professional development. Teacher leaders rose to the challenge and worked hand in hand with leadership at CCSP. One campus noted how newer teachers that were more adept with technology took on leadership roles to teach seasoned teachers how to set up Google Classroom and manage the related online video platforms. Teacher meetings included some form of technology takeaway as well as relevant content review and planning.

Dr. Schneider, the district director of curriculum and instruction, led an effort to increase the amount of synchronous teaching to have daily lessons taught on each grade level throughout the spring. This effort focused on tracking student completion of work. Teachers conducted daily reviews with students in Google Classroom settings for completion of work, and students who missed assignments received follow-up calls from teams of educators at each campus to provide support and to encourage student follow-up with the set assignments. Toward the conclusion of the school year, Dr. Schneider shared the following:

> Although the COVID-19 crisis has brought to light the severe
> inequities in education for youth across America, it has also
> demonstrated the unwavering resilience of educators who remain
> steadfast in their commitment to providing the best possible education

for our youth. The depths of this crisis has left educators with no choice other than to reprioritize what matters most for our children. America's historic and long-standing obsession with competition through testing has been taken off the table, and instead we are now looking at the needs of the whole child. The prioritization of social emotional learning and response to trauma will ensure our students have critical life skills that will ensure personal success, and ultimately the advancement of our society as a whole.

In response to civil unrest for the police murders of George Floyd, Ahmaud Arbery, Breonna Taylor, and countless other Blacks, CCSP joined in solidarity with the Black Lives Matter movement. Under the CEO's leadership, the district immediately messaged staff, students, and board members its common stance to fight these injustices and address structural racism that impacts student learning within the school. On an all-staff conference call, leadership provided a space to discuss the ugly realities of racism and provided tools to discuss these events with students. CCSP, with the support of the board of trustees, also took steps to make several changes showing how to make progress with action. Juneteenth, a holiday celebrated on June 19 to commemorate the emancipation of enslaved people in the United States, was declared a formal holiday in the district. CCSP students and staff were encouraged to participate in Juneteenth events or take the day for healing and mental health. Mr. Palmore also announced the establishment of a district-wide Race and Equity Committee whose focus will be to support district-wide discussions and reviews of policies and curriculum as it relates to structural racism. Though these efforts represent very small steps toward progress, they are not reparation or reconciliation. The efforts do, ultimately, reflect the incremental nature of change. What these changes do not do is address the demands of the Black activists, who continue to push for substantial and impactful policy changes made by those in privileged positions of power. However, CCSP is far ahead of many districts in this regard, and the steps the district takes now will no doubt create a more equitable future.

The iLearn Charter School Network, which serves 10,000 students in New Jersey and New York, took a comprehensive approach to support families and students during COVID-19. iLearn's CEO, Nihat Guvercin, stated that "While COVID-19 is horrible and brings many issues, we must see this as a learning experience and constantly be in a position to learn from this experience." With his transformational leadership, he provided guidance and direction for the hundreds of teachers and thousands of students they serve. iLearn has historically had a focus on innovation in education. Their teachers use various online tools through the network and Schoology platforms and have a 1:1 laptop to student ratio across their network. So, the leap to online instruction was a natural progression. However, as the CEO of iLearn explained, "Even though students are not on campus, learning must continue, and students still must feel connected with the school and their teachers."

iLearn prioritized keeping many of the main aspects of their schools in place when they transitioned to a distant learning platform during COVID-19. Daily, those who work at iLearn greeted students in virtual morning assemblies. Teachers were required to provide four hours of real-time instruction with their students, and leaders across the network worked directly with teachers to plan effective strategies for providing online instruction. iLearn's CEO, Nihat Guvercin, contributes the school's success in these areas to their deliberate focus on teacher professional development during COVID-19.

In addition to the adaptive leadership work to promote high academics during COVID-19 at iLearn, the district also sought to address concerns with many families that lacked necessities such as food and water. The district created a program called iCare, which focused on providing food, goods, and water directly delivered to families. The network organized volunteers who worked directly with local businesses and pantries that donated monies and food. The volunteers, amid uncertainty of exposure to COVID-19, went door to door providing food and water donations to families. iLearn also championed their efforts by ensuring that meal distribution would continue at their campuses throughout the pandemic.

In response to addressing structural racism, iLearn is in the process of launching an inclusivity effort to promote dialogues about injustices and issues that act as barriers to access for their school communities. While still in development at the time of this publication, the team's goals are simple: they will convene to discuss strategies to ensure iLearn continually demonstrates inclusivity and that all iLearn community members feel a sense of belonging. This effort will be coupled with network-wide professional development for all staff members in the fall.

College Achieve Paterson is another district in Paterson, New Jersey, spotlighted for adaptive leadership moves during the COVID-19 pandemic. College Achieve Paterson is the newest school district in the city, which serves over 500 students in kindergarten through 8th grade. Led by Dr. Gamar Mills, the district's response to COVID-19 identified common district-wide domains for virtual learning. As noted by Dr. Mills, he sought to provide clarity with the changing roles of all the stakeholders at College Achieve, including leaders, teachers, support staff, families, and students. It was important to stress the changes and provide the right guidance and professional development for teachers to adjust accordingly. Second, the district stressed communication as a guiding principle to effectively "take away any potential hurdles for progress." Therefore, communication in this district was done through multiple mediums that included daily check-ins and communication about student participation rates and meals served, and student, staff, and parent surveys.

The additional domains for their COVID-19 strategy focused less on structure and more on the collective belief patterns that would guide student teaching in learning. For example, at College Achieve, Dr. Mills championed a belief in his district that all teachers could successfully adapt their instruction to meet any of the demands with synchronous teaching (the College Achieve model mirrored formats found at CCSP and iLearn schools). He referenced that his district professional development for online teaching was a linchpin for his effective rollout. The other domains used by College Achieve provided teachers and students with simple and easy-to-use tools throughout the transition to distance learning. Particular focus was also paid to reflecting on and improving the approaches taken by district and teaching teams. Dr. Mills reiterates that his district's focus on the guidance and support provided to his leadership team by larger Charter Management Organizations, including Success Academies in New York and UnCommon Schools, which operate schools in New York, New Jersey, and Connecticut.

College Achieve Paterson also took an out-of-the-box approach to address the crises that materialized during COVID-19. Dr. Mills launched an effort to raise funds for the families to promote running and healthy eating. The Social Distancing Run Challenge, created through ingenuity and the Nike Run App, virtually united hundreds of people around the United States during COVID. Over 7 days, participants were encouraged to run 75 miles. Runners across the country raised $5,000 for families struggling with COVID-19. Dr. Mills, himself a COVID-19 survivor and a participant in this challenge, shared that "I became more human and closer with the school community and was forced to engage in community in a real meaningful way. Our collective efforts helped to provide folks in NJ resources they don't have, which is amazing!"

IMPACT ON CORE VALUES

We are called to plan for something none of us have seen before. There is no success metric, but the leaders and teachers we interviewed turned to their personal or schools' core values to become the North Star. While in the initial planning stages in early March, leaders felt paralysis, uncertainty, or disorganization of resources as the weeks went on, revision of the initial plans was underway. These planned iterations were grounded in an aching desire for equity, engagement, and joy in learning. Leaders in each school context looked to core values as their anchor for planning. They also were compelled to put a strategic focus on equity. Dr. Schneider discussed the flexible synchronous and asynchronous learning experiences and the impact on participation and equity. She also identified that severe inequities and the resilience of educators remain focus areas to support our youth:

The depths of this crisis have left educators with no choice other than to reprioritize what matters most for our children. America's historic and long-standing obsession with competition through testing has been taken off the table, and instead, we are now looking at the needs of the whole child. The prioritization of social emotional learning and response to trauma will ensure our students have critical life skills that will ensure personal success, and ultimately the advancement of our society as a whole.

Leaders and teachers said they found it important to flex their creativity and think outside normal paradigms constantly. Prior to COVID-19, they may not have conceived a world without standardized testing. Now they ask the questions: do these tests even matter? How can we create more meaningful ways for students to showcase their learning? Leaders could not easily answer the "how" for the questions, but there is great passion and excitement for discovering what is possible. One Two Rivers network leader, Maggie Bello, shared her feeling of this moment with "it has provided a movement that we have to reflect and say what we are doing, why are we doing it and how can we do things better? We can't go back, and I am not sure what the answer is, but I'm excited about the prospects."

SHARED LEADERSHIP

COVID-19 and the impact that this will have on our district is unknown. We don't have a playbook or policy to follow moving forward. However, we have an opportunity to re-envision what it means to provide high-quality teaching and learning to our 900 plus students. It's important that we all lean on each other in the days and weeks to come.

This was part of the Superintendent introduction at the All Staff conference for the Community Charter School of Paterson. The Community Charter School of Paterson is a three-campus public charter school district that serves over 900 students in Paterson, New Jersey. On this call, Mr. Curtis Palmore, the district CEO, provided encouragement for the future while uncertain about what was to come.

While talking to these leaders about what emerged as most important, they each had examples of how they were forced to share their load. The immense burden of leading without having answers and sometimes only getting answers five minutes before a meeting, while coping with their struggles, made shared leadership a critical key in how they maneuvered working during the pandemic. Who is most proximate to the work? This is the question network leaders grapple with. They shared that they made choices to allow for more conversations and decisions led by teachers and school leadership. Network leadership recognized they are not the ones on the ground day to day living the impact of those decisions. Giving ownership to teachers and principals in deciding what school will look like in the coming months emerged as critically important to network leaders.

Additionally, principals discussed the importance of having multiple voices at the table when decision-making happens. Resultantly, decision-makers are more intentional about democratizing decisions through a larger stakeholder input. Principals found that creating spaces and structures for those additional voices built trust and more team alignment.

Loss

As we mentioned previously, we lost three CCSP family members to COVID-19 related illness. Since many of the CCSP families live in communal homes that house extended families, the loss and level of trauma was especially difficult for the community. During this time a host of staff members also contracted COVID-19. Daily stakeholders across the school community shared stories of COVID-19 related losses. Dr. Ford, a campus leader at CCSP, shared anecdotally that all the teachers on his team had multiple family and friends infected and/or impacted by COVID-19.

During the pandemic, school districts across the country felt the impact of the staggering COVID-19 death toll in America. Each school referenced in this section dealt with the loss of loving family members, teachers, administrators, and support staff alike. These losses have a lasting impact on the fiber and future of schools moving forward. Schools also experienced loss through the lens of identity, as noted by interviewed school leaders. Mr. Palmore describes how "not having the ability to connect with my school communities directly brought about much despair. Weeks into the pandemic I yearned to see smiling beautiful brown faces in my classes and to interact with teachers and leaders directly. Zoom calls did not drive my passion for this work." Loss also reared its ugly head with leaders who felt immobile while seeking to find direction as they navigated through complex decisions and structures with transforming their schools to distance learning platforms. A Philadelphia school leader told his school that no one could imagine or prepare for schools to close down completely. It was unthinkable. Without any formal directions from bureaucrats and policymakers, school leaders traveled a lonely, never-ending road while navigating COVID-19.

Educators and leaders across all contexts felt the loss of the community and the inability to connect directly to colleagues. This significant finding became one of the cornerstones of how we might empower communities to thrive through the COVID-19 pandemic. The anticipation of continued navigation through the virtual space provides educators with challenges that impact connection and contribute to the feelings of loss of community, school, and teachers and students.

Connection

The entry point question with each leader was "What has emerged that really matters to you?" The answers were each full of passion and thoughtfulness. One theme that emerged across all responses: the importance of connection. Through this pandemic, school leaders found that the connections with students, their own families, and teachers became a unique priority. Many of the leaders interviewed are also parents, and they all shared that while being home with their children and trying to work posed many challenges, they were enlivened by the quality time they were able to give their own families. Maggie Bello said, "The ability to spend time with my family and the flexibility to not be harried and crazy and just breathe for a minute has been really nice. Connecting with my family and just the flexibility in not having to be at a job from seven to five every day and being able to go put a load of laundry in the wash. That matters." Each leader shared their version of this gratitude for the ability and privilege to have more time and flexibility with their family. There is also a deep desire to find ways to make sure that they continue to prioritize spending time connecting with family as we move beyond this pandemic and back into traditional workdays.

Overall, the emphasis on connection is not limited to leaders' families. They are also thinking about how to remain more intentionally connected to their teams. We acknowledge how hard it is for everyone through this remote schooling, but leaders need to stay constant even when people are feeling down. Principals shared that they scheduled regular Zoom meetings with their teachers and assistant teachers to stay connected. It was important to them to nurture those relationships and communicate that we are in this together. There is a plan and they can count on their principals for constant and steady leadership. As Chelsie Jones, a Two Rivers principal, put it, "I got their back, and we are going through this together. I valued that [connection] anyways, but it has really been amplified."

Jeff Hyke-Williams, director of Curriculum and Instruction at Two Rivers PCS, shared that remote learning has pushed his leadership around personal interactions:

> Every interaction right now must be so intentional. There are no spontaneous interactions throughout the day. You have to set up virtual meetings for a certain time during the day, and they have a finite time blocked off. Every interaction in the professional sphere is because somebody set up a time for me to come, connect with them . . . and while that is ok, now I have to intentionally ask how

you're doing, because we need to do that. The transactional element is so heightened because there is a feeling that I've got to accomplish x y z before the end of the meeting. Work suffers because of this.

He shared that because he can't just walk into someone's office and check on them, he has to leave space in meetings to check in with people and decide if something is urgent or essential.

The most important components cited, first by John Getz, high school mathematics teacher, then by Rosemary Gephardt, principal, Glen Meadow Middle School, then by elementary speech teacher Aimee Hamilton and high school English teacher Vicky Smith, were compassion and connection. All four faculty members cited regular best practices pre–COVID-19. Seeing body language, facial expressions, or even how students enter a school building help educators understand children and what they may need. Identifying peer groups or whether peer groups changed helped administrators assess what was going on with individual students. Teachers could then differentiate based on the social emotional needs of individual children. Zoom (virtual) meetings or, in some cases, posting assignments to platforms allows for very little interaction. Faculty felt they could not "build that bond" through virtual instruction as they could in person. Leaders reflect that no amount of phone calls home, virtual conferences, or messages on interactive platforms or emails can substitute for the interpersonal and intrapersonal relationships that impact students (and building climate) daily.

School leaders reflect on the opportunities that were present in school pre-COVID. Messaging for all stakeholders throughout the district was a key part of the distant learning strategy during COVID-19. Given the shortcomings of communication models, the district leadership sought alternative ways to communicate directly with all stakeholders. Social media became a significant lever for maintaining connection. Districts used Instagram, Flipgrid, and YouTube channels for parents and students that provide daily video updates, including the traditional schoolwide morning announcements, community meetings, teacher and student profiles, and highlights of student work. These alternative forms of communication were welcomed and important for keeping the district together as a community. As indicated in the leadership vignette, the healing opportunity through prayer groups and other purposeful, compassionate connections allowed leaders to build bridges to remain connected to families and their needs.

Family Partnership

The pandemic forced many school communities to center families in a new way. In Two Rivers Public Charter School, engagement with families has always been critical to our schools' work. Leaders and teachers both shared how they overhauled their engagement with families' needs. Moving school to a remote platform meant that families were central and not the school. Teachers now need to be invited into a child's space and context. Before COVID-19, students and families were invited into the school context with a superficial merging of the two worlds. Losing the connections with families in the brick-and-mortar building was initially devastating. Principal Chelsie Jones shared a realization that what her school did pre-COVID for families was not helping them. She wanted to find ways to "pull them in tighter." When we don't have walls, how do you pull people in and hold them together?

The Two Rivers leadership answered this question through monthly Zoom meetings with families and bi-weekly listening sessions broken down by different groups of families and their needs. Specific listening sessions took place for families of students of color or families of students with IEPs. These intentional interactions created groups in the school community that needed to be heard and otherwise on the margins. Seeking family connection in more intimate ways became necessary when issues were not brought forth to the leadership team. For example, when a parent asked multiple questions during a meeting, it signaled the importance of sending a private email asking if they wanted to talk. For parents who miss a meeting, receiving personal email "pulls them in" and indicates an added level of care and compassion. Leaders and teachers have become more available and responsive to parents in the context of remote schooling. Most of this connection revolves around supporting families through their own fear and uncertainty. The availability of this emotional connection—when we don't have the technical or intellectual answer—is critical for how these educators build authentic partnerships with families

The iterative process was also necessary to connect with children and provide support. We were impressed by the drive that each educator demonstrated to achieve one's objective. When teachers couldn't reach a child, phone calls, emails, texts, and even a knock on the door (with a mask on) were impactful strategies that increased connection with students who had fallen into the COVID-19 abyss of depression. Both leaders and educators interviewed grew more and more concerned about students who went "missing" or no longer "checked in" online. Strategies like the ones used in the Two Rivers Charter School happened across contexts and schools. Emergency Zoom calls became commonplace to engage families.

Philosophical beliefs about education also come into question during these times. With parents as paraeducators supporting their children at home during COVID-19, how school administrators might assess children for levels or placement becomes a topic of serious discussion. What role will parent input and evaluation of their children play in identifying the needs of students if/when they assimilate back to brick-and-mortar classrooms? We also need to consider the role of parents in discussions on race. Two of the four faculty interviewed from Vernon specifically mentioned how parental beliefs and statements influence children in school.

Mr. Getz, a math teacher at Vernon Township High School, also realized the troublesome nature of not knowing what is going on with students and being forced to develop a "one size fits all" approach. He remains concerned about students who have lost family due to COVID-19 and various inequities, specifically regarding socioeconomic challenges. Mr. Getz feels that meeting social-emotional needs is "far more important than what is done in the math classroom." It is no surprise that educators craved the ability to "pull families in tighter." We always knew that partnering with families was essential for student success pre-COVID. However, through this pandemic, we realized that the home-school connection was necessary to ensure engagement and an essential fabric for the future of communities everywhere fighting a pandemic and racism.

Uncertainty

Through the pandemic, experiences of flux manifest themselves in a variety of ways. Flux showed up in uncertainty, experiencing the unknown, doubt, and even fear. Principal Muronji Inman-McCraw says, "I was consumed by my fear. I considered the magnitude of what was happening and how not having a roadmap for success would impact my leadership moves." Chelsie Jones said, "I found that every time I widened my aperture and considered what was just beyond my issue, my pain, it became a little smaller. What was immediately in front of me was dwarfed enough so I could see to put together pieces and trends and put together another perspective." Educators identified the need to gain perspective from a vantage point of being within the pandemic was resounding.

Several leaders shared the idea that moments of pivot came in the form of not knowing. This uncertainty, while challenging, translates to opportunities for growth and grace. Giving each other grace in these moments has been critical, while leaders all acknowledge the urgency in figuring out how to proceed and how to identify and fill gaps students may have due to lost instructional time. Grace also provides the opportunity to slow down and reconnect with the bigger vision of schools. Leaders and teachers do far more than merely filling in gaps. Investing in connection and emotional support is essential to the future. This investment is the future.

The depth and breadth of pedagogy and the discomfort that White educators feel while discussing pedagogy and racism is evident. Statements such as "There is so much going on with trying to get students back to school during COVID that race has taken a back seat" or "It feels taboo to talk about it" or "I'm not the person who can say 'this is how we fix it'" are all statements made from uncertainty and doubt. Doubt remains among White educators that they will do the wrong thing. Yet, doing nothing at this time is the most "wrong thing" we can do.

Responding to Systemic Racism

How racism is taught through parents' opinions and heard through children's minds creates the conditions for generationally entrenched dissemination of structural racism woven into the fabric of America. Addressing the generational dissemination of racism now is critical. Kenneth McCants-Persall, Chief Academic Officer at Two Rivers PCS, shared that as a Black leader, he has trouble in a position that requires him to use his voice to talk about race. While managing the narrative of pain associated with his racial identity, he is to lead his schools during crisis. There is a deep knowing that we can no longer look away and remain quiet; it is also deeply painful for Black leaders who are expected to shoulder the burdens of White guilt through their voices. Caroline Mwebda-Baker, a principal at Two Rivers, discusses the urgency of creating spaces, for even the youngest students, to share their experiences and how they intake the world. These youngsters look at the existing structures critically, prompting educators to include more time and space for discussions about race. Younger generations know what is happening and offer hope to school leaders and empowerment toward a necessary shift to achieve equity.

White leaders express doubt. They wonder if they are the right leaders during this time. They ponder, "What is my value, and what do I have to offer during this time?" They are grappling with their value as leaders when organizations are turning their focus to being antiracist. This dichotomy begins the exploration into the continuum of racism in our country. During discussions regarding race, the common elements cited among four White faculty members (three teachers and one principal) were uncertainty, confusion, and doubt. "Racism is a system, not a person. If I'm part of that system, then I guess I'm (racist) . . . I don't take that with a badge of honor. I take that as a slap in the face, but I don't know what to change." This statement, by John Getz, is evidence of the uncertainty White educators feel. Further, Aimee Hamilton, pre-kindergarten speech teacher, says, "We need to figure out what we are doing wrong at the Preschool level because up until now, I have been kind of oblivious to it. It is eye opening."

Yet, the location of Vernon on the continuum struggles to shift racism. Even the most "woke" educator in Vernon is uncertain of their role with the necessary racial reckoning in our county. In comparison, other contexts we researched were active and bold with their leadership. Curtis Palmore, CEO, inspired leaders, educators, community members, and families. His direct discussions on racism and leadership toward activism were evident through communications. He also strived for inclusivity about injustice and established a district-wide Race and Equity Committee. Likewise, in Washington, DC, the steadfast action toward being an antiracist school, defining that mission, and embarking toward the future under the leadership of Principal Muronji Inman-McCraw, exemplify necessary leadership moves against racism and where her DC community identifies itself on the continuum.

Across three contexts, racism exists. The racial composition of each community, core values, and community/school beliefs all contribute to the change necessary for our country to provide equity and access for all students. Each community requires unique methods and strategies of implementation. How leaders and educators navigate this future space will take brave conversations, adapting to new norms, and bold leadership moves.

REFLECTIONS

Throughout these interviews, we gained perspective of our adaptive leadership moves during COVID-19. Themes that emerged throughout the research were impact on core values, shared leadership, loss, connection, family partnership, uncertainty, and systemic racism.

Leaders provided evidence, strategies, and examples of courageous, bold moves to unify communities, enhance communication, embrace the value of connection, and inspire the possibilities of the future of education. We hope these experiences offer other leaders affirmation, guidance, inspiration, and hope to lead in their context, even outside of COVID-19.

As Chelsie Jones, principal at Two Rivers, considered the future of education, she said, "I want to say it's about restoration, but restoration is the wrong word. I don't want to fix something that is broken. I think there is something around the idea of rebirth. I want to teach our children about being human, how they should love, what they should reach for and rage against. We have this opportunity to sow into the community." Her position encourages us to be bold about the way we envision the future. We have an opportunity to reimagine something new by considering what is possible for children.

We don't claim to be leadership experts, and we know the road to systemic change is long and challenging. We intend to offer hope as conceptualized by the late renowned civil rights activist John Lewis: "Do not get lost in a sea of despair. Be hopeful. Be optimistic. Our struggle is not the struggle of a day, a week, a month, or a year, it is the struggle of a lifetime. Never, ever be afraid to make some noise and get in good trouble, necessary trouble." We hope that educational leaders and policymakers get into good trouble by boldly using these takeaways to drive systemic change in school districts across the country through the pandemic and beyond.

RAPID-CYCLE INQUIRY

Rapid-cycle research design

Goals: To learn a range of perspectives of adaptive leadership moves through COVID-19; to learn lessons from and for ourselves and our peer leaders.

Rapid-cycle data collection

1. Rapid-cycle interviews. Interviews, conducted over a 2- to 4-week time frame on Zoom with 11 leaders and six teachers. Interviews lasted between 30 and 90 minutes.

Rapid-cycle analysis

1. Rapid-cycle member checks/participant validation. For some interviews, transcriptions were sent to participants for member checks/participant validation.
2. Rapid-cycle data reads and data visualization. Immediate coding occurred and review of interviews for facilitation purposes were used to identify important questions to refine the interview process. Interviewers reviewed interviews and identified themes in order to extrapolate evidence to write about.
3. Informal inductive coding was used. We were in communication with each other to identify themes that emerged and debriefed after interviews concluded. We collaborated about questioning strategies and successful questions.

Inquiry Outcomes

1. Weekly call with leaders interviewed to discuss the navigation of in-person instruction.
2. Created structures for teacher voice on a regular basis than prior to the interviews.
3. Took more time off from work and encouraging people to do so in regard to self-care as a part of successful leadership.
4. More regular (monthly) workshops and meetings to communicate with parents.
5. More apt to utilize a leadership strategy where stakeholder input is solicited, considered, then acted upon.
6. More confidence in conducting interviews for the dissertation process. This was a good exercise to boost confidence in informal inductive coding for the dissertation.
7. Reflection on how leaders are cared for during these critical moments and during difficult leadership times (such as COVID) and how they support others during critical moments.

CHAPTER 11

Crisis Leader Literacies in K–12 Independent Schools During COVID-19

Jessica Flaxman, Christopher J. Hancock, and David Weiner

EDITORIAL FRAMING

In this rapid-cycle inquiry, three doctoral candidates take up the call to investigate what crisis leadership looks like within the K–12 independent school context. Their hopes in conducting these semi-structured interviews with six independent school heads across the country included an examination of crisis definitions as well as various leadership approaches and styles in crisis. As we discuss in the flux leadership chapter (Chapter 3), a leader's learning agility in crisis or crisis agility mediates the impact of the crisis on everyone in the organization. Learning agility in crisis is complicated within educational contexts because a crisis often lands on our diverse stakeholders in different ways and requires a response where emotions remain in balance. As readers can imagine or have experienced themselves, this flux tenet is crucial—leadership communities need stories to better understand what crisis agility looks like for educational leaders who must balance an array of needs and demands. These authors rise to the occasion and investigate how this looks in real time: how crisis leadership is enacted within the context of independent schools in hopes of uncovering those leadership moves.

Rapid-cycle inquiries like this are essential in times of crisis. While these can be difficult to conduct, the affordances of these stories are undeniable for the purposes of knowledge sharing within the educational leadership community. By being embedded within a particular educational context, educational leaders from similar contexts can use these narratives to reflect on their own site of practice in new ways. In this chapter, readers can witness these strategies and approaches around crisis agility from all angles, including the emotions embedded within these leadership practices. The authors mentioned one leader describing his role in comparison to that of a duck: "I may be paddling furiously underneath, but I'm going to try to project a sense [that] we're going to be okay." Anecdotes like this one should resonate with many educational leaders and prompt larger inquiries on how we can cultivate and model crisis agility within our leadership teams.

We saw in Chapter 3 that crisis agility requires an appropriate leadership response that focuses on collective school improvement. These authors dig into this aspect—what we call being a reflexive visionary—a leader who allows organizational vision to evolve, emerge, and build through humanizing collective circumstances and situations in crisis. Through their intentional focus on understanding these types of leadership practices, this chapter provides a more holistic view of what crisis leadership looks like within the independent school context. It is also important to note that this chapter works to utilize data analysis as a holding ground for nuggets of wisdom for school leaders across all contexts. Within their thematic sections, stories emerge embedded with wisdom, such as handwritten letters written to faculty at the beginning of the crisis. Rather than crisis leadership feeling abstract, readers can better understand how educational leaders made sense of their leadership practices in real time and how a flux leadership approach can better serve all of us in these situations

INTRODUCTION

COVID-19, a novel, easily transmitted, and deadly illness, within 6 months touched nearly every community around the globe, causing economies to shut down, institutions to halt operations, and supply chains and transportation routes to stall. Since March 2020, institutions serving the public, such as libraries, theaters, and schools across the United States, have closed their doors. While post offices, grocery stores, and gas stations—deemed "essential" to sustain a bare-bones economy and social nexus—remained open, institutions serving the public moved their operations online to stem the spread of COVID-19. In this context, educational leaders have had to adjust and adapt their leadership modes, methods, and goals to lead effectively in this time of flux, when daily expectations and experiences of faculties, families, and students have radically pivoted. Flux leadership, like flux pedagogy, brings radical compassion for students, staff, and self with "high-yet-humanely-calibrated expectations for their learning, behavior, and performance" (Eren & Ravitch, 2021; Russo, 2018).

In response to this crisis, as independent school leaders ourselves, we formed a leadership inquiry group to understand how other K–12 independent schools leaders adapted to and managed this unprecedented crisis. Independent schools are mission-driven, private organizations typically led by a head of school who reports to a board of trustees. To learn directly from leaders, we conducted semi-structured interviews with sitting heads of K–8 and K–12 independent schools in different parts of the country. Four female and two male heads of K–8, 5–12, and K–12 independent schools were selected by convenience sampling. Two (one male, one female, both White) were long-standing heads with over 15 years of experience; three (one male, two female, all White) were seasoned heads with between 4 and 7 years of experience; and one (Black, female) was in the second year of her first headship. Representing schools in the Northeast, Midwest, and western United States, these heads of school provide insight into their respective crisis definition, their leadership approaches and styles in crisis, and their communication practices within the context of COVID-19.

CRISIS LEADERSHIP

Crisis leadership is an evolving area of organizational behavior and industrial psychology wherein typical hallmarks of leadership, such as vision or a bias toward action, are insufficient for the immediate challenge. Petriglieri (2020) defines crises as unanticipated tests of the internal and external systems created previously. He states, "Crises always test visions, and most don't survive. Because when there's a fire in a factory, a sudden drop in revenues, a natural disaster, we don't need a call to action. We are already motivated to move, but we often flail. What we need is a holding so that we can move purposefully" (p. 1).

The concept of *holding* interests us. The heads of school we interviewed all describe the work of the independent school leader during this crisis characterized by the need to contain emotion and chaos, calm others, and communicate with clarity and support.

A crisis is a seismic event defined and experienced differently by leaders. For example, one head of school describes a crisis as "a situation that disrupts or upends the systems and operations of a school and threatens its future survival." Another head believes "a crisis is a thing that changes you as opposed to a problem, which you solve and move on, or a dilemma which you live with, make part of you and again, you move on . . . a crisis changes you." A crisis is "an out-of-control feeling situation" or "an acute event, a situation that impacts the health and safety of the community, and that can be emotional and psychological health and safety as well." A crisis is "the one thing that, if it happened, it would blow your school apart." These statements evince the powerful felt experience of crisis leadership; each comment speaks to an understanding of how impactful crises are to defining a leader, and how important it is for leaders to be responsive in crisis as a protective factor for people in the school community (Imad, 2020).

Heads of school who occupied the role during a previous national crisis, such as the national crisis of 9/11 and the Great Recession of 2008, noted that these earlier crises, while challenging, were substantively different. September 11, 2001, had a more emotional and far-reaching social impact as terrorism became a worldwide concern. Some schools dealt with the loss of loved ones, and, subsequently, discrimination against Muslim students (Fine & Sirin, 2007). In independent schools, 9/11 caused considerable disruptions to teaching and learning, but for a relatively short period of time. Though teachers, students, and families were upset and traumatized, school communities could resume daily operations relatively quickly. During the 2008 recession, the landscape of independent schools changed dramatically; many experienced economic hardships for the first time in their histories, and some schools closed. Over time, however, schools weathered the crisis as the economy recovered.

Neither 9/11 nor the 2008 recession disrupted schedules, assessment, program, employment, or school culture as much as COVID-19. As one head shares, COVID-19 "upended so many of the structures that have endured for so long in independent schools." These structures are both physical and symbolic and include school buildings, desks, theaters, gyms, teacher–student communication and relationships, learning processes and structures, how grades are given, and many other elements of education. In powerful contrast to the 2008 recession and 9/11, COVID-19 has changed the very nature of what it means to be a school. To be a teacher. A student. A community. A leader. Every aspect of schooling has changed this time around, and leaders find themselves without blueprints.

CRISIS LEADERSHIP APPROACHES IN FLUX

To gain insight into the impacts of the COVID-19 crisis on independent school leaders and their leadership approaches, we asked six heads of independent schools to reflect on their leadership approaches in relation to the crisis. Some felt that their leadership approach did not significantly change but deepened. Leaders discussed how they felt they "leaned into their strengths" as leaders by being more empathetic and understanding of their employees or focusing even more than usual on finances to ensure that the school could absorb moments of financial flux. Other heads noted they felt compelled to leverage multiple leadership approaches at once—for example, to take up elements of authentic leadership, relational leadership, transformational leadership, and embodied leadership approaches—calling on aspects of these different approaches for situations as they arose.

Notably, the heads described a process of adjusting their leadership approaches gently rather than explicitly or abruptly. This sentiment was striking. They shared that they are intentionally working to evolve their approach during the crisis in ways that are felt, not announced. As one head said, "I think if you start to overthink how you lead, you lose your leadership capacity. It's more that my leadership style has evolved. It's more like sanding a piece of wood than it is choosing a different piece of wood." This is important, as leaders often mention the "paralysis of analysis" that can ensue if they lead without a clear forward vision in a crisis.

Most, if not all, heads self-identified as adaptive and authentic leaders (Heifetz, Grashow, & Linsky. 2009) who value distributed leadership and are also comfortable giving direction during a crisis. Distributed leadership acknowledges that the work of improving student learning requires that leadership is distributed among followers and situations (Spillane, Halverson, & Diamond, 2004). These leaders shared that both distributed and directive leadership are necessary in such chaotic times.

Embodied Relational Leadership

As Ravitch (2020) asserts, "Leaders must be quite intentional about saving focus and energy for teachers and be outwardly caring and positive (and real) when engaging with them. Intentionality is critically important to their sense of safety, belonging, engagement, and to their sense of belonging" (p. 7). The six independent school heads interviewed shared that they focus their crisis leadership on building dynamic relationships within their specific school contexts, wherein interpersonal, intergroup, and intragroup relationships are critical to individuals' health, well-being, and the learning organization as a whole.

One head shared her view that "a school should be viewed as an organism that needs to be tended to ensure that employees make their mortgages, pay their rents, and take care of themselves physically, mentally, and emotionally." This attention to the human needs within their organization was echoed by other heads as well—that these are not just schools but are also places where employees make their livelihood and that both matters deeply to equity and social justice. This same leader shared what we view as a North Star question for all crises: "How do we create systems of care?"

When the news of COVID-19 hit, this leader made sure to "be out everywhere," walking the hallways, going in and out of bathrooms, and standing at the bottom of the stairs to be sure to be present to listen. She made sure to see and genuinely communicate to employees that she cared and that, as a community, they would get through this crisis together. For her, crisis leadership is all about the face-to-face: "It's face-time, it's 'How are you? It's good to see you this morning. I saw that thing. Did you get your lunch?' It's that kind of thing. You're just there. You need to be."

All the leaders we interviewed foregrounded the relational aspect of crisis leadership above all else and discussed the need to physically embody that relational leadership during the first moments of the current crisis.

The value of and need for educational leaders to be physically and visibly present during times of crisis—to embody their leadership presence—is irrefutable (Hanson, 2018). During the COVID-19 pandemic, this has been both important and challenging due to radical limitations on in-person interactions, which undoubtedly help build relational trust in independent schools (Batiste, 2012). Embodied leadership describes how a leader's physical actions consistently reflect their values and commitment especially amidst stress and pressure (Hamill, 2013). In good times and bad, said one head, "leadership communication is not about what you say, it's about what you do." Another head, in the second year of her first headship when the COVID-19 crisis occurred, spoke at length about their relational leadership style and how she has cultivated relational trust with her administrative team and families in the school. For this head, "leadership is a relational exercise." From these leaders, we learn that crisis agility is relational agility (Hanson, 2018) and that socioemotional learning matters for everyone in schools, especially during crisis (Walker, 2020).

Authentic and Pastoral Leadership

In times of crisis, the need for educational leaders to be authentic and transparent is heightened (Hanson, 2018). Within the context of the COVID-19 crisis, because information itself has been in a constant state of flux, a leader's ability to take decisive action has been unusually difficult. The pressure on educational leaders to address their respective communities and to "have answers" mounts each moment of each day. Specifically, questions around when in-person schooling will resume and under what circumstances, as well as questions about employment status and job security, echo and reverberate in endless circles of worry swirling around school heads.

In response to this acute level of uncertainty, one head redoubled her transparent leadership style of speaking honestly and directly to people's concerns. In a past crisis, she made a decision that the local media caught wind of and covered. Her approach addressed her faculty by saying, "I'm really sorry if that was the wrong decision. It felt like the right decision at the time. I still think it might've been the right decision, but I apologize for putting us in the middle of a controversy." Ownership in this way shows us that even small disruptions can feel seismic within a school community and that a leader's relationship with employees are strengthened through transparency and authenticity.

Humor can be an expression of that authenticity. One head shared how she uses humor to connect with people: "I always try to use some humor, even if it's gallows humor, because we have to laugh sometimes at the absurdity of it all." It is well known that while a crisis is a serious matter, within some contexts, humor and laughter can mitigate anxiety and create connection through tension (Bell & Pomerantz, 2016). This same head employed another authentic leadership method of writing handwritten letters to her faculty and staff during the opening weeks of the COVID-19 crisis. "It feels like a very old-fashioned and in some ways more meaningful form of communication," she said and described how her employees felt happy to receive personal notes demonstrating that they were on her mind and that they mattered. For this head in this crisis, there was an aspect of performative leadership within her expression of her authentic leadership: "I had to model for the faculty that I was braver than I may have actually felt." This profound example embodies crisis leadership.

One of the most impactful leadership approaches one leader discussed as vital during the crisis is pastoral leadership, a servant-leadership framework wherein care, and care systems are prioritized and foregrounded (Focht & Ponton, 2015). As one leader shared,

> People are quite desperate for something that feels like church, something that gives them a sense of the larger purpose of all of this, and somebody who can speak to what it means to be human and why we learn, why we gather together in a community, what it means to respect other people, why diversity matters, how you grow from all of these encounters and difficulties and challenges in life.

Both authentic and pastoral leadership require keen self-awareness from a leader. This leadership mindset and set of related behaviors are built on positive psychological competencies. It is no surprise that their authentic leadership led to articulate, self-reflective expression during the interview and the belief this style sustained positive feelings within the organizational culture during crisis (Focht & Ponton, 2015).

Never Worry Alone: Teams in Crisis

The heads we interviewed formed their crisis teams in response to the pandemic and spoke about their importance as part of their crisis leadership. One head shared that she made sure to have "20-minute check-ins every day, and longer, 2- to 3-hour meetings each week to manage the early stages of this crisis." They shared how important it is to have "some pretty nimble decision-making that was still collaborative" instead of going solo or only consulting a limited coterie of colleagues. One head shared the similar importance of swiftly and thoughtfully bringing her team together: "My leadership literacy would include now, get out of your own head and use what's around you. Quickly. And benefit hugely from the wisdom in the group." Another head spoke about the importance of "cross-functional" teams whereby employees who have different areas of expertise must come together to lead an independent school in crisis. In response to COVID-19, heads of schools spent a lot of time structuring, organizing, and empowering their teams to succeed. This stands out as their top crisis leadership strategy and good leader reason (Hanson, 2018).

"Be Like a Duck": Strategic Planning in Crisis

One leader described his role during a crisis as that of a duck: "I may be paddling furiously underneath, but I'm going to try to project a sense [that] we're going to be okay." As part of being calm, a leader needs to be the "community focuser" during a crisis. Especially during COVID-19, so much changed so quickly that it's up to the head to sit down with their leadership team and establish priorities. They must ask as a team: *What needs to be done now? What can wait? What long-term goals do we need to start thinking about?* As another head of school noted, "planning is our friend." Heads need to think slowly but act quickly. In practice, this means spending a lot of time with their leadership team to sus out the details of decisions and anticipate responses from their constituents (parents, students, faculty, board) while ensuring that you respond to crises promptly. As one head said, "I want to do it, I want to do it right, and I want to do it right now. I think that allows us to make things better, and that permits us to take care of our people as best we can."

COMMUNICATION, THE CORE COMPONENT OF CRISIS LEADERSHIP

Perhaps expectedly, but still poignantly, the importance of clear and warm communication during crises emerged as a dominant theme. The word communication itself was mentioned more than 60 times within the six interviews and touched on by every participant, just as one quick indicator of its salience to leader crisis thinking. While many heads acknowledge that the frequency of communications to their constituent groups has not increased, they are focused on communication as their priority, "the number one thing." Specifically, leaders shared their distinct crisis leadership philosophies, their crisis modes and methods, and the impact they believe their crisis communication had on their communities' well-being. As one head shared, "This crisis has the unique gift of removing our ability to connect while increasing the need for precisely that. And so, communication becomes so important." So we learn from these leaders that communication—proactive, personal, clear, and ongoing—is the main strategy of organizational care in these scattered times.

Philosophy

Interviews revealed that their own emotions undergirded heads' communication philosophies. Whether a head appeared emotionally wound up by the unfolding events or expressed an emotional distance from their decision-making and crisis communications, their emotional proximity to the event was linked to their communication and action philosophy. For example, one head who expressed, "I don't find, and this may just have to do with my eminently pragmatic nature, I don't find the doom loop helpful," also shared "a bias for action" for their communications during the current crisis. Their philosophy was, "Do it right and do it right now." This leader juxtaposes their emotional response to the current crisis to that of some team members: "I understand that some people cannot do that because . . . their fears have to go somewhere . . . but there's this part of me that's saying it isn't helping, I think, right now." This head's pragmatism moved them to communicate and act seemingly detached from the emotion of the moment. However, this detachment emerged as an indicator of a head's communication philosophy. A head's ability to gauge their emotional proximity to the crisis proved critical to shaping a compelling, authentic crisis communication philosophy.

In further support of this emergent theme, another head offered a contrasting emotion and response. In their first engagement with a crisis as a head of school during 9/11, an experienced head shared, "I think I had more of a fight-or-flight reality in my head then. My instinct was to flee. Not that I could or would . . . It was like, oh shit. Now, what do I do?" They continued, "As a lead communicator, I would get anxious and try to buy more and more time, so I know more so that what I communicate would never be seen as lacking comprehension of the situation . . . and . . . I have procrastinated or waited because I wanted more information and then gotten heavily criticized." They shared that they felt their emotions ran too heavy early in their career, creating communication and action paralysis. Since 9/11, they expressed an increased ability to identify emotion during an active crisis. This leader identified their alertness to "the emotional consequences of world events" and marshaled a more collaborative communication approach, sharing that "I brought in the people that I needed to be around . . . I would say my leadership literacy would include now: get out of your own head and use what's around you quickly, and benefit hugely from the wisdom in the group." Their emotional proximity to the crisis required them to "convene wisdom, grab it quickly, and move into action." They learned to lean on those around them to collaborate on communication to advance action they might otherwise be too paralyzed to do.

The self-awareness of one's emotional response to/in a crisis can better prepare heads of school to marshal the resources necessary to communicate effectively and do so in harmony with their own emotions and leader values. "As a leader," one head said, "you develop a code. I think those are the leaders who are coherent." Another echoed, "I want to lean on my strengths. In a crisis, I don't want to try to become a new kind of leader. I need to lean into what I'm good at." For these leaders, this code, or covenant, or leader stance keeps them in touch with themselves, their emotions, and how they communicate—a seemingly clear path to successful and enduring relational leadership (Hanson, 2018).

Modes and Methods

As emotional proximity shaped communication philosophies, it also mediated a leader's mode of communication. Communication proved the physical manifestation of a head's crisis philosophy because it worked as both a mirror and a window. Half of the leaders interviewed noted that as soon as the crisis unfolded in late February and early March, their priority shifted to caring for their faculty, students, and parents in significant distress. One head eloquently shared their philosophy, "to relate a feeling of care, emotion, and empathy in every communication" governed their chosen methods and modes of communication. "The best form of communication during this pandemic crisis is the fireside chat approach. Now, that could be Zoom," one head elaborated. Another self-identified relational leader put the want for face-to-face communication more bluntly, "You can see the damn people you're talking to." Their attention to the emotional exchange needed between leader and community led to a more interpersonal philosophy when choosing communication modes. Those who identified this exchange were more likely to leverage applications like Zoom to communicate rather than utilize email and written word.

Heads focused on emotional connection through email. While historically seen as distancing, email has been leveraged by heads to buoy a community's spirits. "I send out Sunday messages to families. That's a homily, frankly. What they want is a pastor," one head shared. Another reiterated, "I always try to have a little bit of a parable in there for parents." Yet, most heads who identified as relational leaders were challenged by the shifting modalities of communication, particularly email, where they could no longer sit, talk, build intimacy and convey empathy through embodied means. Those who "try to relate a feeling of care, emotion, and empathy" indeed shared struggle to "get a sense of how your communications are landing or not in our current circumstances." This same head expanded the thought: "It's impossible for me to have the perfect communication that's going to meet the needs of every family in the school. That's always the case for a leader, but it seems like you know when you're hitting the mark when you're in the school, when you're walking the hallways, when you're seeing parents at drop off in the morning and pick up in the afternoon. You kind of get a sense of how things are landing for folks." That is not the case during COVID-19, which is felt and being strategized actively by leaders.

In fact, and some ways surprisingly, given the glut of social media, email emerged as a more suitable vehicle for the pragmatic, less emotionally proximate leader. Their expressed duty of care to their employees was equal to the more emotionally connected, emotive leaders, yet, they shared, "We have to rely on email more." Another shared, "I'm deeply pragmatic, and I want to do the best that I can now (email), rather than describing the problem, which is what we excel at in schools." They continued, "I think that allows us to make things better, and that permits us to take care of our people as best we can." For the pragmatist, the shift to written expressions of their care was a self-identified strength and reflection of their emotional presence rather than those typically done in-person.

Impact

This inquiry did not seek out community members to explore how their respective communities received each mode of communication selected by heads. Identifying those individuals' impressions of the impact of a heads' choices during a crisis is ground for further research. Still, it was clear that all heads possessed a self-awareness that allowed them to utilize various modes of communication, each suited to their emotional proximity to the crisis, to attempt to support their communities. Some even offered humble insights on how it might have been received like, "It's nothing but mistakes over here," and,

> I don't think people are very good at knowing how they come across. They can sometimes imagine they come across a certain way. And then it can sound, oh what is it, self-centered or conceited . . . So I would say people say that I am . . . direct, which engenders confidence. I know that I can exhibit passion, which I think also can be energizing for people. People suggest that I speak well and present well. So, I think my style is that I'm an effective communicator, both in person and in writing.

Another offered it's "been a learning curve for me in terms of making sure that I have a right balance of communications that are empathetic, and understanding that different people are in different places, but also there are some moments where people just need the facts now. And that's been an important lesson for me to learn."

This crisis amplified the importance of the performance elements of a head's role on the impact felt by community members. The duty to bury one's insecurities or emotions, or at least deftly navigate them, to bring calm and clarity to the chaos of a pandemic was felt more strongly by some heads. "These videos are going to be somewhere, so you feel really verklempt about it. It's just sort of strange. You want to communicate fluidly, and naturally and this is unnatural and permanent. Weird," one head shared. Caution was also offered: "If you are not comfortable with the performative nature of this role, you won't last in it." Yet, all believed their authenticity was received well by their constituencies, including a head early in their tenure: "I've only been leaning into, like I said, what I know how to do and I think that I do well . . . and that's been well received. I think that's been felt." One head chose frequent virtual town halls to share information and express care. Another shared the challenge of adequately expressing their grief, loss, pain, and anger via email. A third introduced the yearly auction online through video dressed in a dark brown suit with a black top hat encouraging participants to "dig deep into their pockets," and, if possible, "their neighbors' pockets," attempting to inject humor into a moment wrought with sadness and unease for everyone. Each head understood their central role as a stabilizing presence for their community no matter how they chose to communicate. That self-awareness is a beacon for the most significant impact.

CRISIS LEADERSHIP LITERACIES

Bob Johansen, when thinking about the future of organizations and the prevalence of both distributive leadership and crisis, posited in 2017 that "in the future, disruption will become the norm for most people, as the scope, frequency, nature, and impact of disruption explodes" (p. 6). In his book he identified five "new leadership literacies": a willingness to engage with fear; a commitment to creating positive energy and momentum; a special level of attention to "being there," even when it's impossible to; an understanding of organizations as "shape shifting"; and an ability to envision the future and take action in the present moment from that future-vantage-point (p. 7). The heads that we interviewed leveraged and even embodied many of these leadership literacies, probably without knowing they had been identified.

Crises such as the current one present independent school leaders with challenges beyond their previous imaginations, but which nevertheless give them opportunities to strengthen their existing leadership styles and approaches while developing crisis literacies. Ravitch (2020) writes:

The COVID-19 pandemic and emerging social transformation movement of 2020 offers wide-ranging opportunities for the co-construction of new critical literacies—opportunities to read, re-read, re-write, and re-enact education as an agentic, collectivist project of freedom-building and to reject oppressive structural constraints sedimented into the education system long before coronavirus." (p. x)

The heads we interviewed actively engaged with questions about which literacies they felt were most important to their leadership during crisis and radical flux, signaling a resonance and an area for future research. They were intrigued and, in one case, perplexed by questions about which literacies they were leveraging and developing during the COVID-19 crisis.

The qualitative interviews conducted for this inquiry reveal that crisis literacy involving communication privileges candor over charisma. It obliges leaders to think creatively about how clearly and how often they share information. Crisis communication, specifically during the COVID-19 pandemic, also requires new modes through which independent school heads communicate and reflect their own emotions. Many such modes are newly developing literacies for school heads and fertile ground for future study. Unease with the permanence of these new forms of communication and their impact on the performative elements of a head's work in crisis is unambiguous within the research. Despite, or perhaps because of how these adaptations created discomfort among heads, care for others and communicating with them emerged as their primary leadership literacy.

We noted a strong refrain on the need for financial literacy from many of the heads we interviewed. Before the current crisis, independent schools were already highly concerned about their financial sustainability as tuition and expenses have continued to increase over the past decade. Now, with a radically shrinking economy and continued shifts to enrollment and full-pay students, independent schools, particularly those with small or no endowments and with student bodies of less than 300, are on high alert. That said, our interviews revealed that school heads with strong enrollment and endowments were more likely to see crisis and disruption as an opportunity to innovate and improve their systems. This helps us understand that all educators are innovative at heart and will, if able, use disruption as an opportunity.

PRACTITIONER REFLECTIONS:
FINDING NEW OPPORTUNITIES IN CRISIS

How we live and grow and stay purposeful in the face of constant change . . . determine[s] both the quality of our lives, and the impact that we can have when we move into action together.

—Adrienne Maree Brown (2017, p. 69)

Leading in a time of crisis and constant change like COVID-19 can result in unforeseen opportunities. For example, when the pandemic started in earnest in mid-March, one of the authors formed a Teaching and Learning Committee consisting of three full-time teachers, the school's learning specialist, and an international coordinator and EFL teacher. At the time, the committee was responsible for researching best practices in distance learning and recommending pedagogical changes to best support students and families. As time passed during the spring, however, the committee discussed the very nature of teaching and learning: *What's best for students in a time of crisis? Does the traditional grading system make sense given the current crisis?*

After much discussion, the school decided to continue Pass/No Credit grading for students in 6th and 7th grades during the 2020–2021 school year, piloted in the spring of 2020 in response to the pandemic. As a result of these discussions, faculty and administration have now a movement to remove traditional grading altogether. *How can we focus on mastery as opposed to achievement against an external standard?* When it was formed, the Teaching and Learning Committee did not intend to change the grading system, but COVID-19 encouraged the committee to think deeply about how our students learn and chart a path forward that makes the most sense academically, socially, and emotionally.

RAPID-CYCLE INQUIRY

Rapid-Cycle Research Design

Goals: To understand the specifical leadership practices and literacies that heads of school used to respond to the COVID-19 pandemic. Closely related to this, we probed heads of school about their previous experiences with crises, including 9/11 and the Great Recession, among others. Finally, we wanted to understand more about the specific technologies and media that heads of schools used to communicate their leadership during the pandemic.

Rapid-cycle data collection

We reached out to heads of school whom we knew from our professional settings. The interviews were semi-structured, and we developed an interview protocol beforehand. Each interview lasted for approximately 30–45 minutes.

Rapid-cycle analysis

We each conducted informal inductive coding and then met to see which patterns we saw in the data to analyze the interviews. From there, we identified themes and then split up the work of writing the articles accordingly. Unfortunately, we did not have time to do member checks with the heads of school we interviewed or other independent school administrators.

Indeed, we are currently living in a world of constant change—one that affords new opportunities for innovation and leadership. Educational leaders should therefore look for opportunities in times of crisis and embrace new modes of communication and new leadership literacies.

Based on our research, we are left with some lingering questions: *What new leadership styles and literacies have emerged as a result of COVID-19? Will these be used after the pandemic is over?* Our research indicates that embodied and relational leadership is paramount and will become even more essential as independent school heads navigate the second wave of infections. What is new about this approach is the context. Now more than ever, heads must demonstrate empathy and understanding but without being there in person.

Furthermore, heads' modes of communication will, arguably, be forever changed. After the pandemic, leaders may record video messages using Loom instead of writing emails to communicate with their communities or plan hybrid meetings where some participants attend in person while others are online. Digital literacies are becoming essential for running an independent school. More research needs to be done to establish what these look like in practice and how heads can incorporate them into their leadership approaches.

REFERENCES

Batiste, H. E. (2012). Toward an understanding of the role of relational trust for new heads of independent schools. Unpublished doctoral dissertation, University of Pennsylvania. ProQuest: UMI 3530065.

Bell, N. D., & Pomerantz, A. (2016). *Humor in the classroom: A guide for language teachers and educational researchers*. Routledge.

Brown, A. M. (2017). *Emergent strategy: Shaping change, shaping worlds*. AK Press.

Eren, N. S., & Ravitch, S. M. (2021). Trauma-informed leadership: Balancing love and accountability. In K. Pak & S. M. Ravitch, *Critical leadership praxis: Leading educational and social change* (pp. 187–200), Teachers College Press.

Fine, M., & Sirin, S. R. (2007). Theorizing hyphenated selves: Researching youth development in and across contentious political contexts. *Social and Personality Psychology Compass 1*, 1–23.

Focht, A., & Ponton, M. (2015). Identifying primary characteristics of servant leadership: Delphi study. *International Journal of Leadership Studies*, 9(1), 44–61.

Hamill, P. (2013). *Embodied leadership: The somatic approach to developing your leadership*. Kogan Page.

Hanson, R. (2018). *Resilient: How to grow an unshakable core of calm, strength, and happiness*. Crown.

Heifetz, R. A., Grashow, A., & Linsky, M. (2009). *The practice of adaptive leadership: Tools and tactics for changing your organization and the world*. Harvard Business Press.

Imad, M. (2020). Trauma-informed teaching and learning. YouTube. April 13, 2020. 57 minutes. http://artjournal.collegeart.org/?p=15236

Johansen, B. (2017). *The new leadership literacies: Thriving in a future of extreme disruption and distributed everything.* Barrett-Koehler.

Petriglieri, G. (2020, April 22). The psychology behind effective crisis leadership. *Harvard Business Review.* https://hbr.org/2020/04/the-psychology-behind-effective-crisis-leadership

Ravitch, S. M. (2020). Why teaching through crisis requires a radical new mindset: Introducing flux pedagogy. *Harvard Business Publishing Education.* https://hbsp.harvard.edu/inspiring-minds/why-teaching-through-crisis-requires-a-radical-new-mindset

Russo, A. (2018). *Feminist accountability: Disrupting violence and transforming power.* New York University Press.

Spillane, J. P., Halverson, R., & Diamond, J. B. (2004). Towards a theory of leadership practice: A distributed perspective. *Journal of Curriculum Studies, 36*(1), 3–34.

Walker, T. (2020). Social-emotional learning should be priority during COVID-19 crisis. http://neatoday.org/2020/04/15/social-emotional-learning-during-covid

CHAPTER 12

Rituals, Routines, and Relationships

High School Athletes and Coaches in Flux

Steve A. Brown

EDITORIAL FRAMING

Flux pedagogy reminds us that we must humanize the learning spaces for and with our students in times of change (Ravitch, 2020). Within this last doctoral candidate chapter, Steve Brown, a champion for student athletics, works to better understand how aspects of student life and learning are impacted for student-athletes. While teaching and learning is an essential component of schools, flux pedagogy reinforces the idea that enacting critical and humanizing pedagogies means we must see schools as holistic ecosystems and communities for students. For many youths, this means seeing school as the place where being elected captain of the varsity soccer team, making the state playoffs for volleyball, and beating the school record in the 500-meter freestyle means everything. Flux pedagogy views classrooms and schools as complex systems of care; ultimately, student passions like sports fall within these systems, and during COVID-19 these rituals were upended. In times of crisis, these stories of how students grapple with these losses or changes cannot be ignored.

During COVID-19, budgets were getting slashed left and right due to the sociopolitical and financial circumstances of the pandemic. Many individuals making resource allocation decisions seemed to forget that students are living out the results of these budgetary decisions and that their overall school experiences will inevitably and powerfully be shaped by these choices and opportunity costs. People making these impactful decisions often do not see the look on student faces when they wear their basketball team jerseys or the look of pride when a student walks out during the school pep rally wearing their school colors. Flux pedagogy reminds us that students are the beating hearts of schools and that it is necessary to pause to explore and identify how students cope with change in a holistic manner. In this chapter, there is a foregrounded commitment to not only search for student-athlete perspectives but to center their voices in more validating and generative ways. This final practitioner-scholar chapter is a reminder that making time for student focus groups, participatory collaboratives, and collective thinking about new decision-making models such as student board members is worth consideration. As Brown makes clear: "While the perspectives of athletic directors remain a central focus during the COVID-19 pandemic, the power of this inquiry is its effort to decenter traditional figures of authority." This chapter reminds us that during crisis, it is worth taking the time to uncover and foreground the stories of students to help us make better decisions on their behalf. These stories of youth, full of wisdom and intentionality, are exactly the data points leaders cannot overlook in times of crisis and ever-evolving change.

INTRODUCTION

Nationally, COVID-19 has adversely impacted recreational and competitive sports both economically and emotionally. This inquiry examines the impact of the pandemic on the experiences of high school student-athletes. To shed light on the nuanced experiences of high school student-athletes, I interviewed high school athletic directors, administrators, coaches, and parents during the spring and summer of 2020. These individuals reside within many social, cultural, economic, geographic, and school contexts— independent/private and public schools in Alabama, California, the District of Columbia, Florida, Georgia, Massachusetts, New York, North Carolina, and Rhode Island. While the perspectives of athletic directors remain a central focus during the COVID-19 pandemic, the power of this inquiry is its effort to decenter traditional figures of authority. To do this, I center student voices, which provide essential insight into how schools might prioritize resources and support for student-athletes now and in the future. The inquiry sought to answer the question, *How does the mindset of student-athletes allow them to respond to sudden shifts in their lives?*

The impact of athletics on American culture has long been evident. The ways that COVID-19 continues to impact sports across the board, then, should not be surprising. Impacts on franchises, colleges, and organizations are not only economically but also emotionally based. Economically, how sports and sports culture bring revenue into communities became increasingly evident when the pandemic halted life as we know it. The absence of tourists, minimal ticket sales, reduced travel, nonexistent league fees, and elusive sports equipment sales all adversely impacted a $19-billion industry (Wood, 2019). Yet, less obvious are the social impacts on athletes— specifically high school athletes—relationships, rituals, and routines (Brown &

Hoins, 2020). The absence of a discussion on the emotionally based impacts of COVID-19 for athletes fuels my passion for inquiry. I approach this work as a former high school and collegiate student-athlete. My positionality provides me with a keen understanding of the commitment required to succeed in the classroom and on the playing field. I carry this interest and aspects of my identity into my doctoral program, which continually challenges me to understand student-athletes and the systems of power that influence them with nuanced criticality.

Through quantitative online surveys and follow-up interviews, student-athletes conveyed mixed feelings toward virtual learning. While many enjoyed a different pace of instruction and the flexibility with completing assignments, athletes also expressed their frustration that not much learning took place. Though there are many reasons for this, athletes specifically identified the impersonal approach to teaching by some instructors. Student-athletes also shared the impact of canceled practices, training sessions, team meetings, and competition seasons. Powerfully, the data indicate that conditions associated with the pandemic often increase student-athletes' motivation to improve in their sports. This motivation occurs through constant reinforcement from various support systems, which play an integral part in student-athletes, well-being when experiencing limited social interaction with peers. Finally, data show that educational leaders must continually reiterate the role that co-curriculars, such as athletics and the performing arts, have on the second half of the school day.

METHODOLOGY AND PROCEDURES

To better understand the lived experiences of high school student-athletes during the spring and summer of 2020, I asked high school athletic directors, administrators, coaches, and parents from independent/private and public schools in Alabama, California, the District of Columbia, Florida, Georgia, Massachusetts, New York, North Carolina, and Rhode Island to help gather student stories. This inquiry employed two instruments: a survey questionnaire (quantitative) and a semi-structured interview protocol (qualitative).

Surveys gathered demographics, sport(s) played, reasons for becoming an athlete, and long-term goals. Open-ended questions focused on life post–COVID-19: the learning of new training methods (if any); difficulties with training; new practices; any changes in their belief in their sense of their ability to succeed; and the impact of the pandemic on their motivation to succeed. I also asked students about their support systems, including parents/guardians, coaches, personal trainers, teammates, and family members.

Of 26 student-athletes, 25 self-identified as male, and one self-identified as female. COVID-19 constrained the sample to our immediate networks. In this case, the data is overwhelmingly skewed male, and future research should investigate how being female and an athlete during COVID-19 presented its own set of unique socioemotional challenges. Across the board, themes began to emerge. Athletes shared the impact of canceled practices, training sessions, team meetings, and competition seasons. As a whole, the group of athletes participated in 10 different sports: baseball, basketball, cheerleading, crew/rowing, football, ice hockey, soccer, swimming, tennis, and track and field. Sevenathletes agreed to follow-up, semi-structured interviews. Vulnerability, through their candid responses added an unexpected level of depth to the data. It was thus imperative to develop rapport and establish credibility with the students to feel comfortable and be authentic in their responses (Bogdan & Biklen, 2007; Maxwell, 2013).

Questions investigated athletes' motivation and initiative, ability to seek out and ask for support, perseverance without the traditional athletic schedule, structures, and facilities, as well as variability in different student-athlete resources and perspectives. In times of constant change and uncertainty, the surveys and conversations also examined the pandemic's emotional impacts on student-athletes' self-efficacy, mindsets, and motivation. Students shared a range of emotions and interpretations of online learning and their time away from school, their teams, and their coaches. Athletes sought to satisfy their physical, emotional, and mental needs on their own, with parents' and coaches' support, in a range of ways. Here, the ways that we understand athlete's difficulties and barriers to asking for help begin to emerge (Gulliver, Griffiths, & Christensen, 2012). Still, adults strived to reach and support these student-athletes through the framework of social support, including emotional, tangible, and informational support (Schaefer, Coyne, & Lazarus, 1982). From this process, generative themes emerged, which are shared below.

VIRTUAL LEARNING: BENEFICIAL TO SOME, NOT TO OTHERS

Two student-athletes with diagnosed learning differences expressed appreciation for the instruction pace that virtual learning and an amended school schedule allowed. One athlete shared that working separately with his tutor during designated times of the school day allowed them to more intentionally talk through important and upcoming writing assignments. It also afforded focused, quality time for a young student-athlete who admittedly expressed his difficulty remaining focused with the multitude of electronics at his disposal. One-on-one time with his tutor seemed easier to schedule with the new, flexible school day.

> For me, it wasn't too hard. My tutor did stay in contact with me, and she would ask me whenever there would be a big project coming up or anything like big assignments writing-wise. We would like schedule a time after school, like during the tutorial time, to see her . . . like have an hour where we'd sit down and kind of walk each other through (the) Google Docs, or anything like that. So, it wasn't too hard. Um, it wasn't like bad. And for me, I have a hard time focusing when there is a lot of electronics around me. I mean, that was the only thing that was a little bit limiting or not limiting, but like, challenging for me to stay on top of it. —12th-grader

Another student-athlete, also diagnosed with learning differences, talked about how he appreciated the longer built-in breaks of the laidback virtual schedule. These longer breaks contrasted the experiences of his peers at neighboring schools, who maintained their same schedule online as if everyone was physically present on campus.

His assessment of schools trying to mimic a full day's schedule in front of the computer screen was "brutal." In this way, schools underestimated how campus variables—changing locations from one period to the next, interacting in hallways with peers en route to class, experiencing the scenery both inside and outside of the building—broke up the monotony of sitting in front of and staring at a computer screen in the same setting for hours. Maintaining a regular schedule with the same focus and enthusiasm while virtual during a crisis is both an uncaring and unrealistic ask for anyone, especially a teenager.

> Personally, I love the whole online learning thing. I mean, I preferred to be around my classmates and my friends at school talking with them every day, but besides that and missing baseball in the spring . . . that's the only two things I was really missing because to me, we started Advisory at 8:30 a.m. I was able to wake up at 8:25 a.m., I mean roll out of bed, brush my teeth, and go sit in front of a computer screen; and it was good too because everyone (else) had just woken up, and it was like expecting anything differently than just fresh out of bed. We sat through our three classes. If you needed to go to tutorial, you could go to tutorial after class if you scheduled an appointment with a teacher. Then it was just kind of naptime for about an hour, and then (I'd) wake up, go hit (batting practice), come back, and do homework. And that was really what it was for however long we did (virtual) for a month or two. So, I mean, I personally loved it.
> I thought the teachers did a really good job not piling on a bunch of stuff, um because they knew sitting in front of the computer screen like that was hard. I mean, like the three classes were not that bad, but then we knew we'd come back and do homework later in the

night. I mean, I know schools like Bennett, Wilson, and Michaels (pseudonyms), their schedules were brutal. My girlfriend, I mean, she got to wake up at like the same time kind of sort of, but she, I mean, her (classes) started like at 9 a.m., we started at 8:30 a.m., but they were not done until like 2 p.m. or something like that. They were like an hour-long class, 5-minute break, hour class. Like lunch, was like 30–40 minutes. It was a full day basically in front of the computer. —11th-grader

Not all students agreed, however, that the virtual experience benefited their learning. Two student-athletes and the parents of two additional student-athletes, attending schools in different states, expressed that teachers guaranteed a student's overall grade would not be negatively impacted when the pandemic forced schools to go virtual through graduation. Students and parents alike voiced that teachers would communicate the assignment and the student was only required to turn it in by a designated time (i.e., end of the class period, for example). For many, this was the extent of their class instruction.

Further, athletes expressed their struggle to adjust to the lack of rigor and standards in their curricula. Some students said that merely turning the assignment in on time helped them improve by one letter grade. One parent shared their frustration that though their child was earning all A's in his classes before the pandemic, there was no incentive to continue doing schoolwork for the remaining 2 to 3 months left in the academic year. Instead, this child's parent was forced to find supplemental material outside of class to keep engagement levels high. One student-athlete expressed his wish for greater accessibility to teachers, for questions and discussions about the assignments, in student-friendly ways:

I feel like they handled it (online learning) better. Well, as best as they could, because I mean, everything was so sudden, um, one thing that I wish that some of my teachers could have done would be probably following up with students about questions on assignments and projects. —11th-grader

Another student expressed the following:

Well, first off, they made it so that we just went on to online learning . . . they made it so our grades could not drop. They could only go up. So, that made it easier to get (better grades). I went from having like, a C, an A, and a B to having a B, an A, and an A. (I) got all A's and a B because of that. But then also, there was way less information. It was hard to learn stuff . . . No, like, I passed everything, even in my Chemistry class at the end I got it up to a B, but like if someone were to quiz me on this stuff, I would not pass it. I just got the information and put it in. —10th-grader

This impersonal approach to learning frustrated many student-athletes and their parents. Administrators and school leaders were generally unaware of this lack of instruction because many were trying to maintain teacher morale and make it to the end of the school year while also reducing the number of positive cases in their school buildings and on their respective campuses. The few administrators I spoke with expressed the inconsistency of accountability toward basic teaching techniques. They could not confirm or deny that some teachers' shortcomings existed during a unique and hectic time.

MOTIVATION AND INITIATIVE:
INCENTIVIZED BY MORE TIME TO TRAIN

One of the open-ended survey questions asked, "How has COVID-19 and school closures affected your motivation to succeed at your sport?" Forty-two percent of the respondents expressed that this experience improved their motivation to work harder. These student-athletes attributed the renewed desire to be better to have more time to train:

It has greatly improved it, as I have had time to think about what is truly important to me. It has increased my desire to return to the sport and work hard.

My motivation has only increased. I have a once in a lifetime opportunity to train with no school to interfere.

Helped, I have gotten better at my sport while training at home than I would have at school.

Student-athletes spoke of how increased flexibility in the day (without school serving as a barrier now) allowed them to work out daily, often multiple times a day. Every student-athlete mentioned the support they received from parents, coaches, and personal trainers.

I don't like want to let my teammates down. I want to be able to go out and work harder or like just as hard or harder than all of them and push them because I want our team to be great. I don't want to be that the weak link. —10th-grader

Competition for playing time within the ranks of one's team caused many of these athletes to continue to strive to get better to either maintain their starting position or earn one. Athletes commented on not wanting to let their teammates down, wanting to be the best they could be, and wishing to perform at their highest capability. Admirable is an athlete's ability to compartmentalize tumultuous experiences through understanding the temporality of difficult situations. As a former athlete, I leaned into Dr. Norman Vincent Peale's *Power of Positive Thinking* (1952) to get through injury, setbacks, and difficult times while competing. Moreover, the idea of positive thinking resonated with the young people I interviewed. Their outlooks, full of hope and inspiration, translated an athletics mentality to the pandemic. They vocalized their beliefs that this situation will improve and that we will return to normalcy. When we do, they will be ready! Through an understanding of this mentality, we begin to comprehend and recognize that this is a natural segue to discuss the importance of support systems in youth resilience.

NEED FOR A CONSISTENT, STRONG SUPPORT SYSTEM

When examining support systems, I utilized social support as a multidimensional construct, divided into different types. Schaefer and colleagues (1982) describe three functions of social support: emotional support, tangible support, and informational support.

> *Emotional support* is to feel loved and cared for, which one achieves through reliance and confidence in other persons.
> *Tangible support* involves more direct aid through loans, gifts, driving one to venues, and so forth.
> *Informational support* is when one provides information or advice and gives feedback to the athlete.

"To perform well," researchers concluded, "athletes, and especially adolescent athletes without much experience, must recognize and manage competitive and organizational demands constantly, as well as recognize and use the social resources available to them." In our follow-up interviews, the students I spoke with talked about the benefits of having their parents driving them to training venues (*tangible*), reminding the student-athlete to believe in themselves, and always asking "how I [the student-athlete] was feeling" (*emotional*). Coaches had regular Zoom meetings to check-in with their student-athletes, provide virtual workouts, and even competitions (*informational*). One high school student involved with his crew/rowing team spoke of having competitions against a university team in the United Kingdom on the erg machine. These innovative alternatives kept these student-athletes' identities intact and helped them to feel good about themselves. Most important, support networks remind athletes they are not alone during times of crisis.

DISCOVERIES AND TAKEAWAYS

At the start of the 2020–2021 academic year, our school and many of the schools these student-athletes attended researched and implemented a protocol for limited school opening if/when possible. Administrators described various benefits to learning virtually. Among them were alternative opportunities for meetings with colleagues, added flexibility for additional tutorial sessions outside and during class time, and creative ways to stream athletic competitions and practices to possible college recruiters, parents, and other family members. Yet they still recognize the need for personal interaction for humans' social well-being.

One student-athlete expressed his disdain for school. Not because he did not care or appreciate his teachers. For him, school, in its most traditional sense, felt like something he was forced to do. The ways we instill in our youth linear knowledge dissemination to prepare students for future endeavors compounds resentment. An 11-grade crew/rowing athlete spoke of the ways that mundane, memorized instruction and stoic classroom settings contribute to frustration with school attendance:

> The bleak nature of attending classes from 8 o'clock to 3 o'clock followed by 3 to 5 hours of homework takes a toll on the teenage psyche. Personally, rowing gives me something to look forward to after the bell rings at 2:45. It is a break between the mindless workloads we're told to endure from age 5 until our late 20s, and all of it just for the slight chance of success in adulthood. The meaning of athletics stretches far beyond just existing as an extracurricular to write down on a college application. Athletics are an escape from a world where numbers on paper judge kids. Athletics care for the real physical student instead of the name on a transcript. After reading what I had just stated on athletics, you may ask me: What is the meaning of athletics to you once the academic aspect is removed? Athletics become a place to bond with teammates and nurture the inner-competitive spirit. It teaches kids to physically push themselves after they have told themselves they have nothing left. I believe athletics to be critical in the development of teenagers. That's why I row. —11th-grader

Youth are our teachers now. They know how to engage in and live out flux. We can learn from and with them while also supporting them through ongoing questions and challenges they will inevitably confront.

RAPID-CYCLE INQUIRY

Goals: To examine the impact COVID-19 has had on high school student-athletes' experience. As a former student-athlete in high school and college, I fully understand the commitment required to succeed in both the classroom and on the playing field. The inquiry sought to answer the question, How does the mindset of student-athletes allow them to respond to sudden shifts in their lives?

Rapid-cycle data collection

1. The online survey (quantitative) lasts about 10–15 minutes and was sent to high school student-athletes in seven states: 25 males and 1 female participants, representing 10 athletic disciplines, from football to cheerleading.
2. Semi-structured interviews lasted 30–45 minutes. Of the 26 students-athletes who completed the online survey, seven elected to complete a follow-up interview.

REFERENCES

Bogdan, R., & Biklen, S. (2007). *Qualitative research for education: An introduction to theory and methods.* Allyn and Bacon.

Brown, S., & Hoins, K. (2020). Rituals, routines and relationships: High school athletes and coaches in flux. *Penn GSE Perspectives on Urban Education.* https://urbanedjournal.gse.upenn.edu/archive/volume-18-issue-1-fall-2020/rituals-routines-and-relationships-high-school-athletes-and

Gulliver, A., Griffiths, K. M., & Christensen, H. (2012). Barriers and facilitators to mental health help-seeking for young elite athletes: A qualitative study. *BMC Psychiatry, 12*(1), 1–14.

Maxwell, J. (2013). Qualitative research design: An interactive approach. *Applied Social Research Methods, 41,* 90–96.

Peale, N. (1952). *The power of positive thinking: A practical guide to mastering the problems of everyday living.* Prentice-Hall.

Ravitch, S. M. (2020). Why teaching through crisis requires a radical new mindset: Introducing flux pedagogy. *Harvard Business Publishing Education.* https://hbsp.harvard.edu/inspiring-minds/why-teaching-through-crisis-requires-a-radical-new-mindset

Schaefer, C., Coyne, J., & Lazarus, R. (1982). The health-related functions of social support. *International Journal of Behavioral Medicine, 4,* 381–406.

U.S. Government Accountability Office (2017). K–12 education: High school sports access and participation. www.gao.gov/assets/gao-17-754r.pdf

Wood, L. (2019). Youth sports: Market shares, strategies and forecasts, worldwide, 2019–2026. Wintergreen Research, Inc. https://apnews.com/press-release/pr-businesswire/76a1e6e0c8ea421987a1f5ded46e589a

CHAPTER 13

Story-Based Frameworks and Practices for Educational Change

Sharon M. Ravitch and Chloe Alexandra Kannan

FLUX PEDAGOGY AND LEADERSHIP FOR CHANGE

While COVID-19 was a moment of entry for these conversations and ideas, the 25 students in the Mid-Career doctoral program clamored for frameworks and tools that could translate diversity, equity, and inclusion into action for their schools and districts. Even before the pandemic crisis of COVID-19, educational leaders constantly experienced unforeseen—sometimes unwelcomed—change. After COVID-19, we know that rapid change is here to stay. Alston (2005) reminds us that the ever-evolving changes and rapid flux our educational leaders contend with reside within larger sociopolitical forces around race, class, gender, and injustice. School demographics continue to evolve rapidly, budgets are slashed, communities are still caught in the middle of polarizing views on education, and leaders are continually pressured to make decisions on decontextualized data provided by outside sources.

Flux pedagogy, discussed in Chapter 2, is an actionable framework for humanizing and equitable learning to transpire within school ecosystems. To support this pedagogical shift, we argue that flux leadership must be exercised to allow for flux pedagogy to become a living and breathing force in schools. An educational leadership framework, flux leadership guides leaders in making humanizing and culturally responsive decisions in times of rapid change. Flux leadership offers mindsets, frames, and practices that support responsiveness to emergent school and community needs and help leaders humanize every aspect of school. This mindset and its corresponding strategies also provide an approach to capturing real-time, contextualized data in ways that promote long-lasting educational change and uplift stakeholders.

As these leader-led inquiry chapters illustrate, educational leaders need frames, approaches, and supports to make sense of new realities. Specifically, it is crucial to employ tools and frameworks that can grapple with how new realities implicate leadership, teachers, staff, communities, and colleagues, and for the field of education as a whole. Educational leaders must be willing to counter the deep structural inequity, hyper-individualism, greed, and neoliberal transactionalism of the U.S. education system—with its sidestepping of racial equality and systematic marginalization and dehumanization of Black, Brown, Indigenous, and Asian students and communities—by leaning into constructively critical, transformational leadership, and pedagogical approaches (Love, 2019). In these moments, in both educational leadership research and practice, we need models that help leaders feel willing and able to consider and approach these complexities in new ways and provide alternatives in how to think about leadership in crisis and times of radical flux.

Radical flux also demands a reorientation to how we view teaching and learning as a humanizing endeavor rather than one focused merely on transactional gains. Flux pedagogy engages in this reorientation by centering engagements like healing-centered, trauma-informed pedagogy and balancing radical compassion for students (and teachers) (Eren & Ravitch, 2021; Russo, 2018). This multifaceted moment—and all the ones to come—necessitate that leader build new mindsets and skills for inspiring transformative pedagogy and the co-construction of dialogic spaces to make sense of crisis moments toward more equitable organizational development. Equally important to creating the conditions for flux pedagogy to flourish within classrooms and learning spaces, flux leadership brings humanizing and contextualized decision-making to the forefront. In doing so, it acknowledges an urgency for educational leaders to utilize everything in their toolbox to make data-driven decisions that are bespoke to, and best for, their school communities. Flux leadership, like flux pedagogy, integrates relational and critical pedagogy frameworks into a humanizing and contextualized leadership approach. It's constructivist, adaptive, and reflexive; it is a humanizing framework that helps leaders examine the systems and processes of schooling toward the goal of fomenting transformative teaching and learning. Flux leaders support their teachers in enacting flux pedagogy—teacher pedagogy cultivated in and for adaptive, responsive, racially literate, critical inquiry mindsets and ecosystems.

Flux leadership, discussed in Chapter 3, is guided by the belief that stories are an under-utilized and vitally important set of data points that can and must guide school improvement, whether in moments of change or crisis. While school improvement has often been guided by the stringent demands imposed on educational leaders, flux leaders ask whether other data points can guide schools forward during times of imminent change and through crisis. And every day. They might ask: What insights can be gained from the long-standing members of our communities healing from decades of racial injustice in their neighborhoods? How are students experiencing this moment? What is happening that no survey or standardized test can tell us?

Utilizing insights from stories is not a novel concept. Educational leaders can—and we argue, must—create the collaborative groundwork to build spaces where stakeholders can feel safe sharing their stories authentically.

Flux leaders do not engage in their leadership practices alone. They engage a radical leadership approach that requires and relies on distributive wisdom to shape fundamental school improvement decisions. This collective and relational approach is generative as it pertains to organizational learning. Flux leadership centralizes shared wisdom to support the enactment of culturally responsive schooling structures and classroom processes, emergent design curriculum, resonant communication structures for meetings and learning spaces, and maximally supportive professional development. Inquiry-based learning allows for a range of knowledges and kinds of expertise to be uplifted and amplified in these environments. Through inquiry-based learning in school contexts such as professional development and family engagement, the approach challenges top-down hierarchies regarding decisions around teaching, learning, and leading.

RAPID-CYCLE INQUIRY

The rapid-cycle inquiries in this book illuminate the expansive possibilities of story-based inquiry processes enacted within spaces that allow flux pedagogy and flux leadership to flourish. The leader-authored chapters (Chapters 4–12) constitute counter-narratives to top-down narratives that deficitize students and teachers of color, flatten identity complexity, and make growth, healing, and belonging secondary to transactional goals like efficiency, standardization, and strict measurement. These leaders enacted collaborative rapid-cycle inquiry during crisis to story the gaps in information they needed to serve their stakeholders and other educational communities that could benefit in the best ways possible during unimaginable suffering. Rapid-cycle inquiry became a collaborative data-driven mechanism for these leaders to make responsive decisions for and with stakeholders in real time.

As Chapter 4 describes, the educational leaders at the heart of this book were new doctoral students in an executive leadership research seminar when COVID-19 hit. Rapid-cycle inquiry became a collaborative method of story-based inquiry, used in real time to answer emergent questions and surface stories traditionally silenced or erased in their contexts (Chapter 5). Alongside the rapid-cycle inquiries that explore what happened to educational stakeholders during the pandemic, we present Chapters 2 and 3 as well as editorial framings of each of the subsequent chapters to capture how flux pedagogy and flux leadership were employed as equity-oriented frameworks in order to support leaders in their work. We fundamentally argue that inquiry-based storytelling approaches, such as rapid-cycle inquiry in this book, are models for how educational leaders can begin to think about gathering data to inform their own contextualized decision-making. Appendixes A–D offer process considerations and templates to begin your own rapid-cycle inquiry processes.

The individual and collective power of these place-based stories humbles us and fundamentally requires cultivating the conditions for brave spaces to flourish in order for stakeholders to feel safe to share their stories on behalf of educational change. While rapid-cycle inquiry can be crucial for data gathering in schools, it cannot happen without flux pedagogy and flux leadership. A sole and narrow focus on data without humanizing the educational context could lead to disastrous outcomes for schools. Flux pedagogy and flux leadership provide better and long-lasting alternatives for considering the purposes of data and school improvement by shifting the focus: *What can story provide to understanding where we are and how we move forward? How can we create the conditions to gather story-based data in humanizing ways on behalf of educational progress and change?*

As a living leadership framework, flux leadership assists leaders in cultivating the kinds of story-based inquiry and brave-space work that school communities need to enact now more than ever. These inquiry-based stories, and the storytelling processes that elicit them, renew a commitment to institutional justice born through shared critical inquiry, constructive critique, and intentional reflection in/on practice. In the service of equality, today's school leaders must critically examine their mindsets, implicit beliefs, and internalized knowledge hierarchies in actionable ways and help those around them do the same. Without this, these stories cannot be unearthed in ways that are ethical and sustaining. Creating brave spaces in order to support inquiry-based story work requires leader reflexivity: critically reading and adjusting self in real time with disciplined, curious, and compassionate humility. *Brave-space inquiry* is at the heart of this work and requires disrupting the power dynamics as we inquire into a bolder and more equitable futures for our students.

As discussed in Chapters 1, 2, and 3, taking an inquiry stance (Cochran-Smith & Lytle, 2009), foundational to flux pedagogy (Ravitch, 2020), requires that practitioners embody a reflexive learning stance on identity, mindsets, practices, and the contexts—near and far, personal and societal—that shape practices in organizations. As each chapter illuminates, rapid-cycle inquiry helps leaders to understand normative knowledge hierarchies critically and make room for more equitable education possibilities. Working from an inquiry stance means that leaders show up as reflective, curious, and engaged learners who engage in humble inquiry about their mission mode (Schein, 2013) rather than as unilateral experts. This intentional shift in power dynamics around expertise, when leaders centralize the wisdom of everyone around them and leverage shared wisdom to push into knowledge hierarchies, constitutes a *distributive wisdom approach*. In a distributive wisdom approach, all wisdoms are foregrounded, brought into the conversation, and hybridized. Co-creating intentional processes for individual and shared knowledge generation elevates everyone in school communities, as we see in Chapters 8 and 9. Educational leaders must create the conditions—through enacting brave-space inquiry—for people to be agentic in sharing their perspectives, experiences, ideas, and concerns, as doing so is vital for learning, healthy development, and positive educational experiences and outcomes (Khalifa, 2018; Ravitch, 2020).

WHY WE NEED TO STORY THE GAPS IN EDUCATION

As the leader-authored chapters make clear, school communities—alongside those who lead and teach in them—must learn how to story the gaps in schools and classrooms. As we see in Chapters 6 and 7, the political nature of schooling creates these gaps in contextualized information, assets-based understanding, and humanizing pedagogy. As these chapters elucidate, one powerful antidote to missing critical information and actionable contextual understanding is storytelling. When situated as an enactment of a brave-space inquiry stance, storytelling helps organizations to become communities of practice engaged in shared inquiry, reflection, and meaning-making, as seen in Chapters 10 and 11. As storytelling through inquiry processes is introduced in schools, leaders should be attentive to the long oral traditions of Indigenous peoples, BIPOC communities, as discussed in Chapter 1.

Story-based inquiry is transformational for leaders, teachers, and school communities. It provides a framework for schools to engage in the most critical tenets of storytelling by centrally acknowledging unequal power dynamics in school communities marked by race, class, gender, religion, culture, and other identity intersections. Further, story-based inquiry allows for the centering of equitable process and communication norms. When enacted with critical attention to issues of equity and identity, as we see in Chapter 8, story-based inquiry offers possibilities for restorative learning and growth, the building of personal and group authenticity and resiliency, self-learning, relational learning, and world learning. Stories, when engaged within a brave-space inquiry stance, as we see in Chapter 5, become a pedagogical and relational portal into contextually engaged insight generation and knowledge production, as well as racial socialization and positive identity and history affirmation (Stevenson, 2014).

As discussed in Chapter 1, a *brave-space inquiry stance* is an intentional approach to cultivating intra- and interpersonal awareness, racial literacy, and actionable communicative accountability, and radical compassion for oneself and others (Ravitch, 2020) by learning into experiences through stories. Storytelling within a brave-space inquiry process helps leaders create the conditions for critical examination of our belief systems and the broader social, cultural, political, and structural forces and narratives that shape them (Solórzano & Yosso, 2002). When situated within brave spaces, story-based inquiry offers a means of learning, confirming, and contesting reality. Through intentional storytelling processes, leaders learn to identify, reflect on, examine and re-examine experiences, histories, and values (Khalifa, 2018). Finally, as we see in Chapter 5, intentional storytelling processes help leaders examine how context and history inform thought and behavior patterns in both visible and tacit ways in the daily life of students, teachers, and school communities (Solórzano & Yosso, 2002).

There is an ethical imperative for educational leaders to fill existing gaps of understanding with meaningful and contextualized data rather than top-down metrics, especially in moments of crisis and ever-changing classroom, school, and district conditions. There are tremendous equity gaps in who is heard—often, it is not practitioners; more often, it is not even students, as we see in Chapter 5, on a racial and social class bias. As we see in Chapters 10 and 11, even educational leaders are often not heard, given the primacy placed on academic versions and visions of leadership has made more authentic leader narratives hard to find (Pak & Ravitch, 2021).

CONCLUSION: BRAVE-SPACE LEADERSHIP
FOR EQUITABLE CHANGE

In an educational landscape where school leaders are bombarded with so-called experts who dictate school improvement priorities, the voices of children and teachers and other important stakeholders are often silenced or missing from strategic priorities that shape teaching and learning, as Chapter 5 makes clear. In these times of ever-evolving change, we must all work to center these voices for data-driven school improvement. The act of utilizing stories as a crucial data point for strategic initiatives, as we see in Chapter 5, works to humanize data and provide the pathway for leaders to make data-driven decisions rooted in context and actual need and resource.

Brave-space leadership is a key driver of flux leadership because it supports leaders in gathering and immediately analyzing authentic data from stakeholders. The other seven tenets of the flux leadership model must be exercised regularly for a leader to create the conditions for this space to operate and flourish. Additionally, the cultivation of brave spaces requires leader and group bravery as well as ongoing leader modeling and engagement. These processes create spaces where people feel comfortable enough to discuss educational, social, and group-dynamic issues in ways beyond what is typically discussed. This pivot is particularly necessary when identity-privilege-based norms, so-called "safe spaces," marginalize people of color and undermine equality in groups (Arao & Clemens, 2013; Ravitch & Carl, 2019). Brave-space leaders use these spaces to gather data in the form of people's stories for school improvement and decision-making.

Storying the gap requires research methods rooted in the practitioner context—attentive to educational leaders who are on the frontlines doing this work alongside their communities. In times of rapid change or emergent crisis, data-driven school improvement must have tools and methods that leaders and educators can utilize quickly and humanely. These tools must be attentive to the dimensions of power that circulate within a school setting and braid the sociopolitical in a manner that feels ethical. As discussed in Chapter 1, rapid-cycle inquiry is a collaborative method and process. This inquiry approach is generative because individuals from various stakeholder positions engage in the inquiry work—generating questions, collecting stories within brave spaces, and engaging in collaborative data analysis. This method also fully acknowledges that time is a constraining factor for practitioners on the ground, especially in times of rapid change.

Rapid-cycle inquiry leverages the power of stories as data that can help leaders engage in collaborative decision-making that is better contextualized to the moment. *Flux Leadership: Real-Time Inquiry for Humanizing Educational Change* offers alternatives for thinking about data in school improvement, as standard metrics are not always the answer. The leaders centralized in this volume knew essential voices must be heard to create effective initiatives and policies in real time. In order to do so, they examined emerging questions and realities arising in their contexts by employing rapid-cycle inquiry through a collaborative approach from start to finish. Most important, leaders were able to use tenets of flux leadership to create brave spaces for their stakeholders in order for them to share their stories in ways that felt humanizing and authentic.

While rapid-cycle inquiries are by no means a replacement for other data-collection methods in schools, this approach combats deficit perspectives through surfacing the complexity in people's lives and wisdoms they possess, which can shape school initiatives for the better. Flux leadership centers the humanity of leaders and the people they lead through engaging story-based inquiry processes like rapid-cycle inquiry. We hope that both flux pedagogy and flux leadership can create the brave-space leadership spaces that schools have been searching for in times of change. We also hope these models and corresponding narratives prompt educational leaders to enact and support these approaches within their sites of practice to affect equitable and humanizing educational change.

As we close, we return to Arundhati Roy's (2020) "The Pandemic Is a Portal," which inspires us to continue to unlearn and remake forward in times of change in transformation:

> Historically, pandemics have forced humans to break with the past and imagine their world anew. This one is no different. It is a portal, a gateway between one world and the next. We can choose to walk through it, dragging the carcasses of

our prejudice and hatred, our avarice, our data banks, and dead ideas, our dead rivers, and smoky skies behind us. Or we can walk through lightly, with little luggage, ready to imagine another world. And ready to fight for it.

We must work together to affirm, converge, and amplify our individual and collective stories, spheres of influence, and wisdoms as we shake the knowledge tree of education down to its socially reproductive, deficit-oriented, top-down-policy roots. Together, we must work to rebuild education as a practice of freedom (hooks, 1994)—the generative convergence of liberatory policies, stories and critical inquiries, and humanizing practices. This convergence is the promise and the hope of equitable education and schooling. The time is now. Let's learn together.

REFERENCES

Alston, J. A. (2005). Tempered radicals and servant leaders: Black females persevering in the superintendency. *Educational Administration Quarterly, 41*(4), 675–688.

Arao, B., & Clemens, K. (2013). From safe spaces to brave spaces. In L. Landreman, (Ed.), *The art of effective facilitation: Reflections from social justice educators* (pp. 135–150). Stylus.

Cochran-Smith, M., & Lytle, S. (2009). Teacher research as stance. In G. Anderson, and K. Herr, (Eds.), *The SAGE handbook of educational action research* (pp. 39–49). Sage.

Eren, N. S., & Ravitch, S. M. (2021). Trauma-informed leadership: Balancing love and accountability. In K. Pak and S. M. Ravitch (Eds.), *Critical leadership praxis: Leading educational and social change* (pp. 187–200). Teachers College Press.

hooks, b. (1994). Confronting class in the classroom. In A. Darder, M. P. Baltodano, and R. D. Torres (Eds.), *The critical pedagogy reader* (pp. 142–150). Routledge.

Khalifa, M. (2018). *Culturally responsive school leadership*. Race and Education Series. Harvard Education Press.

Love, B. L. (2019). *We want to do more than survive: Abolitionist teaching and the pursuit of educational freedom*. Beacon Press.

Pak, K., & Ravitch, S. M. (Eds.). (2021). *Critical leadership praxis for educational and social change*. Teachers College Press.

Ravitch, S. M. (2020). "Flux leadership: Leading for justice and peace in & beyond COVID-19." *Penn GSE Perspectives on Urban Education, 18*(1).

Ravitch, S. M., & Carl, M. N. (2019). *Applied research for sustainable change: A guide for education leaders*. Harvard Education Press.

Ravitch, S. M., & Carl, M. N. (2019). *Applied research for sustainable change: A guide for education leaders*. Harvard Education Press.

Roy, A. (2020). The pandemic is a portal. *Financial Times, 3*(4).

Russo, A. (2018). *Feminist accountability: Disrupting violence and transforming power*. New York University Press.

Schein, E. (2013). *Humble inquiry: The gentle art of asking instead of telling.* Berrett-Koehler Publishers.

Solórzano, D. G., & Yosso, T. J. (2002). Critical race methodology: Counter-storytelling as an analytical framework for education research. *Qualitative Inquiry, 8*(1), 23–44.

Stevenson, H. (2014). *Promoting racial literacy in schools: Differences that make a difference.* Teachers College Press.

Rapid-Cycle Inquiry Framing and Process Template

RAPID-CYCLE INQUIRY: FRAMING

Who can do rapid-cycle inquiry?

Rapid-cycle inquiry is for leaders, teachers, students, staff, parents, and communities. Anyone can engage in these processes, in which equitable representation is a goal. This real-time inquiry method supports the cultivation of person-centered organizational learning and humanizing processes in schools. *Flux pedagogy* creates the conditions for knowledge to flourish in humanizing ways, whereas *flux leadership* creates the conditions for leaders to enact equitable education through leading and creating the conditions for story-based inquiry.

What constitutes data?

Traditional modes of research limit the generative possibilities of applying real-time, story-based data into practice. The rapid-cycle inquiry process makes this possible. Rapid-cycle inquiry creates the conditions to gather data in the form of stories that are often silenced, missing, or flattened; it brings stakeholders together to make meaning in ways that guide decisions, programming, and practice in schools, classrooms, or groups.

Possible data sources in rapid-cycle inquiry are numerous. Since data need to be contextual within a school or classroom, *stories are centered as the primary form of data.* As a first step, ask: *What narratives can inform existing data? What everyday processes and experiences generate data useful to rapid-cycle learning processes?*

Why are brave-space norms important?

In rapid-cycle inquiry, data are collected within the brave-space tenet of flux leadership and analyzed collaboratively within the brave-space tenet of flux pedagogy. Because of the nature of these data, traditional analysis is not adequate. A brave-space analysis is needed to expose how realities are circumscribed by structural, societal, and organizational biases and discrimination. This is essential because of the hierarchy of voice in schools. The purpose of this method is to gather vital data for equity in times of rapid change.

What does the process look like?

Following is a template you can use to map your own rapid-cycle inquiry process. In the section on data collection below, choose among these possible data sources based on the goals, resources, and bespoke contextual factors. It is not necessary or even advisable to do them all; choose the ones most generative to the issues at hand. The process is laid out below.

RAPID-CYCLE INQUIRY: PROCESS TEMPLATE

Rapid-cycle research design

    a. Goal or problem of practice (e.g., to understand student stress)
    b. Issue/s addressing in real time (i.e., critical context and action questions)
    c. Existing knowledge, rapid-cycle literature search (i.e., Google scholar)
    d. Equitable representation (i.e., identities, roles, experiences, perspectives)

Rapid-cycle data collection within the principles of flux leadership

    a. Rapid-cycle interviews
    b. Rapid-cycle storytelling
    c. Rapid-cycle focus groups
    d. Rapid-cycle observational field notes
    e. Rapid-cycle surveys
    f. Rapid-cycle participatory methods: Photovoice, multimodal data elicitation, priority/resource/need/issue/crisis mapping
    g. Existing data (e.g., documents, artifacts, social media)
    h. Data students and teachers produce (e.g., lesson plans, student work, free-writes, portfolios)

Rapid-cycle data analysis within the principles of flux pedagogy brave-space work

    a. Rapid-cycle participant validation/member checks (data validity)
    b. Rapid-cycle data reads

   c. Rapid-cycle data visualization
   d. Rapid-cycle thematic analysis and discovery
   e. Rapid-cycle meaning-making session

Rapid-cycle knowledge sharing and dissemination

   a. Rapid-cycle discovery debriefs
   b. Rapid-cycle dissemination across channels (e.g., newsletters, town halls, reports, social media)
   c. Rapid-cycle process for equitable stakeholder engagement (i.e., participatory methods, brave-space norms for dialogue)
   d. Rapid-cycle participatory feedback loops (i.e., for stakeholder groups)
   e. Designated messengers representing stakeholder and social identity groups

Rapid-Cycle Inquiry Design Process Template

Goal or Problem of Practice	• What is the primary goal of this inquiry? • What does the inquiry seek to improve or rectify? • Why is this goal/topic important and to whom? • How could this inquiry improve pedagogy, practice, experience?
Guiding Inquiry Questions	• What are the guiding inquiry questions? • How do these guiding questions reflect the goals of the inquiry? • What do these questions suggest to intended changes/outcomes?
Existing Knowledge	• What does the team already know/need to know about the topic? • What documents, data, or resources already exist? Will we need to collect? • What wisdom and expertise exists in the group? In the setting overall? How do we build on this? Tap into it?
Connection to Existing Data and Policies	• How/does the inquiry build on/inform existing data points? • How does the inquiry relate to organizational policies, culture, values? • How can the inquiry explain existing metrics/data?
Methods	• What data sources and collection methods does the team plan to use? • How will data be recorded? (e.g., interviews recorded by Otter.ai) • How will these methods be sequenced? • Who is responsible for the forest and the trees of data collection? • How can we analyze together through a brave-space process?
Participants	• Who will be included as participants in the inquiry? Not included? How and why are these decisions made? • What processes will the team take to protect confidentiality? • How will people's pain or struggle be affirmed?
Validity	• What will the team do to ensure their findings are accurate? • What are ways to resist imposing interpretations or desired outcomes? • How can data analysis be collaborative? Generative?

Time and Resources	• How can this inquiry be most effectively accomplished? • What resources are needed to ensure its success? • How can the process be incorporated into existing structures? (e.g., team meetings and professional development)
Action Plans	• Where does the team see the potential for informed action? • Who are the different stakeholders and audiences of the inquiry? • Who should be involved throughout? In dissemination?
Timeline	• What is the timeline for conducting the inquiry? Sharing the findings? Using the findings? Is adequate time built in to check in with participants on accuracy of the analysis and findings?

Team Selection Considerations for Rapid-Cycle Inquiry

Goals and Topics	• What is the topic or issue is focus? • Why is this topic important and for whom? • What are the different social identities and roles/perspectives to include on the inquiry team? • What individuals in the school, community, and/or elsewhere should be on the inquiry team? • Why them? Why not others?
Organizational Equity Factors	• How do we achieve equitable representation? What does that mean in our context? • Who are the influential voices on this topic? • What kinds of influence do they have and why? Should they be on the team? Why/why not? • What resistance might there be to this topic in general? • How can we understand resistance from multiple perspectives and vantage points? • What are primary equity considerations as we begin the inquiry? To consider throughout the process? • Whose experiences and perspectives are left out, unheard, or marginalized? How can they be pulled into the team and/or participant pool?
Basic Considerations: Size and Time	• What is an ideal size for the inquiry team so it is small enough to be efficient and representative? • Is there a dedicated time that all these individuals can meet? When and for how long? Should subgroups be organized that way? Focused on tasks related to the inquiry process? • Do any individuals have knowledge of practitioner inquiry or qualitative methods? Access to people who do? Is there a university partnership in place to offer support? • What range of roles, perspectives, and social identities need to be included and why?

Skills and Resources	• What skills should members of the inquiry team have? • Is there a person familiar with research approaches, skilled in facilitation, organizational development, dissemination? Are there people who have strong emotional intelligence to foster effective team dynamics? Brave-space pedagogy? Trauma-informed approaches? • What other skills do we need to pull this off effectively? • What resources can we use for the development of research skills? (e.g., video tutorials, quick lessons from team members)

Existing Educational Data in Schools

(With thanks to Dr. Torch Lytle)

Data	Examples
Student	• Student demographic data • Enrollment and attendance records • Report cards, progress reports, evaluation reports • Portfolios, transcripts • Discipline records • Attendance records • Student assignments (e.g., class work, homework) • Student proficiency scores • Standardized test scores (SAT, ACT, ERB) • Student growth on assessments • Disability/special education accommodations • Individualized Educational Plan (IEP) data and meeting minutes • 504 accommodation plans • English Language Learner (ELL) student proficiency on assessments • Percentage of students on free and reduced-price lunch • Participation/performance in AP and IB coursework, CTE programs • Percentage of students on track to graduate based on credit attainment • Transportation services eligibility • Parent contact/emergency contact information • Social media • School publications (newsletters, yearbooks) • Awards and recognitions
Employee	• Personnel files (school, district office) • Attendance records • Demographic information • Sign-in sheets/time-accounting records • Payroll • Teacher grade books, observations, and lesson plans • Teacher credentials evaluation ratings • Professional developments attended

Data	Examples
	• Certification/Highly Qualified Teacher • Professional portfolio • Social media • Awards and recognitions
School	• Curriculum materials • Code of conduct • Student, teacher, and parent handbooks • School website/social media • High school graduation rates • School environment (e.g., posters, appearance of building) • Grading policies • Faculty meeting agenda and minutes • School budget and expenditure records • Teaching and student schedules (e.g., teacher planning time; student ability grouping) • Student-to-teacher ratio • Counseling and nurses' office records • School yearbook and newspaper; alumni magazines • Parent/guardian attendance at events • School surveys • Preexisting action research studies • Teacher inquiries • Awards and recognitions
District	• School board agenda, minutes, policies • Administrative meeting agenda and minutes • Operating, categorical, and capital fund budgets • Program evaluations • Union contracts • Grievance decisions • Curriculum guides • Census block/school catchment areas • Connectivity to agency IT systems (e.g., court access to school records) • Attendance records • District website • College matriculation and retention rates • "Big data" school management platforms (e.g., SchoolNet) • Awards and recognitions

Radical Student Check-Ins as a Form of Radical Self-Care

William N. Thomas, IV

During the past year I have worked to make sense of the many challenges that face Black educators. From our health pandemic to the increase in racial tension, I as a Black educator have had to both lead others during these difficult events as well as attempt to take care of myself in order to support my family. The many intersections of health, criminal justice, education, and race collide, particularly as I attempt to complete a dissertation during a health crisis.

After taking several courses with Dr. Ravitch and receiving ongoing research advice, I started to process one aspect of her key themes in flux pedagogy (Ravitch, 2020). This idea of radical self-care started to resonate with me as I began pushing myself to consciously process the traumatic events of the last year. As a result, I began writing about my "radical self-care" experience and sharing it with the community educators across the country. I was asked to join a panel of educators to discuss how teachers and parents should prepare for the new school year among the many social and health anxieties that seem to dominate those preparing students for learning. The Jacob Blake incident (Blake, a 29-year-old Black man, was shot and seriously injured by a police officer in Kenosha, Wisconsin) sparked me to write a chapter focused on the importance of Black Male Educators practicing radical self-care using what I call the 3 Ms: self-management, self-monitoring and self-motivation. After attending Dr. Ravitch's talk on flux pedagogy, I was inspired to write again but on the importance of "radical self-care" for all educators through "radical student check-ins."

RADICAL STUDENT CHECK-INS

The difficult balancing act of work life, home life, and school life can sometimes cause foreigners to the Ivory Tower (like myself) to lose focus on the important role to play in expanding the craft of teaching and the strategies for navigating the political landscape of education. As I continue on my path to completing my doctoral studies in educational leadership, I am often reflective on the many experiences with my students during my teaching years—mainly whether I have had a positive impact on their ability to navigate the world in these challenging times. During the start of my data collection this summer, I received a message on LinkedIn from a student who I taught when she was in the 5th grade. She was now a college student and was excited to reconnect with me after a very paradigm-shifting 8 years:

> Hey Professor Thomas! I'm not sure if you remember me but I'm Tiana from 5th grade at CAPCS. I searched the internet for hours looking for a way to contact you. You honestly had the biggest impact in my life, out of my 12 years of being in school. I will always be grateful to have learned from you!

As an educator, I was immediately reminded of the "teaching mystique" of being a teacher, which brings us so much motivation and optimism for future generations. My current administrative role in the central office puts a certain degree of distance between those deep, impactful relationships developed on the campus level. I wrote back with a sense of renewed purpose as an educator and felt reaffirmed that my sometimes extreme educational techniques did not traumatize all my students:

> So great to hear from you! I hope you have been well there in Columbus. Are you still swimming? I am honored to hear that I impacted your life knowing how hard I was on kids. I have been feeling guilty some days when I think of ways I could have been a better teacher, so this means the world to me! How is your mother and grandmother? What about your little niece? Please give them my best. I hope you have been staying healthy and safe during this time. Please feel free to reach out for anything you might need! So glad you found me!

My experience interviewing (for my dissertation) Morehouse College alumni who were current and former teachers promoted me to reflect on my own motivations as a teacher and now an educational leader. I was able get over 100 survey responses and interview brothers who I had deep personal relationships with as well as those whom I was meeting for the first time. Regardless of the level of relational proximity, we were able to generate knowledge based on the activation of life milestones that connected to their experience as a teacher.

These interviews became therapeutic for me, especially as I had to watch the acts of racial injustice that took place over the year. I was proud that men from the institution of higher learning that developed me into the educator that I am had produced countless stories of Black men who defied the odds, took the road less traveled, and committed to the upliftment of underserved communities through the vehicle of teaching. Ironically, as I was concluding my data collection, I received a second message from my former student, which reminded me of the impact teachers have on racial literacy and identity:

> The only way you could have been a better teacher was if you paid for everyone to go to college lol. Don't be hard on yourself! You were the only teacher who taught me to love myself and to be confident in the skin that I'm in. You taught us to be pro Black before we could find out that the world was built against us . . .

As I thought about a response, I couldn't help but think about some of the other students in her class that I was particularly proud of and how they have positioned themselves to be successful and grounded in culture and positive identity. One student from the class fulfilled an unwritten aspiration of many Morehouse alumni who were K–12 teachers: He was accepted into Morehouse and enrolled as a chemical engineering major. The dream of teaching a student and having an impact on a decision that you feel can change the trajectory of their life opportunities as a Black man

Figure E.1. Student Connections Over Time

One student from the class, pictured at two different ages below left, fulfilled an unwritten aspiration of many Morehouse alumni who were K–12 teachers when he was accepted into Morehouse, enrolling as a chemical engineering major.

fuels my passion for giving young people a better educational experience than I had. I had been meaning to call this student to see how the pandemic was impacting his experience at Morehouse but had not carved out the time to do so.

As a form of self-care and an active reminder of purpose, I have decided to conduct Radical Student Check-Ins with former students who have taken the initiative to keep in contact with me, along with other educators and their former students. I feel that the infinite energy that former students bring can propel even the most stressed doctoral student and others to push through the pandemic demands of 2020. I have started to internalize the very necessary critical analysis of scholars like Dr. Sharon Ravitch who have articulated various survival strategies through researched theories that can support educational leaders during this time when education is experiencing an accelerated evolution that is exposing inequities that have existed for generations.

WHAT ARE RADICAL STUDENT CHECK-INS?

A *Radical Student Check-In* is a relational inquiry form of radical self-care (Brown, 2007), one of the many theories within Ravitch's (2020) flux pedagogy. These check-ins act as a space for educators to remember, reflect on, and reactivate impactful shared experiences with students. This semi-structured interview between the moderator, teacher, and student serves as a mechanism for self-motivation and affirmation for a life committed to developing lifelong learners and independent thinkers.

WHY DO EDUCATORS NEED RADICAL STUDENT CHECK-INS?

The current context presents opportunities as well as challenges as it relates to retaining quality educators who are motivated to remain in the profession. One core experience in education, for an educator, is the growth and development of students. While some educational leaders remain in the classroom, those who have chosen roles outside of being a teacher can sometimes get distracted by the political and economic impact of education and detour necessary professional reflection time on the experience of the student. Some students remain in contact with their former teachers whether they are in college or active in their profession. In order to leverage these strong relationships, Radical Student Check-Ins give these teacher–student relationships an opportunity to affirm the intentions and the benefits of the educational interaction. This affirmation and recognition acts as an instrument to remind both of the expectations and confidence they had/have for one another.

FRAMEWORK DESIGN ANCHORED IN
RAVITCH'S FLUX PEDAGOGY

How do you develop empathetic kindness toward the self? The examination of social and political power and systems of dominance can be overwhelming for educators, but Dr. Sharon Ravitch from the University of Pennsylvania's Graduate School of Education has identified key elements of *flux pedagogy* that are critical to consider when navigating the changing landscape of education. Activating past success with students can help position educators to rehumanize themselves through communal re-storying of their impact and purpose as an educator. What follows is a summary of those key elements and how they support Radical Student Check-Ins.

Trauma Context

The educator's experience of the COVID-19 pandemic and the graphic coverage of racial injustice has been penetrating and personal. Radical self-care addresses both the intergenerational trauma that educators experienced prior to the pandemic as well as the added emotional anxieties that have formed as a result of this heightened awareness to race and health. These traumas weigh heavily on both educators and students, who are attempting to learn as well as understand their identity in a brave new world.

Inquiry Entry Point

As initiators of radical self-care, as a result of the traumatic context, educators can and should situate themselves as learners to sharpen their craft and generate knowledge that will help build the self-motivation muscle that educators use to innovate and sustain in the school setting. Taking an inquiry stance toward not only oneself but also the students you have impacted transcends the moment in history and becomes knowledge for refinement.

Shared Student-Centered Experience

These check-ins are designed to center inquiry on the pedagogical approaches taken to develop students as lifelong learners and independent thinkers. Students should be at the center of any educator's experience, and reorienting oneself to the genuine reasons that education exists is critical for educators, particularly the best practices that have resulted in student success and achievement. The narratives of how students were transformed by teachers through the educational curation of learning feed the educator's psyche with nourishment that builds self-esteem, confidence in their craft, and patience in the face of changing educational expectations.

Figure E.2. Radical Student Check-Ins anchored in Ravitch's Flux Pedagogy

Radical Student Check-ins as a form of Radical Self-care

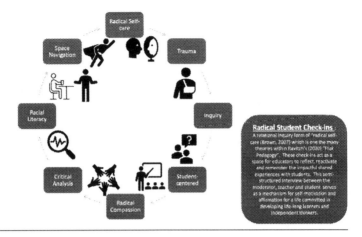

Reciprocal Radical Compassion

Understanding suffering within an equity-oriented lens is easier said than done. This form of compassion toward oneself as well as toward the former student builds a reciprocal transformation through the activation of verbalizing shared experiences.

Critical Collective Analysis

Part of this process of radical self-care is a layer of critical questioning relating to the student's experience and the circumstances that contributed to the context. Both the student and former teacher are expected to interrogate their shared experience in a way that shows radical compassion through an inquiry stance. This allows the shared visualization and articulation of milestones in the student's and teacher's experience that can act as a source of motivation and intellectual guidance for all participants.

Revealing of Racial Literacy

Giving a space where educators and students can reflect on the racial context of their shared experience and how the climate has evolved is healthy in the process of radical self-care. Teachers sometimes act as real-world role models for students on how to navigate race and identity within a professional and sometimes community setting. As educators process and determine the best ways to support future students with the new challenges of the day, they can also learn from those students who were able to turnkey lessons and then benefit from them.

Brave and Safe Space Navigation

While race can sometimes dominate the lens through which students are processing the world, it is important that they have an opportunity to understand the interrelated relationship between identity and culture. This overlapping experience of culture and identity typically comes in various degrees of safe and brave spaces. But how do students navigate these spaces that are now infiltrated with radically polarizing truths that dress themselves within a binary code of philosophy and fake news? The reconnecting of students with teachers who have profoundly influenced their perception of the world can be a starting place for self-reflection and reciprocal radical self-care for former students and educators.

The value of a strong teacher–student relationship is priceless. This bond can last beyond the lives of both the student and teacher as it creates a fund of knowledge that others can learn from, build on, and refine. The leveraging of today's technological capabilities and relations dynamics positions all participants as learners of the relational literacy being produced in these check-ins. The exchange of this shared reflection becomes new knowledge that can be used as a tool for self-motivation and self-rediscovery of one's educational philosophy and purpose.

REFERENCES

Brown, A. M. (2017). *Emergent strategy: Shaping change, shaping worlds*. AK Press.
Ravitch, S. M. (2020). Flux pedagogy: Transforming teaching and leading during coronavirus. *Perspectives on Urban Education, 17*(4), 18–32.

About the Contributors

Sharon M. Ravitch is a professor of practice at the University of Pennsylvania's graduate school of education. She is principal investigator of *Semillas Digitales*, a school-based education program in the coffee-producing regions of Nicaragua that cultivates a holistic model of educational innovation focused on pedagogical and curricular enrichment, inquiry-based teacher professional development, digital literacy, and community partnership. Ravitch has published six books: *Critical Leadership Praxis: Leading Educational and Social Change* (with Katie Pak, 2021); *Applied Research for Sustainable Change: A Guide for Education Leaders* (with Nicole Carl, 2019); *Qualitative Research: Bridging the Conceptual, Theoretical, and Methodological* (with Nicole Carl, 2016/2021); *Reason and Rigor: How Conceptual Frameworks Guide Research* (with Matthew Riggan, 2012/2017); *School Counseling Principles: Diversity and Multiculturalism* (2006); and *Matters of Interpretation: Reciprocal Transformation in Therapeutic and Developmental Relationships with Youth* (with Michael Nakkula, 1998). Ravitch earned two master's degrees from Harvard University and a doctorate from the University of Pennsylvania. She is a GIAN Scholar of the Government of India and a Fulbright Fellow (2021–2022). In 2021, she was selected as a faculty recipient of the Recognition of Outstanding Service Award to honor her dedication to providing a nurturing and supportive environment for students.

Chloe Kannan Chloe Kannan earned her EdD in reading/writing/literacy from the University of Pennsylvania Graduate School of Education in 2021. In her dissertation research, she studied the experiences of first-generation students of color in a college access alternative that focused on issues of equity. She continues to be a practitioner-scholar in her tribal homeland. Kannan is currently the Literacy Coach and the Native American Creative Writing instructor at Joseph K. Lumsden Bahweting, a K–8 Anishinaabe public school academy in Sault Ste. Marie, Michigan. Kannan has her master's in educational leadership from Columbia University Teachers College. During her time at Penn, she worked as a project director for a community-based research team, liaison director supporting schools with strategic plan initiatives around mental health, and qualitative methods writing coach in the mid-career doctoral program. Chloe taught middle school language arts for

7 years: in public schools in the Mississippi Delta, and in Mumbai, India at the American School of Bombay, an international school. She has experience supporting teachers, principals, and instructional coaches in the areas of curriculum, instruction, and educational leadership.

Manuela Adsuar-Pizzi is a lead ELA, literacy, and writing instructor at The Lang School, an alternative K–12 independent school for twice exceptional students. She graduated from Hunter College with a BA in philosophy and a minor in English and holds three MSEd degrees as well as certification in adolescent education for grades 7–12 (ELA) from St. John's University, school building leadership from Fordham University, and adolescent literacy (5–12) from Hunter College. She is currently a doctoral candidate at the University of Pennsylvania.

Steve Brown is director of financial aid and institutional research at The Lovett School. Steve analyzes financial information of applicant families and implements research design, data collection, archiving, reporting, and analysis of information in support of institutional planning, research, and assessment. He also teaches math. As a competitive scholar-athlete, Steve was an All-American in track, a former professional football player, and competed in the 2000 Olympic Games in the 110-meter high hurdles. Steve holds a BS from Wake Forest University and an MBA from Duke University, and is currently working on his EdD in educational leadership at the University of Pennsylvania.

Deirdre Johnson Burel is a program officer on the U.S. Southern team with the W. K. Kellogg Foundation. In this role, she provides leadership and oversight for the execution of program efforts and designs and implements grant initiatives, place-based work, and multi-year projects that affect systematic change and program strategy in New Orleans. She brings 25+ years of experience in education, having worked in schools and nonprofits and in advancing state-level policy in the public sector. She holds a BA in political science from the University of California, Berkeley, and an MPA from New York University's Robert F. Wagner Graduate School of Public Service. She is currently a doctoral candidate at the University of Pennsylvania.

Amelia Coleman-Brown is an assistant superintendent with the School District of Philadelphia serving Learning Network 11. Amelia has served as a principal, classroom teacher, academic coach, and teacher consultant with the Philadelphia Writing Project, and is currently an adjunct instructor of reading and writing. Amelia holds a BS in early childhood and elementary education from Temple University, a MS in education from the University of Pennsylvania, and an instructional leadership certificate from the University of Pennsylvania's educational leadership program for aspiring principals. She is currently a doctoral candidate at the University of Pennsylvania.

Drew Cortese is a director of experience design at Avenues: The World School. As part of Avenues' Tiger Works, their research and development group tasked with revolutionizing T-12 education, Drew currently leads admissions and enrollment efforts for the Avenues Online, Studio Hamptons, and @ Home programming. He was part of Avenues' founding faculty in 2012, developing their drama program for the middle and upper divisions before becoming head of grade 9 and then dean of students for grades 10–12. Drew holds dual degrees from Duke University in public policy studies and drama and an MFA from NYU's graduate acting program. He is currently pursuing his doctorate in educational leadership at the University of Pennsylvania.

Karen D'Avino serves as superintendent of schools in the Vernon Township School District in New Jersey and is a doctoral candidate at the University of Pennsylvania. She started her career as a music teacher and has served as an assistant principal and principal before the superintendent role, through which she has served for a cumulative 13+ years in three districts. She has worked toward increased student engagement, the improvement of student outcomes based on differentiated instruction, a child-centered approach meeting the needs of the whole child, and professional development that supports teachers in delivering strong instructional pedagogy to students.

Rahshene Davis is an assistant superintendent for the School District of Philadelphia. She served as a director of school partnerships for the Achievement Network and chief academic officer for Children's Literacy Initiative and as a principal in Newark, New Jersey, where she received Administrator of the Year in 2011. Her vast experiences in school change prompted her move into school leadership as a way to effect change. She holds a MSEd, with a specialization in TESOL (Teaching English to Speakers of Other Languages) from the University of Pennsylvania and an MS in education administration from Baruch, CUNY. She attended NLNS (New Leaders for New Schools), a national urban principal training program in 2007. She is currently a doctoral candidate at the University of Pennsylvania.

Michael Farrell is the deputy chief of leadership development for the School District of Philadelphia. Prior to this role, Michael served as the principal of Sadie Tanner Mossell Alexander University of Pennsylvania Partnership School (Penn Alexander School). A Philadelphia native, Michael has worked in Philadelphia district and charter schools as a special education teacher, student support coordinator, assistant principal, and founding principal. He is a founding board member of the GLSEN Philadelphia chapter. Michael's doctoral research explores the racial identity development of White school principals. He is an adjunct instructor and a doctoral candidate at the University of Pennsylvania graduate school of education.

Elizabeth A. Fernandez-Vina is deputy director at the Office of Recruitment, Preparation, and Induction, New Jersey Department of Education. She started her career at New Brunswick High School as an English as a second language and Spanish teacher after earning her BA and MA degrees from Rutgers University. She also completed an MA in school leadership at the University of Pennsylvania while working as the school-based leader at Northeast High School in Philadelphia. Elizabeth served as assistant principal at Universal Audenried Charter High School in Philadelphia before joining the New Jersey Department of Education. She is currently a doctoral candidate at the University of Pennsylvania.

Jessica Flaxman is a founding partner at 120 Education Consultancy. Jessica currently directs a consulting collaborative of leadership practitioners working in independent schools. She began her career as an English teacher and served as department chair, upper school director of studies, and assistant head at multiple independent schools over 20 years. Jessica is a consultant and is the writer and editor of *Klingbrief* and *Well-Schooled*, the site for educator storytelling. Jessica holds an MA in English from Columbia University and an MEd from the Klingenstein Center at Teachers College. She is currently a doctoral candidate at the University of Pennsylvania.

Christina M. Grant is the acting state superintendent of education for the Office of the State Superintendent of Education. Dr. Grant recently served as the chief of charter schools and innovation for the School District of Philadelphia, where she oversaw a budget of more than $1 billion and a portfolio of both district and charter schools. In this capacity, Dr. Grant managed a complex organization, working closely with the superintendent of schools and the president of the board of education and the mayor's chief education officer. Dr. Grant's career began as a public school teacher in Harlem; she has held numerous roles in education, including as superintendent of the Great Oaks Foundation and deputy executive director at the New York City Department of Education. Dr. Grant has a doctorate in education from the University of Pennsylvania; two master's degrees from Teachers College of Columbia University and Fordham University; and a bachelor's degree from Hofstra University.

Kelly Grimmett is assistant head of Lower School Friends Seminary in New York City. For the last 15 years, Kelly has supported leadership teams that promote positive, inclusive schools for all constituents. She endeavors to increase dialogue between school administration and faculty, increasing transparency of decision-making to foster greater trust in leadership. Her research interests include curriculum innovation and design, social-emotional learning, and professional learning communities. Kelly has a BA in English literature and information technology and informatics, and an MLIS from Rutgers University. She is currently a doctoral candidate at the University of Pennsylvania.

Carla Haith is head of lower school at Dedham Country Day School, a suburban independent school in Massachusetts. Prior to her current role, Carla taught in Boston Public Schools. She also served as the co-director of an educator preparation intern program, mentor of aspiring teachers, and kindergarten, 2nd-, and 3rd-grade teacher at the Chestnut Hill School. She holds a BA in early childhood education from Clark Atlanta University and an MEd in education from Lesley University/Shady Hill School Collaborative Program. She is a proud member of Sigma Gamma Rho Sorority. She is currently a doctoral candidate at the University of Pennsylvania.

Christopher J. Hancock is head of school at Benchmark School in Media, Pennsylvania. He began his career in independent schools in 2003 and has worked in special education, Waldorf education, and gifted education. Prior to his current role, Chris served as an assistant head of school, director of development, admissions officer, coach, and tutor at multiple institutions. Chris holds a BA in Economics from Haverford College and an EdM in school leadership from Harvard's Graduate School of Education. He is currently a doctoral candidate at the University of Pennsylvania.

Kiet Hoang is the former chancellor of Broward College, Vietnam. Kiet is currently pursuing a second doctoral degree in educational leadership at the graduate school of education at the University of Pennsylvania in Philadelphia. Previously, at the Institute of American Education, he was the provost at Thanh Tay University (2017–2019), the chancellor of American Polytechnic College, and Broward College, Vietnam (2014–2017). He received his first PhD in statistical physics from Sungkyunkwan University, Korea, in 2008, after completing his diploma at the International Center for Theoretical Physics (ICTP) in Italy in 2003. He is currently a doctoral candidate at the University of Pennsylvania.

Muronji C. Inman-McCraw is a passionate educator and artist and the principal of Two Rivers Public Charter School. She earned an MA in special education and human development from George Washington University and a BA in communications and theater with a minor in African American Studies from Temple University. Muronji taught in Washington, DC, for several years before teaching at Harlem Children's Zone, where she held leadership roles including, special education coordinator, humanities coach, assistant principal of instruction, and director of curriculum and instruction. She is currently a doctoral candidate at the University of Pennsylvania.

Jeannine Minort-Kale serves as a high school vice principal for Waterbury Public Schools. She started her career in education in the South Bronx as a New York City teaching fellow and holds an MST in adolescent education from Pace University, a graduate certificate in gifted education and talent development from the University of Connecticut, a 6th-year degree in mathematics educational leadership from Central Connecticut State University, and certification from the National Board of Professional Teaching Standards. She is currently a doctoral candidate at the University of Pennsylvania.

Felicia Owo-Grant is head of schools at Friendship Public Charter Schools, one of the Friendship Public Charter Schools in Washington, DC. Felicia leads an initiative to develop a professional learning institute for Friendship Public Charter Schools' 16 DC campuses and nationally. Under her leadership, Friendship Woodridge International School has earned a high-performing Tier 1 rating, received International Baccalaureate World School authorization, been named a Leveler School by the DC Policy Institute, and earned a BOLD Performance award by Empower K12 for dramatically increasing student achievement for at-risk students. Felicia holds degrees from the University of Texas at Austin, Trinity Washington University, and George Mason University. She is currently a doctoral candidate at The University of Pennsylvania.

Curtis A. Palmore is the CEO at Community Charter School of Paterson, New Jersey. He started teaching in New York City through the Teach for America program in 1995. He has over 25 years of teaching and leadership experience in traditional and public charter schools, including his turnaround efforts as founding principal at Exceed Charter School. Curtis holds BA and MA degrees from Morgan State University, Fordham University, and Teachers College, Columbia University. He is currently a doctoral candidate at the University of Pennsylvania.

Andrew Phillips is chair of the School of Design at String Theory Schools in Philadelphia. He is an architect turned educator, with degrees from Pennsylvania State University and Harvard University. His design firm received numerous awards and accolades over its 20-year span. Andrew served on the graduate and undergraduate architecture faculties at the University of Pennsylvania before joining the Charter High School for Architecture+Design. As director of design education, he built its design curriculum into a standard-setting model for design education. He has several publications, leads professional developments, and speaks about K–12 design education. He is currently a doctoral candidate at the University of Pennsylvania.

Clare Sisisky is the executive director of the Global Education Benchmark Group, a nonprofit that supports 280 member schools around the world in all aspects of global education. Clare's previous roles include senior administrative roles at independent schools and a large public school district, as well as teaching and teacher training including in Beijing and rural India. Her research and professional work focus on global competency development in students and educators. Clare has an undergraduate degree from George Washington University and a graduate degree from Harvard University and postgraduate research fellowship in Mauritius focused on immigration and religious identity. She is currently a doctoral candidate at the University of Pennsylvania.

Michael Tapscott, assistant principal at De La Salle Academy, has over a decade of experience working with middle school students. He has taught math and science, served as the chair of math and science and as the dean of student affairs, and is currently the assistant principal at a private independent school in the heart of New York City. Michael received his BA from Wesleyan University and his MA in private school leadership from the Klingenstein Center at Teachers College, Columbia University. He is currently a doctoral candidate at the University of Pennsylvania.

William N. Thomas IV has dedicated the past 17 years to service as an urban educator. He received his doctorate degree in educational leadership from the University of Pennsylvania graduate school of education in 2021. His research unpacks the intersectionality of self-motivation, professional development, and young males of color in relation to teacher retention of Black men in public schools. William serves as director of science for all Mastery Charter School campuses in Philadelphia and Camden. Prior to his current position, he was a biology teacher at Ron Brown College Preparatory High School and a restorative justice public school in Washington, DC, founded to support the social and emotional development of young men of color. William holds an MA in middle school science from George Washington University and a BA in English from Morehouse College.

David Weiner is dean of studies and director of college counseling at Barrie School. David has 14+ years working in education. For the past 11 years, he has taken on a number of roles in independent schools, most recently dean of studies, where he leads a division-wide project-based learning initiative and guides the Teaching & Learning Committee. He holds a BA in history and psychology from the University of Rochester, an MA in education from Johns Hopkins University, and is currently completing his doctorate in educational leadership at the University of Pennsylvania.

Index

Note: **Bold** type indicates contributors of chapters to this volume.